JANUSZ PIEKALKIEWICZ

The Cavalry of World War II

STEIN AND DAY/*Publishers*/New York

Picture acknowledgements

Bundesarchiv Koblenz: 195
Imperial War Museum, London: 59
Sikorski Institute, London: 9
Établissement Cinématographique et Photographique
  des Armées Fort d'Ivry, Paris: 17
Sotatieteen Laitos, Helsinki: 3
Department of the Army, US Army Audio-Visual
  Activity, Washington: 3
Archives for the History of the Army, Athens: 1
N.T.B. Norsk Telegrambyrås, Oslo: 3
Novosti, Moscow: 2
J. Piekalkiewicz: 41

First published in the United States of America in 1980
Copyright © 1976 by Südwest Verlag GmbH & Co. Kg, München
English language edition © 1979 by Orbis Publishing Limited, London
All rights reserved.

Printed in the United States of America
Stein and Day/*Publishers*/Scarborough House, Briarcliff Manor, N.Y.10510
Library of Congress Cataloging in Publication Data

Piekalkiewicz, Janusz.
    The cavalry of World War II.

    Translation of Pferd und Reiter im II Weltkrieg.
    Bibliography: p.
    Includes index.
    1. World War, 1939-1945—Cavalry operations.
I. Title.
D794.P5313   1980   940.54'1   80-5800
ISBN 0-8128-2749-X

Contents

Foreword

In all the countless publications about World War II in all possible languages, there is still one yawning gap: man has forgotten about his faithful servant, the horse. Perhaps I should first give a word of warning to anyone who expects this book to contain a series of tear-jerking stories, in case they are disappointed. This book is not like that. 'The Cavalry of World War II', as its title suggests, is a book about the War, the War on horseback, and it includes reports of the action seen by the mounted units of the nations involved; it is the first book ever to be written about this subject, although a whole age, a generation, has elapsed since then. This is one of the reasons why I found it so difficult to gather together the information I needed for this book. But in any case, the photographs, many of which are very rare, give, perhaps, a clearer idea of the war on horseback than any text could: each says more about man's friend the horse than a thousand words. The British officer, Major G. Tylden, declared that the horse was above all a true companion – even when wounded, or half starving, he would never shirk his duty until he was simply unable to take another step forward. Loyal and patient, the horse carried on whether with friend or foe, in stifling heat or in the bitter cold of a northern winter, on hard tarmac roads or on rough paving, across furrowed fields or knee-deep in mud – often without enough food, rarely properly stabled and unprotected from enemy action. In all these circumstances, the poor dumb creature was always there – only his enormous eyes sometimes revealed his indescribable sorrows.

These creatures, endowed by nature with an uncanny sense of direction which even today remains unexplained, were at the mercy of modern military armament and were sacrificed wholesale at the hands of the men they served. And never in the long history of the horse were they used more recklessly than in World War II. They were ridden against tanks, and used in mounted attacks with entire regiments facing massive machine-gun and artillery fire. The horse would be the first to be hit; there was seldom any cover or any way of escape if it was being used to draw a field cannon or a baggage cart. In the hard Russian winter, the horses often stood in temperatures of -50 degrees outside peasants' shacks, eating rotten roof-shingles or decaying straw from the eaves. Compared with World War I, nearly twice the number of horses – 2·75 million of them including mules – went into the field of battle for the Führer and the German Fatherland. The Red Army, true to its cavalry tradition, sent a good 3·5 million horses into the war. We shall never know how many of them survived the carnage which lasted from the first hour of the war to the last; on average, 865 horses died each day for the German Reich. Anyone who was involved in World War II will carry the picture of the many horses' bodies which lined the sides of the roads indelibly printed in his memory. In the siege of Stalingrad, around 52,000 horses, as well as their two-legged comrades, lost their lives; and every new muddy period, every Russian winter, brought the spectre of death for the unfortunate animals. But the tragedy on the Crimea overshadowed all these lesser perils.

When the German 17th Army at last received the order to evacuate the Crimean peninsula early in 1944, this amounted to a death sentence for the horses which the Germans could neither transport away nor leave over for the Russians. The entire stock of the Army's horses, tens of thousands of them, were led in rows to the edge of the steep cliffs; there they were systematically shot and hurled into the abyss.

Janusz Piekalkiewicz

The life of a cavalryman during the war

This letter from a cavalryman in Germany's 1st Mounted Regiment shows the difference between the life of a cavalryman and that of a soldier in any other arm of the services, perhaps better than any straight description – and it is representative of all the cavalrymen of World War II.

'... You don't seem to have any idea of what our operations on horse-back are like. They expect the same daily output from us as they do from the motorized troops ... if a motorized unit travels 150 kilometres, it takes them maybe from ten in the morning to three in the afternoon. When they reach their destination for the day, they can park their cars and that's that. But if we cover 90 kilometres, we need 14 to 16 hours – and that means from four in the morning to ten at night. Then at the end of all that, we have to look after the horses, which takes at least an hour, and at night be on stable watch for another one or two hours. An infantryman nowadays can march maybe 50 kilometres in a day. If he's given a 20 minute break, he lies down on the grass verge and takes it easy. But the cavalryman has to water his horse, fetching the water from as far as 200 metres away. In the infantry, two hours' rest are two hours' rest; but we need an hour and a quarter for the horse, what with unsaddling and saddling up again, fetching the animal water, food and so on. And if we want to eat, we still have to hold the horse. What's more, if we travel 90 kilometres, we'll probably ride for only 40 – we have to lead the horse the rest of the way ... which means that on top of what the infantry does, we still have 40 kilometres in the saddle, and that's no trifle either.

'The infantryman's feet may ache, but so do the cavalryman's – for he's had to walk 50 kilometres too, in boots made for riding, not marching. It's not only his feet that hurt, though – his shoulders and hips are bashed about by his rifle, his buttocks feel as if they're in shreds, and after a ride lasting several days he feels as if he's got no bones left in his body. The infantry soldier's free to walk as he wants, whereas the horseman always has to lead his mount when he's on foot. After a while he has to pull it because it's had enough. Then he has to halt, because it's stumbling forward. When an infantryman has a rest, he can get his own things in order. But for the cavalryman, first he's got to look after the horse's gear and saddle – he has to leave his own things to do in his own free time! What about an airman? He's in great danger for hours maybe, though one might wonder whether it's really any more dangerous than elsewhere in the forces. But every day he goes back to his old furnished home – whereas we have to be eternal gipsies. As cavalrymen we're never billeted in towns, only in villages. We always avoid big cities. What's a detour of five kilometres matter? The horse does what you ask of him. For cavalrymen, the roughest country tracks are good enough ...'

A word of thanks

I should like to express my cordial thanks to the following for their kind help: Dr M. Haupt and Mr H. Walther, of the *Bundesarchiv* in Koblenz; everyone at the Photographic Library, Imperial War Museum, London; Mr J. S. Lucas and Mr P. H. Reed, of the Imperial War Museum, London; Commander J. Wronski, Captain W. Milewski, Captain R. Dembinski, Captain St Zurakowski, Sikorski Institute, London; Mrs v. Gersdorff and Dr Fricke, *Militärgeschichtliches Forschungsamt*, Freiburg; Mr M. Meyer, of the *Militärarchiv*, Freiburg; Colonel R. Cruccu, of the *Stato Maggiore Dell'Esercito*, V Reparto-Ufficio Storico, Rome; Colonel M. Lappalainen and Major A. Juutilainen, *Sotatieteen Laitos*, Helsinki; Captain P. Darnóy of the former Royal Hungarian Honvéd Army; Captain I. v. Emilian of the 2nd Calarasi Cavalry Regiment; Captain A. Bojtschewskij of the 15th Cossack Cavalry Corps; Captain Brignone, *Chef de la Division Photographique*, Fort d'Ivry, Paris; Major V. R. White, US Army Audio-Visual Activity, The Pentagon, USA; Colonel M. W. Zebrowski, 7 *plk. Ulanow Lubelskich*, London; Mr G. W. Jeffke, *Kameradschaft 8. Reiter*, Münster; Mr R. Spiering, *Spiegel Verlag*, Hamburg; Mr M. Marić, Belgrade; also the military and cultural attachés and their staff in Bonn and Bad Godesberg; Colonel De Rill and Mr C. Kesteloot, Belgian Embassy; Colonel E. Raunio, Finnish Embassy; Brigadier-General Sionta, Mr Karageorgiou, Mr Karachalios, Greek Embassy; Colonel R. Aoto, Mr Opiolka, Japanese Embassy; Colonel A. Viviani, Italian Embassy; Mr I. Ivanji, Mrs D. Alavantić, Yugoslav Embassy; Lieutenant-Colonel R. Kristiansen, Norwegian Embassy; Mr Alan Dodds, Mrs I. Köpf, United States Embassy; Mrs Elizabeth Vickus, member of the *Fedération Equestre Nationale* (FN); Mr Günter Bornheim, member of the *Besitzerund Züchtervereinigung für Vollblutzucht und Rennen*.

Uhlans against tanks

'It's war – don't you understand?'

Extract from the diary of Corporal Karpa of the German 1st Mounted Regiment, September 1, 1939:

'We were awoken at 2 AM by a bugle call. At 3.05 AM we were given our marching orders. It was still pitch dark. The whole squadron rode in the close formation of a flying column. We passed through many villages, each time wondering: "Are we already in Poland?"'

4.45 AM, and the early morning mist on the fields held out the promise of a beautiful summer's day to come. The units forming the spearhead of the German force started off from their overnight positions. At precisely 4.55 AM, the telephone rang for Captain Szacherski, adjutant of the Polish 7th Mounted Light Infantry Regiment, positioned immediately behind the Polish–German frontier to the east of Poznan. The Polish captain takes up the story:

'I heard the voice of General Wlad, saying: "Good morning, Captain. The Germans have just crossed our frontier along its entire length. There's already fighting at the frontier posts and among the advanced units. Your orders are that it is up to the regiment to do its duty."

'I immediately telephoned Major Kalwas. On the line came the voice of the duty NCO. "Wake the major and tell him that the Germans have crossed our frontier," I told him. "The regiment has been ordered to do its duty." "What was that again, sir? I didn't quite catch," murmured the NCO. I repeated the message, but still he failed to grasp my meaning. "It's war, you idiot, WAR – don't you understand?" "I see, captain. So we really are at war."'

The German cavalry

The only sizeable mounted fighting unit on the German side, the 1st Cavalry Brigade, consisting of two regiments, was given the task of protecting the eastern flank of the 3rd Army as it advanced from East Prussia. Preparations for crossing the frontier were made on the night of August 31/September 1. The 1st Mounted Regiment, positioned in the Fürstenwald forest, was made ready and ordered to attack Mysienice; the 2nd Mounted Regiment was to follow up in the rear echelons. At 4.45 AM came the signal for the attack: a few shots directed at the Pelty customs post, from an advanced gun of the 'Nelke' battery. The brigade then advanced further along the Ostrolenka road. Meanwhile the 1st Mounted Regiment remained in Mysienice, and the 2nd Mounted Regiment stayed to the east, having made virtually no contact with the enemy. As the Heights of Zalesie were apparently strongly garrisoned, the brigade drew up to the right of the main advance road, waiting to attack after a brief preparatory artillery bombardment. The enemy forces quickly weakened and pulled back, surprised by the accurate fire of the cavalry guns and mortars.

Lance-Corporal Hornes, of a mounted reconnaissance unit of the German 14th Army under General List, recalls his experiences as he and his comrades advanced from the south:

'Around 10 AM we came to the frontier, near Mikula. We halted at a stream, unsaddled the horses, watered and fed them and we too were given a chance to grab a quick bite of bread and tinned sausage. Then suddenly we were given the order to get saddled up again. Everything went faster than usual. We'd heard a host of rumours – like "These hills are still occupied by the enemy", "There's a line of pill-boxes over there", and so on. Everyone was aware that this was the outbreak of war at last. But was it for real this time? Well, the lieutenant came out with the order we'd got so used to in peace-time. "Muzzle caps off! Load! Safety-catches on!"'

The first cavalry attack of World War II

The Polish Army failed to match up to its attackers in either numbers or equipment. The bulk of the Polish cavalry – over 20,000 men – was spread out conventionally in the last days of August along the entire 1,500 km length of the border between Poland and Germany. The Polish Army was under the command of 53-year-old Marshal Edward Rydz-Smigly, who was renowned as a crack shot.

At noon on September 1, in the so-called Polish Corridor, the German 20th Motorized Division was making its way from the west towards Chojnice. At about 2 PM, battle was raging between the German vanguard and the Polish 18th Uhlan Regiment of the 'Pomorska' Cavalry Brigade, along the railway line from Chojnice to Naklo. The Uhlans received the order to counter-attack to enable their own infantry to retreat. In woodland near the village of Krojanty, the horsemen arranged them-

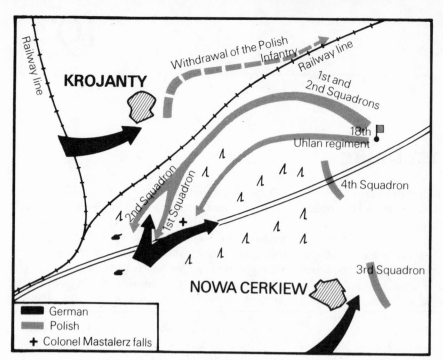

KROJANTY

Withdrawal of the Polish Infantry

Railway line

Railway line

1st and 2nd Squadrons

18th Uhlan regiment

2nd Squadron

1st Squadron

4th Squadron

NOWA CERKIEW

3rd Squadron

■ German
■ Polish
+ Colonel Mastalerz falls

selves in open formation. It was late afternoon when the 1st Squadron of the 18th Uhlan Regiment emerged on the wing of the German columns. When the regiment's adjutant, Captain Godlewski, heard the order to attack, he queried whether it might not be better for the cavalry to dismount before attacking. 'Young man,' answered the regimental commander, Colonel Mastalerz, 'I'm quite aware what it is like to carry out an impossible order.'

At about 5 PM Major Malecki raised his sabre and at this signal, the cavalry launched its assault – the first cavalry charge of World War II.

Even before leaving the wood, they came under machine-gun fire from the German vanguard. The chain of riders put their horses into a trot, then a gallop – moving swiftly forward and away from the open field with its sparse cover. Bowed low over the necks of their horses, they charged with their heavy cavalry sabres held at arm's length. The first dead and wounded fell from their horses. Despite this, the impetus of the charge built up, the more so after the 2nd Squadron joined the attackers. A broad wave of cavalry, consisting of around 250 men, tore over the open field, sabres glinting in the sun; the German infantry, caught off guard, tried to save itself by pulling back. Suddenly, round a bend in the highway, a long column of tanks and motorized troops appeared. At first, in the heat of the battle, it went unnoticed by the Uhlans. The Poles were then hit by a hail of fire from the armoured cars, and before they were even able to turn their horses, the carnage began. Horses crashed heavily to the ground, while others bolted, dragging their riders with them by the stirrups. Figures in khaki uniforms fell from their saddles. A faint bugle call was to be heard, to the accom-

paniment of the anguished groans of wounded men. Here and there, isolated groups of riders stormed over the field, and dark heaps lay strewn over the road. Riderless horses raced over the fields, their stirrups swinging loosely and their reins awry. Captain Swiesciak, who had led the charge, plunged to the ground with his horse, and the regimental commander, Colonel Mastalerz, was himself killed as he hurried to his help with a few Uhlans. In the space of a few moments, half the Uhlans had been hit.

With this cavalry charge at Krojanty on September 1, 1939, was born the legend of the Polish cavalry, armed only with sabres, challenging the German Panzers. But in fairness, it must be said that the Polish Uhlans were not bent on suicide, nor was it in any way a deliberate move on their part to launch a direct attack on tanks. Later in the war, needless to say, there were several other cavalry attacks on German infantry which led the Germans to call in tank reinforcements; what is more, there were some cases of Polish cavalry being attacked by tanks. But for the Uhlans at Krojanty, the only chance of survival was to attempt a breakneck manœuvre as quickly as possible, in order to get past the enemy column. They had not expected the German armoured column to arrive on the field of battle, and when it did, they were completely surprised. From now on, the Polish cavalry forces had met their match.

'Herzog' gives up

Until September 1, 1939, the role of mounted troops had been decisive in every single battle on Polish soil. But from that Friday morning onwards, tanks were the masters of the battlefields. The Polish cavalry, although superbly trained, was totally powerless in a war in which tanks formed the spearhead of the enemy onslaught. The cavalry charges, one after another, would be dissipated in a hail of shells fired by the Germans. And with their antiquated weaponry, this élite cavalry had to rely on skill alone to inflict equally heavy losses on their enemies.

An entry in the dispatches of the German 1st Cavalry Brigade for Sunday, September 3, 1939, reads as follows:

'This morning at approximately 0400 hours, following preliminary reconnaissance, part of the 1st Regiment took the bridge over the river Orzyc. After crossing the bridge, which had been temporarily improved, the 2nd Mounted Regiment advanced to reach the Przasnysz road at Klin. Here, the regiment received an order from Brigade to head southwards from Przasnysz, the 1st Regiment to proceed likewise, and to advance to Czernice-Borowe. At Frankowo, the regiment encountered a strong Polish cavalry unit, the 7th Uhlans, whose presence had already been reported by reconnaissance patrols. After an outflanking attack, the Uhlans were forced back and driven off to the south-east. During the course of this battle, mounted Polish patrols attacked the regiment's battle headquarters but were dispersed.'

The turning point in the entire campaign came on September 3, the third day of the German invasion of Poland. The Polish supreme commander, Marshal Rydz-Smigly, remarked on this day: 'The entire Polish front has collapsed and there is no alternative but to withdraw immediately beyond the Vistula, if this is still possible.'

The German 14th Army, under General List, was marching irresistibly eastwards, to the south of Krakow, with the support of Slovak troops. Lance-Corporal Hornes noted in his journal:

'We were in enemy country, two scouts had gone on ahead with the rest of the group following. We rode along a stony path by the side of a mountain stream, twisting and turning through big rocky outcrops. We were encircled by the wooded hills of the Carpathian countryside. Above us the sky was a deep blue. After a rest of about one hour, we pressed on once more. A broad, sandy road led onwards up through a high pass. The riflemen were cursing and swearing because our horses were throwing up so much dust. It seemed the hills would never come to an end. It was already deep twilight when we reached the highest point. Beyond, the ground sloped sharply away downhill. I was angry because in spite of the incline we were having to trot. I felt that my horse, Herzog, could take no more of it. He was stumbling constantly. I called out to the section commander – "Herzog's had as much as he can take!" I'd scarcely got the words out when the poor beast fell to his knees. There's no doubt that he was in severe pain, though he wasn't lame.

'I wasn't surprised at his tiredness. We'd gone 70 km on the first day, then 60 on the second. And on top of that, we'd had the trek over the mountains and early this morning with the advance patrol about 20 km up and down hill – galloping, what's more – and now another 40 km on top of that. All in all, that meant we'd gone nearly 200 km in three days without any proper rest! Meanwhile the mountain seemed endless. Night had long fallen, and we were still riding. Finally at 10 PM, we overtook the furthest advanced riflemen, and came to a halt in the village.'

Polish cavalry in East Prussia

At 10.45 PM on September 3, a spokesman for the government in Warsaw made a special announcement to foreign correspondents: 'Polish cavalry units have thrust through the armoured German lines and are now in East Prussia, on German territory.' It was the only news from Warsaw that night to contain any cheer for the western allies. The report from the German Wehrmacht shortly before midnight also made mention of the attack, adding however that the cavalry which was attempting to push forward northwards to Olecko had already been repulsed.

On the night of September 3/4, the Polish 1st Cavalry Brigade received the order to report for special duties with the Army Corps, to form the left wing of the army. In the small hours of September 5, the Polish News Agency (PAT) announced: 'Strong Polish cavalry units have entered East Prussia along a broad front. Several towns are already in our hands. The offensive is going especially well for us, and is already standing out as a turning point in the war. Similar offensive actions on other sectors of the front are imminent.' For a while in Warsaw it was hoped that the cavalry would score a victory over the German Wehrmacht.

What had happened? On the night of September 2/3, a squadron of the 10th Uhlan Regiment of the 'Podlaska' Cavalry Brigade (attached to the Narew Army) had led an offensive across the German border, advancing into the province of East Prussia. The weak German *Landwehr* – territorial reserve – with little artillery support, had put up no more than a token resistance. So the 'Podlaska' Cavalry Brigade was ordered to press on with a renewed offensive into East Prussia.

On the east wing, three squadrons of the 9th Mounted Light Infantry Regiment attacked, with the support of a battery of horse-drawn 75 mm artillery; on the west wing was the 5th Uhlan Regiment.

The Uhlans edged forward as far as the edge of the forest, now clearly visible in the early sunlight. Suddenly they came up against a group of bunkers protected by deep trenches. Ensign Strzelczyk pulled out the pin of a grenade: 'There you go, my lad, let 'em have it!' Masked by the smoke of the explosion, they stormed the trenches. The 9th

Mounted Light Infantry, however, beset by powerful German artillery fire, remained in the forests along the frontier line. The 5th Uhlan Regiment approached the village of Sokoly, but was soon forced to withdraw. Moreover, the 10th Uhlans, who had originally been meant to advance behind the 5th Uhlans, were also rebuffed in fighting around midday, coming to a dead stop in the face of the steadily increasing barrage. At this point, the brigade commander gave the order to retreat. 'We took a few dozen prisoners at the frontier, silenced between five and seven machine guns, and captured a few tanks.' The brigade's own casualties were about 55 dead and wounded.

So ended the Polish cavalry offensive which had been greeted with banner headlines by the newspapers of England and France.

On the night of September 5/6, the German 1st Cavalry Brigade had the Rozan–Pultusk road rapidly reconnoitred by the 2nd Mounted Regiment. During the night, the brigade was attached to the 12th Division and instructed to cross the river Narew. The brigade made its plans for action at Brzuze, deciding to use the 2nd Mounted Regiment in the Narew operation. At 6.40 PM, they reached their target of Michalowo Nowe, on the east bank, capturing the bridgehead by the light of the burning houses and farm buildings.

After the brigade, forming the vanguard of the 3rd Army, had crossed the Narew, one squadron of the 1st Mounted Regiment proceeded to the Rozan–Ostrów road, with the other units following some way to the south. At Czarnowo, it had a surprise encounter with a Polish infantry regiment. A vicious hand-to-hand fight flared up, with the Poles completely outclassed.

Lieutenant von Sperber of the 1st Squadron of the 1st Mounted Regiment reported:

'After crossing the Narew on the evening of September 6, we warmed ourselves on the bank by the flames of the burning village. We thought we would be spending the night there, to cover the units behind us as they made their crossing. But after Sergeant-Major Eder had reconnoitred the way ahead and the village of Kunin had been found to be free of enemy forces, we were given the order – doubly popular at night as you can imagine! – to make ready. So we rode on once more into the darkness. Later, we proceeded on foot, leading the horses. The sub-machine gunners moved forward. The atmosphere became rather tense. There was nothing to be seen, yet we knew the enemy must be near. Suddenly we heard the rattle of wheels ahead. We were only a short distance from the Rozan–Ostrów–Mazowiecki road. The order rang out: "Marksmen and machine gunners forward!" As they ran to their positions, heavy firing broke out. Very quickly, the ghostly presence had vanished into the darkness of the night, with a lot of rumbling and shouting. On the road, and especially to the right and left of it in the trenches and fields lay field kitchens, ammunition and baggage-

waggons, dead and wounded horses. There was a headlong rush to grab anything eatable, or at least cigarettes.'

September 7. As day broke, there was a sudden clamour of fighting to be heard to the rear of the 1st Mounted Regiment. Polish infantry, of battalion strength, were attacking some horses on the left flank. Regimental Sergeant-Major Erwied had several horses tied to trees, and got the men looking after the horses to set about their defence at the edge of the wood. The situation was dangerous, and Captain Priese ordered all secret papers and orders he had with him to be burned.

The Battle of the Bzura: the Poles counter-attack

All the Polish armies which had taken up positions on the frontier, with the exception of the surrounded Poznan Army, were driven back. The Lódź Army was split into two by the advance of the German 10th Army: one half withdrew eastwards towards Radom, while the other withdrew to the north-west. Two Panzer divisions advanced towards Warsaw through these gaps in the line. Further north, the German 4th Army crossed the Vistula and continued its march on Warsaw, following the course of the river. Only the Polish army units in the north were in a position to halt the German 3rd Army. They too, however, were soon forced back to the Narew, the only line where a reasonably strong defence was possible. All this had been achieved in the first week of the Blitzkrieg.

The Poznan Army was joined by those divisions of the Lódź and Pomorze Armies which had been driven back in its direction. Their joint strength amounted to 12 divisions. Away through their southern flank, the German 10th Army was forging on towards Warsaw, covered only by the relatively weak 8th Army. Although the Polish forces were actually already encircled, their commander, General Kutrzeba, resolved to strike at the flank of the main German thrust to the south.

On the night of September 8/9, Marshal Rydz-Smigly signalled to General Kutrzeba: 'The sun is rising' – the signal for the start of the operation, which became known in the history of World War II as the Battle of the Bzura. Thereafter, contact with the supreme commander was totally lost. The bold Polish counter-attack not only put the German 8th Army in a critical position; it also diverted part of the 10th Army from its march on Warsaw, and in addition engaged a corps of the 4th Army. The German press at the time hailed it as the 'biggest battle ever'.

On the Polish side, eight infantry divisions and two cavalry brigades (the 'Wielkopolska' and the 'Podolska') were engaged in the fighting, which raged from September 9 to 18 on both sides of the Bzura, a river which meanders romantically through Mazovia, the countryside to the west of

Warsaw. On Sunday, September 10, the Poznan Army went into the attack and recaptured Piatek. The ensuing assault took the Germans totally by surprise, for they had lost sight of the Poznan Army days before. The 'Wielkopolska' Cavalry Brigade attacked in the area between Sobótka and Glówno. The 17th Uhlan Regiment started its attack at midnight. Under cover of darkness, the Uhlans crossed the marshes of the Bzura valley and stormed the village of Walewice. Throughout the day, the Poznan and Pomorze Armies tried to push home their advantage through from the Bzura towards Radom and Krasnik.

On this Sunday evening, the cavalry group under General Grzmot-Skotnicki began a mounted raid on Lódź. Two squadrons of the 6th Uhlans made a frontal attack on Uniejow. The attack collapsed following losses in the face of heavy machine-gun fire. However, at dawn on the following morning, September 11, the Uhlans, supported by an artillery battery, finally succeeded in forcing a way through into Uniejow. And after the Poles had also taken the bridge over the river Warthe, the Germans withdrew, leaving dead, wounded, and many lorries behind. The 14th Uhlans occupied Wartkowice after a short fight. For some time, the big supply depot which they had captured helped to supplement the Podolska Brigade's inadequate supplies. In the evening, Uhlans entered Parzeczew, threatening the Germans at Leczyca. Two units of the 'Pomorska' Cavalry Brigade, the 8th Mounted Light Infantry and the 2nd Light Cavalry Regiment, pressed on in the direction of Orla without meeting any serious resistance.

'The Polish advance was a total surprise for the Germans,' claimed the Polish reports. 'Small cavalry units flushed out enemy forces from the Bzura area. The enemy went into hiding in the nearby marshland for fear of cavalry attacks. The Uhlans have been able to make good use of their lances ...'

Monday, September 11 was a day of intensified fighting. The forces of the German 8th Army (under an infantry commander, General Blaskowitz) bore the brunt of the strong onslaught by both Polish armies. The German 30th Infantry Division (under Major-General Briesen) was particularly badly hit. Blaskowitz reported to the Wehrmacht high command on the crisis which was looming on account of the unexpected advance from the north by 'considerable enemy forces'. The divisions of the 8th Army which had been held in reserve, together with the main body of the 10th Army (under an artillery officer, General von Reichenau), then appeared on the battlefield. Meanwhile, the Polish cavalry was launching mounted attacks at every opportunity. Waffen-SS General Kurt Meyer (known as 'Panzermeyer') reported: 'The Poles attack with enormous tenacity, proving over and over again that they really know how to die.'

One of these notorious and bloody cavalry charges was actually the result of an error. On the night of September 11/12, the 1st (Legion) Infantry Division was cut off on its way to the Vistula by a German Panzer division under General Kempf. When the Polish column approached the German-occupied hamlet of Kaluszyn, Colonel Engel, marching at their head in the darkness, cried out: 'Cavalry, forward!' As he explained later, his order had been intended for the scouting patrol which at the time was dismounted. It is not hard to imagine his astonishment when, a few minutes later, cavalry thundered past him at full gallop, sabres drawn, vanishing into the night towards the town, which was heavily defended by armoured units. Out of 85 horses, only 33 returned from the attack. The leader of the 4th Squadron of the 11th Uhlan Regiment, Captain Wrzosek, had mistaken Colonel Engel's call for the order to charge. And so another Polish cavalry unit suffered insupportable losses because desperate courage was no match for modern weapons and techniques.

Tuesday, September 12. The first phase of the battle of the Bzura was over. Now it was the turn of the Germans to take the offensive. In spite of local successes, as for example to the north of Ozorków, the Polish armies were stopped, and the noose drawn around them became progressively tighter and more formidable. The initiative was now entirely with the Germans, and the outline of the first great chain of battles of World War II was now becoming clear. Although the Polish assaults had thrown the German Army off balance, it had recovered very quickly.

Thursday, September 14. During the morning, the Poles were edging forward step by step, unnoticed by the tough German opposition. An infantry division crossed the Bzura and captured Lowicz, but their advance was then checked and the German menace loomed even larger. The Polish divisions took up defensive positions along the Bzura. In the afternoon, the Germans launched an attack on the northern flank of the Polish lines. The 4th Panzer Division and the Adolf Hitler SS-Leibstandarte unit were ordered to take the river crossings at Brochów and Solchaczew. The 'Wielkopolska' Cavalry Brigade was rushed at breakneck speed towards Brochów, and the 15th Uhlans were the first to approach the densely-populated town lying on the east bank of the Bzura. In the night the houses of Brochów were like black dots ahead of them, becoming steadily bigger as they approached. The planks of the bridge rattled under their hooves, and the dilapidated structure trembled as they thundered over it at a gallop. Brochów itself was separated from the river by a strip of flat meadowland about 0·5 km wide. Suddenly, enemy armoured cars appeared on the horizon. Their firing forced the Uhlans back over the river. However, when the Germans crossed the Bzura, the 7th Mounted Light Infantry advanced and drove them back beyond Brochów.

A scouting patrol in the Carpathians

The German 14th Army, under General List, was in Galicia, advancing in the direction of Przemyśl – and Lance-Corporal Hornes was with them in his reconnaissance unit. 'September 13. At 6 AM, the squadron came through Sambor. We closed up to start the craziest ride of our entire advance. At first, we moved smoothly forward. The sun shone relentlessly down on the scorching, dusty road. We rode on till midday. Already the Carpathians lay behind us, and the surrounding countryside was as flat as a pancake. We rode through a fairly broad stream to overtake the main column. Then on through a village, with houses burning to left and to right of us. We were scared that the horses might take fright, but they didn't take a blind bit of notice. It was scorchingly hot and we were even afraid that the horses might catch fire. Then we rode 'on through the night. The horses were stumbling, and the heads of the riders were nodding forward from tiredness. And still we kept slogging along that fearful road.

'Now it was pitch-dark, with the sky overcast for the first time since we'd entered Poland. It must have been around 11 PM, when we turned off from the road and into a forest track, where we were finally called to a halt. It was now so cold that we had to cover the horses up. As for us, we had no alternative but to lie down on the bare earth. But regardless of this we were so tired that we fell asleep immediately. I was put on "stable-guard" between one and two o'clock, which meant I had to keep watch on the horses, armed with a rifle. In the distance, the guns of Lvov could be heard thundering the whole night long. The field kitchen happened to arrive during my watch, and I was able to get a dishful of rice from it. It was only the next morning that we discovered that we had spent the whole night right between the lines of a Polish cavalry regiment. By an enormous stroke of luck we had come upon a part of the wood that wasn't occupied by the enemy.'

September 14 was the first rest day for the German 1st Mounted Regiment since the beginning of the war. The recce patrols established that there were weak Polish forces in Radzymin, but no opposition directly facing the regiment. So it was at last possible to get a few clothes clean and for the men themselves to have a good wash. But there were still difficulties over watering the horses: because of the exceptional drought, the springs and the water-courses were dry.

On September 14, the mounted reconnaissance unit of the 14th Army came upon Polish cavalry near Przemyśl. Lance-Corporal Hornes' account continues:

'In the morning, we were at last given a warm dinner. It was rice again, the second dishful I'd been able to get. In the nearby machine gun unit they pulled out an overcooked frog from the pan but luckily someone caught sight of it in time.... Probably for the first time since we crossed the frontier, the horses were groomed today. Suddenly at 10 AM we were ordered to saddle up. Apparently a Polish cavalry regiment was marching out from Przemyśl, trying to break through to Lvov. The hilly, wooded countryside was the type which could produce something unexpected out of the blue at any time, and we were forced to ride on cautiously. Two men were sent on ahead, keeping within eyesight. They would hurry at a gallop from one hill to the next, then wave the troop on. As another precaution, lone horsemen were sent out alongside us on the ridges of the hills. Suddenly, we saw new unfamiliar contours emerging from the thick dust-cloud: small, agile horses with bobbing heads, ridden by Polish Uhlans in their khaki uniforms, their long lances held with one end in the stirrup leather and the other slung from the shoulder. Their shining tips bobbed up and down in time with the horses' hooves. At the same moment, our machine guns opened fire and then came the crackle of rifle shots.'

The most valuable booty of the war

On Friday, September 15, on the orders of von Blaskowitz the Germans launched an operation along the entire Bzura front to destroy the two beleaguered Polish armies. The Polish cavalry was faced with a motorized enemy force of vastly superior strength. Waffen-SS General Kurt Meyer ('*Panzermeyer*') of the Adolf Hitler *Leibstandarte* unit commented later: 'It would not be fair on our part to deny the bravery of the Polish forces. The battles along the Bzura were fought with great ferocity and courage.'

The Polish cavalry, however, was short not only of arms, ammunition and food for both men and horses – it even lacked such basic necessities as maps of the region in which it was fighting. After the battle, Captain Z. Szacherski of the Polish 7th Mounted Light Infantry reported:

'There were dead Germans lying everywhere, on the road and in the ruined buildings. I gave my men orders to go through the Germans' map and trouser pockets in the faint hope of finding the maps which we needed so desperately. At last our search was rewarded: we found a map of the Brochów–Sochaczew area in the pocket of a dead NCO. For us, that was the most valuable booty of the entire war....'

On the small strip of land between the point where the Bzura flows into the Vistula, and the towns of Lowicz and Zychlin, there were now 12 large Polish formations of over 170,000 men in all, plus thousands of vehicles. There were also endless columns of refugees, uprooted by the ravages of the German artillery and Stuka attacks. On September 15, as the battle of the Bzura developed more and more into a defeat for the Poles, General Kutrzeba ordered that: 'Both the "Wielkopolska" and the "Podolska" cavalry brigades are now to form a *Grupa Operacyjna Kawalerii* (independent cavalry formation) under the command of General Abraham. The group is to clear the Kampinos forest and to open the road to Warsaw which has been in enemy hands since September 9.'

September 15. While it was relatively quiet around the 4th Squadron of the German 2nd Mounted Regiment and its neighbouring units, with only the occasional star shell bursting overhead, a great conflagration was raging around Fort XIII, in the Warsaw suburb of Praga. The old part of the city, lying high on the left bank of the Vistula, was lit up by the glare of countless fires. In between were the continuous flashes of artillery fire from the Polish batteries in the citadel and Saxony Park.

Saturday, September 16. During the morning, the 'Wielkopolska' Cavalry Brigade, with its two regiments, moved out from the Brochów area to the Kampinos forest. The 17th Uhlans rode ahead through the sparse birch trees as the spearhead of the main middle column. The ground was soft and sandy, in places giving way to bog. Their first obstacle was the Dembowskie woods. The 18th Uhlans struggled from 11 AM till 4 PM, finally managing to get through the forest and its clearings. On the night of September 16/17, at 1.30 AM, an order came from the military high command for the 1st Cavalry Brigade to assemble in the area of Wolomin. By the evening of the 17th, the brigade had occupied new ground around Ortsbiwak. After the heat of the day, the night air was startlingly cold. The cavalrymen unbuckled their rolled-up coats from their saddles and made themselves comfortable under the birch trees. Most of them, thoroughly exhausted, fell at once into a deep sleep. The sentries, left alone, marched up and down on the edge of the wood, rifles under their arms, glancing wistfully at their watches to see if it was time yet to wake the men who were to relieve them.

Through the Kampinos forest

On Sunday, September 17, the Russian armies were swarming over Poland's virtually unprotected eastern frontier and driving to the west along a broad front. On the 18th, they took Vilna, going on through to meet their German allies at Brest Litovsk. The Soviet troops continued their advance to the line previously agreed with Hitler. On this same day, the Kampinos forest was resounding to the sound of confused fighting as the battle moved hourly nearer to the Polish defenders at Bielany, near Warsaw. 'The Kampinos forest became the graveyard of the Poznan army,' said its commander, General Kutrzeba, after the battle. The heathland was suitable for infantry but not for mounted troops. The few winding forest tracks would often peter out, or suddenly descend into deep ravines. The cavalry regiments, which were hoping to find protection here from the ever-present Luftwaffe, found instead a forest of tall, thin conifers with no undergrowth – baked tinder-dry, and interspersed with broad sandy expanses where the horsemen became sitting targets for air attacks. The Polish troops, who were virtually without any aerial defence, were attacked by 820 planes – ordinary bombers and Stukas – which struck again and again, each aircraft making about five sorties a day. On September 17 alone, 328,000 kg of bombs were dropped during 4,100 raids on the two armies, the Poznan and the Pomorze, stuck between the Bzura and the Kampinos forest.

In the woods, isolated battle grounds were formed, with the cavalry units distributed over the entire area. The 7th Mounted Light Infantry Regiment was one of the mounted units which disengaged itself from the enemy after the battle of the Bzura and then headed in the direction of Warsaw through the Kampinos forest. The 'Wielkopolska' Cavalry Brigade was still moving onwards towards Gorki, where, with the help of a map found on one of the dead Germans at Brochów, it gave artillery support to the 7th Mounted Light Infantry.

Objective: Warsaw

Late on the evening of September 18, the 7th Mounted Light Infantry was positioned near the Dembowskie woods. The new regimental commander, Captain Szacherski, reported:

'At 9 PM I ordered the regiment to fall in at a clearing in front of the Dembowskie woods. I rode along the lines of the regiment, with its silent rows of horses. It was pitch-dark. In the sky above the clearing one could see the flashes of shells exploding in the forest. I had a few words with my men, indicated our objective – Warsaw – and described the difficult way ahead, stressing the need for special caution during the night march. They were neither to talk out loud nor to smoke. Each man was to keep close behind the man in front, and orders were to be passed on quietly from the head of the column to the tail. The squadrons were to provide their own protection for both flanks of the advance. Thus the column rode forward, with the horses nose to tail in close formation. I led on, with the help of the map captured from Brochów, at the head of the 2nd Squadron of the regiment.

'Following behind the 6th Uhlans, we passed through a forest of tall trees. From time to time, the column would gradually break into a trot, only to have to stop abruptly in its tracks a few moments later. It was a tiring business, which strained both men and horses alike. It was unpleasantly obvious that the 6th Uhlans, ahead of us, had no maps.

'The moon rose, bathing the countryside in a shimmering, milky luminescence. Far away to the south we heard the rumble of artillery fire. At each fork in the road, the column would come to a halt to make sure of the route. Holding the captured map and a compass in my hand, I led the regiments as far as the edge of the forest in the area of Stara Dabrowa.'

A miraculous escape

'It was September 18, and day was already breaking. Realizing the exhausted state of the men and horses, I ordered them to take a rest, and split up the regiment so that we would not be spotted in the forest from the air. I gave an order for the horses to be unsaddled, watered and fed as best they could be with what little there was. At 11 AM, the two regimental buglers gave the call for the horses to be saddled up once more. It was the last bugle call the regiment was to hear.

'We were in good spirits – the five hour rest had had its therapeutic effect. We went on our way refreshed. In the village of Cybulek, in the hills, we called a halt for a while – a plane was flying low over the tree tops, but it didn't open fire. Then we proceeded at a trot to the village of Duze Cybulice. As we approached, we heard artillery fire on its eastern side. We rode through the village without halting.

'Before us lay approximately two km of broad, sandy flat country stretching as far as the next village. The Germans were obviously watching us, directing their fire along the road and onto the fields lying on either side of it. I decided to lead the regiment in open formation to the next bit of cover. But it was not so easy for the artillery, and I had to have the guns drawn along the open road.

'I drew my sabre and gave the command: "Squadron follow on at the gallop!" And to the accompaniment of the low thunder of the guns, we raced off like the wind. I glanced to the left. In the distance I could see the steep far bank of the Vistula, dominating the entire region; it was from there that the German artillery was firing. We had put about 200 m behind us when the Germans intercepted the road with their firing, sending up a formidable barrage in front of the village of Czeczotki as we approached.

'I looked over my shoulder: the 17th Regiment was spread out as if on a parade ground, keeping its regulation distances in exemplary fashion. Close behind me at the head of the column were the regimental colours; ahead of me, a formidable screen of fire – a booming, moving wall of sand, dust, flames and iron. The regiment was steadily drawing nearer to this thunderous barrier. Though the horses were tired, the pitch of nervous tension induced the weaker beasts to keep up the tempo and the entire cavalcade careered directly at the screen of fire. We were nearly in their range – another 200 metres, another 150, and already scraps of shrapnel were whistling round our heads, with sand spurting into our eyes at every explosion. Then, suddenly, all was quiet. At the very same moment that we stared death right in the face, the Germans had ceased firing. Confused and disconcerted, we disappeared into the village and the cover of the trees.'

Both regiments of the 'Podolska' Cavalry Brigade reached the village of Czeczotki without a single casualty. Their miraculous escape has remained a mystery to this day.

One of the regiments of the 'Podolska' Cavalry Brigade, under Lieutenant-Colonel Gilewski, was already at the Hungarian frontier by September 19. He reported:

'As we rode along on this autumn morning through beautiful mountain scenery on our way to a foreign land, the atmosphere was overwhelming. My second-in-command, Major Starnawski, was weeping openly. For hours on end we rode without meeting a soul. Here and there would be the occasional overturned car or bus, and crates of burned-up documents as we rode along the gorge leading to the Wyszkowski pass. The regimental adjutant returned by motor-cycle with the announcement that the road was empty for some kilometres ahead. We were only a short way from the frontier when we came upon columns of men on the march and hundreds of vehicles. A few hills and valleys further on and we were facing the border. A Hungarian major came towards us with a greeting, asking us to convey to the Uhlans that they were to make themselves at home on Hungarian territory.'

The next day, the regiment gave up its weapons to the Hungarian authorities. For many Uhlans, this gesture was as emotive as the order to retreat. The 2nd, 3rd, and 4th Squadrons were the only ones which remained even vaguely intact.

'On September 21, we were invited to be the guests of the 3rd Hungarian Hussar Regiment at Mukachevo. There, in front of the barracks, the commander of the 3rd Regiment, the elderly Colonel von Pongratsch, was waiting along with his officer corps in ceremonial array. My regiment was given full honours as it marched on to the parade ground.'

A few days later, when the Uhlans set out for the internment camp at Putnok, the colonel of the hussars bade each Polish officer farewell with an embrace.

'Take the flag!'

The battle of the Kampinos forest raged for three days and three nights. On Tuesday, September 19, the Polish cavalry units under General Abraham reached the easternmost stretches of heath on the outskirts of Warsaw. During the night, his Uhlans and mounted light infantry succeeded in capturing Sieraków after heavy fighting. They then made repeated attacks on the village of Laski – the last obstacle on the road to the capital. But in spite of a battle lasting several hours, at times hard-fought with bayonet and pistol, the two cavalry regiments failed to break down the German defence.

Towards 5 PM, the commander of the 14th Uhlan Regiment, Colonel Godlewski, decided to launch a cavalry charge with the aim of breaking through the ring of German troops at Wólka Weglowa. The regiment took up battle positions in the nearby woods.

'I drew my sabre from its sheath and turned

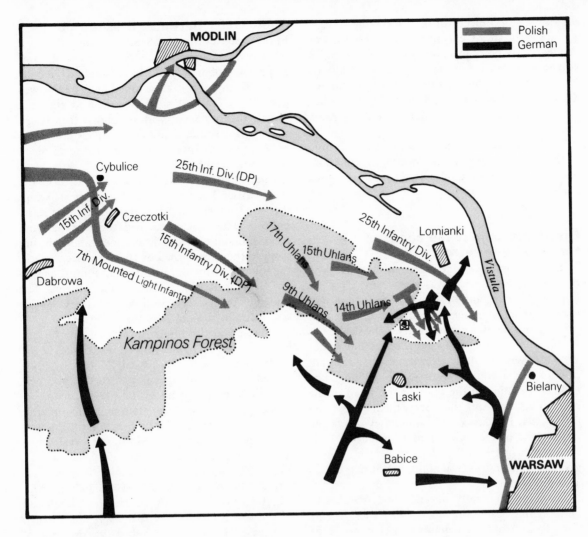

The Kampinos Forest, September 17–19, 1939: movement of Polish troops towards Warsaw.

round in my saddle. There on both sides I saw the pale faces of my men gathered closely round me.'

The standard-bearer, Corporal Maziarski, was galloping closely behind the regimental commander when his horse suddenly plunged to the ground. 'Take the flag!' he yelled out desperately. Corporal Czech, ignoring the hail of bullets, turned his horse round in its tracks, rode back, took up the regimental colours and hurried on behind the regiment. The 14th Uhlans pierced the German lines and in the early hours of September 20 became the first unit of the Poznan Army to reach Warsaw.

The other cavalry regiments of the *Grupa Operacyjna Kawalerii* managed to struggle on through to Warsaw only after heavy and bloody fighting, and the casualty toll was heavy. The cavalry, now dismounted, proceeded to play its part in the defence of the besieged capital.

The bodies of countless cavalrymen and their horses lay along the Bzura, at the fords and the pontoon bridges, along the hedges and in the pine plantations – and with them were the battered wrecks of thousands of military vehicles. By September 18 and 19, the two main Polish armies – the 'Poznan' and the 'Pomorze' – were no longer holding their own. The German generals Blaskowitz,

Kluge and Hoepner took 170,000 prisoners between them. The remaining Polish troops struggled on through the Kampinos forest towards Warsaw, following the lead of the cavalry. A small group managed to force its way into the stronghold of Modlin, which had been staunchly defended for days by its Polish garrison.

On September 20, the German 1st Cavalry Brigade was attached to the Army Corps for special duties. It was ordered to march in the east wing of the Army Corps, and to reach the area of Kaluszyn on the evening of September 20. The same day, the Army Corps turned across the Minsk–Latowice road westwards in the direction of the Vistula. The brigade was divided into two groups, one motorized and one in mounted column.

The last council of war

On Thursday, September 21 at 12 noon, just as Lvov was capitulating to the Red Army, the commanders of the big Polish cavalry units began a council of war destined to be the last in the long history of the Polish cavalry. It was held on the estate of Kraczków, south-east of Zamosc and about 130 km north of Lvov. Assembled there were

15

all the senior officers of the surviving cavalry groups in the area. General Anders – who was subsequently to become commander of the Polish forces in exile and victor at Monte Cassino – chaired the meeting. Another officer present was Colonel Komorowski, the former Olympic rider who was later to become leader of the Polish resistance movement.

'We separated and went back to rejoin our units without a further word. This meeting was our last – and deeply depressing. We could no longer look each other in the eye.'

Discipline amidst the chaos: the cavalry in retreat

In the remaining cavalry units, ammunition was running out and, what was worse, there was no hope of obtaining any more. At the most, it would last out for one more serious engagement. The pain of the long rides was getting worse. The saddle felt as if it were on fire, while both knees and ankles were torn with cramp from maintaining a constant position in the saddle and stirrups for so long. The endless pounding of the trot left the small of the back in agony. And the horses themselves fared little better. For days on end now, they had borne the weight of the saddle and baggage on their sweat-drenched backs, and they were no longer given a respite, not even at night, nor during breaks along the march.

The long, seemingly never-ending marches in the scorching heat of the sun, the scanty fodder and the lack of proper rest drained the last ounce of strength from the horses. Many of them had lost shoes and a large number of them were already lame. There was not a field-blacksmith to be found. From time to time, it was possible to find horseshoes in village shops, while at other times, they were wrenched from the hooves of dead horses. For a considerable period, they had had no proper large-scale maps and instead the troops were having to rely on inaccurate atlases found in village schools or local council offices. The horsemen were dropping with exhaustion; for the last three weeks they had undergone an almost unbroken sequence of forced marches and battles.

Against a background of utter chaos, the Polish cavalry retained its discipline to an astonishing degree – despite losses from air, artillery and infantry attacks. The cavalry struggled through to the end in immaculate order, making for the Hungarian frontier, and even at this late stage managing to score some successes.

On September 21, the German 1st Cavalry Brigade received the special task of taking over the defence of the left wing of the Army Corps, in connection with the siege of Warsaw. Both cavalry regiments reached their new positions that morning. And it was at that point, to all intents and purposes, that the role of the German 1st Cavalry Brigade in the Polish campaign came to an end.

The cavalry battle at Krasnobród

In the early morning of September 23, what was probably the last cavalry battle of the Polish campaign was fought in the fields surrounding the small town of Krasnobród, close to Lublin. The 'Nowogrodzka' Cavalry Brigade approached the area shortly before sunrise, with the 25th Uhlan Regiment as its advance guard. The Uhlans proceeded to engage the German troops who had surrounded the entire neighbourhood.

The situation developed like wild fire: in the thick ground mist, the 2nd Squadron swept through the German defences to advance on Krasnobród. The Uhlans reached the first outlying farm buildings before heavy machine-gun fire stopped them. Surprised by the unforeseen attack, the soldiers of the 8th Infantry Division (Lieutenant-General Koch) evacuated the village. The leader of the 1st Squadron (Lieutenant Gerlecki) sent his Uhlans on in pursuit of the Germans.

The 1st Squadron hurried forward, the Uhlans riding their small light-brown horses, lances at the ready. With a great bellowed 'Hurraaah!' they surged on in a headlong gallop, their flat, steel helmets protecting their necks and the dreaded four-edged spike of their lances glinting in the sunlight. Then, as the Germans sought shelter on the hill near the monastery, a force of East Prussian cavalrymen suddenly appeared. With Gerlecki at their head, the 1st and 2nd Squadrons closed ranks, lowered their lances and rushed directly at the German horsemen, who were just forming up on the hill. A bugle call rang out and there was a roar from the Uhlans: 'Hurraaah!' Drawn sabres flashed over the heads of the German cavalrymen as the bulk of their force veered ponderously down from the high ground with growing momentum. Clearly the Germans, with their heavy warhorses, were simply aiming to run down their enemies in a headlong downhill gallop. But the Poles saw a chance in the manœuvrability of their lighter mounts. A fraction of a second later, the troopers were crashing together in an ear-splitting *mêlée* of sound. The noise of the battle drowned the cries of the wounded animals. More and more horses with empty saddles could be seen wandering around the surrounding fields. The noise quietened and then rose again, punctuated by the crack of isolated revolver shots.

In the midst of the turmoil, a German officer had at the very outset forced Uhlan Lewczuk's light horse to the ground with his own massive stallion, striking the Polish soldier's arm with his sabre as he fell. The German must have been a superb horseman and fighter, for he then proceeded to deal with several Polish Uhlans who blocked his way, with no apparent difficulty, and he then confronted Lieutenant Gerlecki, whom he probably saw to be the leader of the Poles. It is hard to say how the duel might have developed, had not Corporal Mikolajewski come up from behind at the last moment, toppling the German with a sabre-thrust. After that, the German cavalrymen withdrew from the struggle and galloped uphill to the monastery – hotly pursued by the two Polish squadrons.

The confused group of pursuers and their prey clattered past the monastery towards the nearby woodland. For the Poles, this was a disastrous move, for it exposed them to a crossfire from the German machine-gunners. Seconds later, the meadow was strewn with dead riders and their horses. Lieutenant Gerlecki fell to the ground, and the Uhlans were overcome with panic. Corporal Mikolajewski had the presence of mind to lead the remaining cavalrymen to the lee of a small hillock where they were protected from the machine-gun fire. Only 30 Uhlans and 25 horses were saved. The horse's vulnerability to the fire of automatic weapons had been demonstrated yet again.

The phantom squadron

From September 18, the 110th Uhlan Regiment of the Reserve Cavalry Brigade, on its way from the Grodno area, had been riding behind the Germans towards Warsaw, hoping to find a bigger Polish unit somewhere to which it could attach itself. However, on the night of September 23/24, Colonel Dabrowski gave up at Janów, near Lomza, and allowed the regiment to disband. Thereupon, Major Henryk Dobrzanski announced:

'I am taking over the command and will bring the regiment to Warsaw.'

Major Dobrzanski was a lover of fast horses, beautiful women and good wine – and was among Poland's foremost horsemen. He had won the International Horse Tournament at Nice in 1925, and

Poland, September–October 1939: the major engagements of the Polish cavalry.

1. Cavalry charge, near Krojanty, September 1.
2. Cavalry patrols enter East Prussia, September 2/3 and 4.
3. Battle of the Bzura, September 10–17.
4. Battles in the Kampinos Forest, September 18–20.
5. Battle near Krasnobród, September 23.
6. Battle near Morance, September 26.
7. General Anders' troops engage the Red Army near Dernaki, September 27.
8. Battle near Kock, October 1–5.

had later repeated his triumph in London and Rome. He had been honoured by the King of England with the accolade 'he achieved the best individual score out of all the officers of all nations'.

The news of Warsaw's capitulation reached Major Dobrzanski's small force when they had already reached the outskirts of the capital. Dobrzanski and his men reacted to the news by plunging into the woods along the right bank of the Vistula, and then marching to the south-west to cross the river near Lublin. They then vanished into the thick forests of the Kielce region, between the Vistula and Pilica. Their first coup came during a halt near the village of Chodków, when they chanced upon the truck of a German signal-corps unit which had got stuck in difficult going. They charged the vehicle at a gallop; its crew were slaughtered after putting up a desperate defence, and only one German managed to escape. The Polish losses amounted to two dead. From then on, the Germans were never rid of Major Dobrzanski's men. They vowed never to shed their uniforms until Poland was free once more.

Polish cavalry against the Red Army

As from Sunday, September 17, the Polish cavalry were faced with a new and powerful enemy: the 24 infantry divisions, nine armoured brigades, and 15 cavalry divisions of the advancing Red Army. The Red Army horsemen would appear suddenly at any point where poor roads slowed the advance of the Soviet tanks and infantry. The Polish cavalry was under orders not to be the first to open fire when Red Army units came on the scene. For all that, the Soviet forces were capturing any Polish troops they encountered and ruthlessly subdued any who didn't want to surrender.

The *Grupa Operacyjna Kawalerii* led by General Anders was nevertheless pushing forward towards Hungary. On September 26, the 'Wilenska' Cavalry Brigade, which was attached to this group, was caught by a surprise Soviet attack at Leszczesnen. The brigade's commander was severely wounded and taken prisoner. However, one of the squadrons under Captain Lichtarowicz was able to counter-attack and free the prisoners. Next morning, the Russians attacked a patrol of the 1st Uhlan Regiment at Pralnicki, wounding two Uhlans, while the Red Army forces themselves lost a few men. When the Soviets attempted to attack the 'Nowogrodzka' Cavalry Brigade, they were decisively beaten back by the 5th and 10th Uhlan regiments. On Monday, September 26, the 'Nowogrodzka' Brigade, which two days before had been reinforced with the remains of the 'Wilenska' Cavalry Brigade, continued its march to the south-east, encountering parts of the German 28th Infantry Division (Lieutenant-General von Obstfelder). The 25th and 27th Uhlan Regiments tried to break through the menacing ring of enemy forces with an attack on the village of Morance.

However, their charge collapsed in the face of heavy machine-gun fire.

Suddenly, though, the thunder of the guns was interrupted by bugle calls. Three horsemen dressed in field-grey were approaching from Morance with a white flag. The officers with the flag of truce proposed that the Poles should lay down their arms as their position was hopeless and they wanted to avoid further bloodshed. General Anders consented on condition that his *Grupa Operacyjna Kawalerii* should be guaranteed safe conduct through to the Hungarian frontier.

Colonel Schweizer accompanied the German representatives to the staff of the 28th Infantry Division, returning after a while with a written statement from its commanding officer:

'The 28th Infantry Division grants permission to the Polish cavalry to march freely to the south. In return, the Polish cavalry is to allow units of the 28th Infantry free passage to the west. However, if other German forces encounter the cavalry, they will attack.'

The *Grupa Operacyjna Kawalerii* continued on its way without delay. Two days later, it was to be virtually wiped out by the Red Army. The commanding officer, General Anders, was wounded and taken off to the Moscow prison of Lublyanka. General Anders wrote later:

'On September 26, I decided to march southwards. There were German positions around the village of Broszki on the main Jaworow–Jaroslaw highway. A single German shot rang out, followed promptly by the rattle of machine-gun fire. The column had no chance to pull out. I ordered the regiments in front – the 25th and 27th Uhlans – to launch a cavalry charge. The Germans were taken so entirely by surprise that we were able to capture a large proportion of the battalion. The commander of the 28th Infantry Division once more sent out envoys with the proposal that we should surrender. He maintained that it would be impossible for us to continue our march, as the whole countryside was already occupied both by the Germans and by the approaching Soviet Army.

'At sunrise on September 27, I decided that we should nevertheless press on, endeavouring to slip through between the Germans and the Russians. During the attempt, we encountered a strong Soviet force which immediately opened fire with artillery. Then the first tanks appeared. Our 9th Regiment of horse artillery returned the fire, demonstrating their well-known accuracy. The 9th Regiment, together with our anti-tank weapons, succeeded in destroying a good number of Soviet tanks. But by now the heavily-armed Russian hordes barring our way forward were clearly visible. At this point, we were only 40 km from the border with Hungary. The Soviet forces were attacking us ever more heavily from the rear. The artillery fired off their last rounds; likewise our small-arms ammunition was exhausted. There were no field-dressings. The horses had gone without food and water for a long time. We had no alternative but to split up into small groups, and make our way through the forests under cover of night, trying to reach Hungary. The chances of succeeding were slim.'

After eastern Galicia was occupied by the Red Army, the German 14th Army (General List) withdrew westwards, marching through Przemyśl. Lance-Corporal Hornes noted in his diary:

'September 27. We were pleased at not having to get up before 6 AM. It was some time since we'd enjoyed our first march through a sizeable Polish town, but we wanted at least to show off in Przemyśl as the victors. It was a proud moment – German cavalry, leading victoriously through the conquered towns!'

On Thursday, September 28, the defenders of Warsaw under General Rommel capitulated with 120,000 men, General Abraham's cavalry among them. One day later, the Uhlans rode their emaciated horses in long files to the prisoner-of-war assembly points. As the troopers surrendered their arms and were taken prisoner, the horses, having lost their masters, followed loyally behind.

Sergeant-Major Greifenberg and his reconnaissance division reached the German–Soviet demarcation line on September 29.

'We rode off at 6 AM for about a kilometre until we came to the railway bridge over the river San, then made our way to the middle of the bridge. It was blocked by a barrier of barbed wire and tree-trunks. We wanted to see the Russian soldiers for ourselves. Along the river, there was one Russian outpost after another. Most of them were sheltering in caves, willow thickets or behind haystacks. On the other side of the San there were more Russian positions. We gave them a friendly wave.'

Will the cavalry surrender?

On Friday, September 29, the stronghold of Modlin, on the Vistula, under General Thommée, surrendered and on Sunday, October 1, the 4,000 men belonging to the Polish naval units under Rear-Admiral Unrug on the Hela peninsula gave themselves up. Poland's entire territory was now occupied by German and Soviet troops. Polish forces had virtually ceased to exist; a small proportion had been able to escape to Romania, Hungary, Lithuania and Latvia, but the bulk of them were in German captivity, while around 200,000 were in Russian hands.

At this time, the beginning of October, the 'Polesie' Independent Operational Group (SGO) was just beginning its biggest operation. It included both the *Grupa Operacyjna Kawalerii* and the 'Podlaska' Cavalry Brigade. The cavalry units at its disposal were the 1st, 2nd, 5th, and 10th Uhlans, the 3rd Light Cavalry Regiment, the 3rd and 9th Mounted Light Infantry, the cavalry section of the Frontier Guard Corps and the 4th Horse Artillery – a force comprising a total of around 5,000 cavalry-

men. In addition to these, the 'Polesie' group included the 50th 'Brzoza' Infantry Division and the 60th 'Kobryn' Infantry Division, together with a few old sports aircraft of the RWD type used for communications. All in all, it numbered around 1,200 officers and 15,000 men, scarcely more than a single German division.

Battle-hardened by their recent experiences, the troops entertained no thought of laying down their arms. As both cavalry formations tried to make their way through to the Hungarian frontier, they found themselves involved in constant battles with Soviet patrols from the east, and with German units from the west. They were moving against the flow of refugees and soldiers who had been set free by the Germans and were now returning home. All these were astonished at the sight of the advancing cavalrymen, who were singing as they made their way southwards on their emaciated horses, still in orderly formation and with their weapons shining.

On October 2 at Kock, not far from Lublin in central Poland, the 'Polesie' group encountered the German 13th Motorized Infantry Division (Lieutenant-General Otto) which was to support the 29th Motorized Infantry Division (Lieutenant-General Lemelsen) in the last phase of the campaign. In front of the village of Serokomla, there was an extended struggle between the Poles and the German advance guard. The Uhlans dismounted, using bayonets in the hand-to-hand-fighting, and took about 200 prisoners, while three German armoured cars were left ablaze in front of the Polish lines.

On Tuesday, October 3, the Poles as well as the Germans opened up with artillery fire before sunrise. A few battalions of the 50th 'Brzoza' Infantry Division engaged German outposts from the direction of Kock, and at Pojazdów attacked the artillerymen with machine-gun fire Further afield, however, the Poles were right in the German firing line and the infantry was forced to retreat with heavy losses. Later, towards noon, a mounted cavalry charge also had to be abandoned even though it had made some initial headway.

Thursday, October 5. While the German troops were marching past Hitler to the strains of 'Prussia's Glory' in a victory parade in Warsaw, a battle was raging in all parts of the valley around Kock some 110 km to the south-east. It was increasing in ferocity, and the fortunes of the combatants were changing. The Poles – and especially the dismounted cavalry – were making isolated inroads on the German positions, fighting at close quarters. But towards noon, supplies of artillery ammunition began to run out, the soldiers tired, and the Germans began to deploy more and more troops. At 7.30 PM, General Kleeberg gave his men the order to lay down their arms:

'It is one of the privileges of a commanding officer to carry responsibility. Today, in this most difficult hour, I take it upon myself, and order that the battle should be abandoned so as to avoid further bloodshed.'

At first, the commanders of the cavalry units were loath to obey the order to surrender. They argued that for them, there was still a chance of getting through to Hungary. Indeed, the Polish spokesmen negotiating the truce were finally forced to admit that it was uncertain whether the cavalry would in fact capitulate. Thereupon, General Otto declared:

'In that case, I regard these talks as not having taken place – we will fight on!'

October 6, 10 AM. After weeks of sunny weather, the skies were now heavily overcast. The Polish forces marched to the assembly points to surrender their arms. Colonel Grzeszkiewiecz reported:

'On the high ground, protected by a heavy machine gun, were the German general and his staff. General Kleeberg and his chief of staff got out, and I followed. The German general introduced himself as General Otto. He then asked: "Is the cavalry surrendering?" "Yes," replied Kleeberg.'

On the Rhine and in the Ardennes

The phoney war

By September 1939, the French *3e Division Légère de Cavalerie*, under General Robert Marie Petiet, formerly head of the famous Saumur riding school, had already been detailed to cover the Luxembourg border. The cavalry units under the general's command were to reconnoitre the area, smash any minor enemy opposition and – if it came to a retreat – to carry out an extensive programme of destruction to slow the German advance. Most important of all, the reinforced *3e Division Légère de Cavalerie* was 'to carry out a lightning attack (*une action à caractère de raid*) into Luxembourg' if the German Army should endanger that country's neutrality.

In the second half of October, the *3e Brigade de Cavalerie* was moved from the area of Felbach on the Swiss border to the Ardennes near the Belgian border. It was to defend the region between Carignan and Avioth. The dragoons and colonial Spahi regiments placed under the *3e Division Légère* were involved in intensive reconnaissance activity in the areas adjoining the Maginot Line. From time to time they encountered enemy forces, but this rarely led to any serious clash. It was only in two or three sectors that the tacit agreement between the German and French troops to hold their fire was broken with any frequency, as at Apach on the Luxembourg border, for instance, and in the area of Forbach. On the other side the German 16th, 26th and 169th Mounted Reconnaissance Battalions were attached to units assigned to guarding the Luxembourg frontier, while the 6th and 86th Battalions were sent to patrol the Lorraine border. They had instructions to withdraw behind their battle positions if faced with a superior enemy force. They were expressly ordered not to violate the frontier and to use firearms only if the other side opened fire first.

The '*drôle de guerre*', or phoney war, was strongly in evidence during October. The Germans were constantly saturating the French troops on the front with propaganda, using loudspeakers and placards: 'Why die for Danzig, for the Poles, for the British?' 'Don't shoot! We won't shoot if you don't.' The French troops along the Rhine had long since been expressly forbidden to shoot at the Germans. General Gamelin said: 'Open fire on German work parties? The Germans would just fire back at us!' The 'front' itself – north from Basel along the Rhine and then running on to the west of the river to Luxembourg – was normally as quiet as a churchyard. The stillness of the night would only occasionally be disturbed by a sentry on patrol or a grenade exploding.

The French troops were accommodated in miserable quarters in Alsace and in the Ardennes, sleeping in barns on rotting straw. Thousands of cavalry horses died of a mysterious sickness possibly resulting from the careless way they were looked after by the troops. The bad weather proved a good excuse to abandon half-finished manœuvres and to break off defence preparations. The soldiers crowded into the bars with time hanging heavy on their hands.

On September 27, Hitler announced to the Army High Command his intention of launching an attack on the west as soon as possible. The date scheduled for the offensive was November 12, but this was soon altered on account of rain setting in. Hitler was anxious to strike only in good weather, so that the Luftwaffe and tanks could score the same outstanding successes as they had in Poland. The autumn of 1939, however, was appalling. In November it began to teem with rain, the rivers were swollen and the flooded plains made rapid movement impossible for the Panzer columns.

The phantom squadron refuses to surrender

The dismal autumn weather and the endless harrying was also proving wearisome to the 'last' Uhlans under Major Dobrzanski in the woods of Kielce. Their numbers had steadily dwindled, and when the group reached the Zychy forest, near Radoszczyce, only ten die-hards remained. But even these few, riding in full uniform from village to village just like in the old times, left a deep impression on the local inhabitants.

'At the beginning of November 1939, news was circulating of a group of mounted Polish troops in the woods to the east of the Pilica, based at the Holy Cross convent in the Lysa Gara ... in the middle of November, there were further rumours claiming that uniformed Poles had been appearing in forest villages around Kronskie,' reported Dr Heinrich Schreihage, the officer attached to the German 372nd Infantry Division in charge of investigating the enemy position.

Major Dobrzanski, now known as 'Hubal', set about expanding his group. He recruited four men from the district and a village beauty, 20-year-old Marianna Cel ('Tereska'), and from this cadre formed the *Oddzial Wydzielony Wojska Polskiego* (Special Section of the Polish Army). In the middle of November 1939, Hubal decided to establish contact with the official leader of the underground movement. He borrowed a forester's Sunday suit and travelled to Warsaw with false papers. His section was likewise on the move: one part was on leave, while the other made its way into the deep woods near Spala, the headquarters of the German eastern regional commander, General Blaskowitz.

The Winter War begins

A birthday salute

Finland, November 30, 1939. Soviet aircraft appeared over Helsinki, bombing the town without any previous declaration of war. This unprovoked attack by the Soviet Union on a small, peaceful neighbouring country evoked passionate indignation from the outside world. The Soviet attackers then directed their attention to the Finnish frontier defences on the Karelian isthmus – the 'Mannerheim Line' which ran 140 km north to south through forest areas deep in snow. This defence line had a symbolic significance for the Finns.

On December 1, Lieutenant Toiviainen of the Finnish cavalry was celebrating his 45th birthday at the frontier post near Artahuhta. His cavalrymen had come to congratulate him. The officer had just completed his speech of thanks when the sound of machine-gun fire rattled out from Myllyjärvi.

'That must be my friend Molotov ordering the lads to fire off a salute in my honour. Let's go!' said Toiviainen. His cavalry unit galloped off to join up with the 15th Defence Guards at Myllyjärvi. But it soon become clear that they were in no position to halt the Soviet attack. As they withdrew to Artahuhta they strayed repeatedly into the Soviet line of fire. A cavalryman slipped behind the enemy lines, killed the machine-gunner, took his place and fired back throughout the night at the Soviets before his ploy was discovered.

The 'Nurmo' Squadron

On the evening of December 1, Cavalry Lieutenant Kaarlo Parvianinen, commander of the 'Nurmo' Squadron, and his men were also drawn into the war. 'We rode along the edge of the road, passing Karelians fleeing before the enemy – old men, women, and children. The skies were grey with smoke. Our unit had assembled in Oravankyto in the first days of December and in the middle of the month we were transferred to Hirvisaari.'

On December 5, the Soviet forces continued their attack against the isthmus between Lake Suula and Lake Perk. The 'Hämeen' Cavalry Regiment, despatched to defend the isthmus, was forced to abandon its positions after bitter fighting.

Finland, with only 3,500,000 inhabitants, a peacetime army of three infantry divisions, one cavalry brigade, 96 serviceable aircraft and a small anti-aircraft artillery force, set about its defence with determination. Many of its troops were taciturn peasants, who were affected little by the bleak nights in the Taiga at temperatures of between 30 and 40 degrees below zero. They moved around through the trackless countryside on shaggy horses, on snow-shoes or on sleighs; they armed themselves with petrol bombs – molotov cocktails – and sought out any opportunity for close combat using sub-machine guns or daggers. But their supreme commander, 73-year-old Field-Marshal Carl Gustav Mannerheim, a former Tsarist general and an experienced strategist, knew that he could not beat the Russians and that the most the Finns could hope to achieve was to stop their advance.

From the very beginning, the Soviet Union deployed about 45 divisions, comprising more than 650,000 troops, 1,000 vehicles and 2,500 aircraft; and reinforcements were soon added. It was easy for the Soviet division which attacked Petsamo to force back the 700 Finns who were in the area. Generally, however, the attack on Finland's narrowest stretch of territory proved catastrophic for the invaders. The gently undulating countryside was thickly covered with pine forests, there was a thick, hard layer of snow, and the cold was horrific. The Finns were well equipped with skis and warm clothing – both of which the Russians lacked. Moreover the Finns turned out to be eager for battle and brilliant at patrolling the forest terrain. It was the harshest winter there since 1892/93. The bitter frosts and ensuing blizzards were a daunting obstacle for the Soviet army vehicles, while contact between their infantry and air force was frequently hampered by low-lying cloud.

Realizing that the Mannerheim Line as a whole was unassailable, the Soviets then directed their attack along Finland's eastern border, which was more than 1,600 km long, stretching between Lake Ladoga and the Arctic Ocean. On December 17 it appeared as if the Soviet plan would succeed – but nevertheless, the widely-separated Soviet columns were halted. Towards the end of December, the Soviet aim of breaking through the narrowest part of the border past the Mannerheim Line and the Karelian isthmus was finally wrecked. And to the north of Lake Ladoga an attempted outflanking movement by about two Soviet divisions suffered the same fate as the operations in the far north.

The Finnish 'Nurmo' Squadron under Lieutenant Kaarlo Parvianinen celebrated Christmas in Hirvisaari – a small village near to the Mannerheim Line. On Christmas Eve, the paraffin lamps had already been extinguished when the alarm was sounded. Within a few minutes, the squadron was gathered in the stables and saddling up. The full moon was shining in a bright starry sky; the thermometer showed − 44 degrees. It turned out later to be a false alarm. On the second night of Christmas, the squadron rode through Kiviniemi to Sakkola Pannusaari, where they were billeted. The Soviet forces had already advanced through Suvanto towards Kelja.

'It came to nothing, however, for the enemy needed a break just as much as us,' reported Parvianinen. 'We stayed in Pannusaari and set about the necessary defence preparations. A few of us took part in a month-long course on forest warfare held in Konitsa district.'

Stalin now recognized that the Soviet Union was faced with an enemy of a totally unexpected sort. He decided to concentrate his efforts on the Mannerheim Line, where a massive artillery and tank force might in the end be able to gain the upper hand. Such a plan required extensive preparation. So towards the end of the year, action came to a halt along the entire Finnish front.

Christmas in Poland

On December 24, Major Dobrzanski-Hubal returned from Warsaw after meeting the head of the resistance movement, General Tokarzewski. In the Bielawy forest, his cavalry unit sat down to its Christmas dinner, with a great deal of alcohol and music and a richly-laden table – and on the wall, the red and white national flag of Poland. All this took place not far from Spala, the old hunting lodge of the tsars which now formed General Blaskowitz's base. At midnight, a few of Hubal's men marched in full uniform through the deep snow to attend mass in the monastery of Poswietny, a few kilometres away, where German occupying troops also had an outpost. Father Mucha, who was celebrating the mass, was so impressed that the next day he decided to become chaplain to the group.

In the new year, 1940, the Hubal group moved its base to Galki, about 15 km east of Opoczno. The nearby crossroads, where the Petrikow–Radom road joined the Nowe Miasto–Konskie road, offered a good communications network in all directions; the village itself was superbly protected from surprise attacks by the Germans, as it was situated in thickly-wooded countryside, with defence positions in the hills to the north. Heavy snowfalls in December made it unapproachable.

Hubal (nicknamed 'Schimmelmajor' – the white horse major – by the Germans) was the first partisan leader of World War II, although he still regarded himself as the commanding officer of a regular unit of the Polish Army. As he himself said, his cavalry group was to form 'the bridge from autumn to springtime', symbolizing the continuing struggle of the Polish Army until in spring, 1940, the French forces would begin their Rhine offensive against Germany to overthrow Hitler's Reich.

1940

In the forests

Mounted bandits

'At around noon on January 10, 1940, we were in the Smogorzowo area, on our way back to our battalion after buying in provisions from the surrounding villages, when suddenly a group of about nine horsemen appeared from the woods, forcing us at gunpoint to halt our truck,' Sergeant-Major Wolfgang Leirich of the German 650th Infantry Battalion reported. 'The bandits were wearing various Polish uniforms, complete with marks of rank, field-service caps with eagle insignia, and one of them bore the sword straps of an officer. Their weapons consisted of eight 98k rifles, one light machine gun, several German hand grenades, and all the horsemen had Polish-type cavalry sabres. They ordered us to abandon our truck and seized our weapons (three 98k rifles, and 08 pistol with ammunition). They ignored my warning that the possession of any arms by the Poles was punishable by death. Further losses sustained by our unit consisted of: 555 fresh farm eggs, 23 lb of butter, 10 lb of curd cheese, a dish of honey of about 2·5 l. The mounted bandits left us standing there in the open and made off towards the west.'

At the beginning of the year, the Hubal group moved to Anielin, and then, in February, on to Galki. It sent out mounted patrols, riding in extended line in search of weapons and equipment. A great deal had been left behind in the surrounding forests, for it was in this area that the 'Prusy' army had surrendered in September 1939. After the heavy snows of the harsh winter, the remote village of Galki was now starting to resemble an arsenal. It could be reached only by sleigh, and even then the going was extremely tough. Hubal's men began to prepare for a spring campaign.

The daily routine

The group was ruled by the major with iron discipline. He divided it into sub-sections, with sentries and patrols working round the clock. Everyone was under orders to shave daily and to wear clean uniforms; the major himself was the only member of the group to wear a beard. Correspondence and daily orders were sealed with official stamps. Supplies and provisions for the men were organized systematically, with the local people eagerly helping out, even in the most remote areas. The group's operational territory, between Kielce in the south and the bend of the river Pilica in the north-west, covered about 100 km, as the crow flies. The men were under orders not to attack the Germans. The Uhlans, in their borrowed fur coats, were not easy to distinguish from civilians.

One day, as they were drawing three sleighs full of weapons through deep snow along a track no wider than the runners of the sledges, they were confronted by German soldiers coming towards them. They were ordered to move back to make way for the Germans. One of the German soldiers made as if to strike the driver of the leading sleigh with his rifle-butt. Then later, after the Polish group had moved off to fetch their guns, the Germans turned in their tracks as if suspecting something, and hurried away.

The Hubal group's agents in the capital, some 200 km to the north, were two Warsaw girl students. They provided the horsemen with medical supplies, warm clothing and uniforms. These were procured from a big military hospital, where wounded Polish soldiers were glad to exchange their uniforms for civilian clothes which they would be able to use on their release.

There had been no significant activity on the part of the Germans all through the winter. It was not until March, when it became warmer and the snow started to thaw, that occasional reconnaissance flights were resumed by the Luftwaffe. As it turned out, the first member of the Hubal group to be killed did not die from a German bullet; he was struck when two Hubal patrols ran into each other in fog and opened fire.

Life in Galki was starting to take on the routine of a military barracks. Reveille was sounded early, so that the entire squadron was ready for its daily duties and on guard against any possible German attack. Field manœuvres began after breakfast and continued into the afternoon, then came the orders of the day and free time before the Last Post. There was no field canteen, so each man fended for himself in his own quarters, using his allotted rations. The local peasants often lent a helping hand, and, in return, during their free time the soldiers helped out in the fields with their horses. The long winter evenings were spent frequently in heated argument over a glass of schnapps and a game of cards. Many of the Hubal group were keen on photography, and years later, the Gestapo at Radom were to find the numerous group-photos of great assistance in their work.

23

The end of the 'Nurmo' Squadron

By the end of January, the Red Army had succeeded in penetrating deep into northern Finland. But on the isthmus of Karelia, their attempts to break through the Mannerheim Line met with consistent failure. The second Soviet offensive started on February 11 between the lakes of Muolaa and Kuolema, with blanket shelling from a thousand guns. Soviet combat units with cavalry support made nightly flanking attacks, crossing the thick layer of ice on both coasts of the isthmus. At Summa they finally succeeded in breaking through; this forced the Finns to withdraw their southern wing to the area east of Vyborg.

On the south bank of the Vuoksi, the 'Nurmo' Squadron listened to the distant thunder of the Soviet artillery which had been pounding the Finnish positions behind the forests on the main Russian front for hours on end.

'Our squadron was not transferred to Vuosalmi until the end of January,' wrote Lieutenant Parvianinen. 'This time we were in Himotunkangas, where the horses were kept in field stables which gave them no protection from the elements; in addition there were two or three small dugouts. A few days passed, until we were again given orders to march on. The horses, however, stayed behind with their grooms.

'There was a vast amount of snow; we worked our way along the bank of the Vuoksi on skis, then on towards Lake Muolaa. The unit was under orders to cover the retreat of our own troops from Muolaa. And it was there that the "Nurmo" Squadron had its first encounter with the enemy – one from which all the "Nurmo" men of this patrol returned unharmed. In the meantime, however, enemy aircraft had spotted our position and from then on attacked again and again throughout the day. On the evening of March 1, when we left the area on the bank of the Little Vuoksi to move into new quarters, our squadron was still intact, with only one horse wounded by shrapnel.'

On March 3, the Soviet 7th Army launched its big new offensive against the Karelian isthmus, concentrating its attack on the Vyborg area. The next day, the 'Nurmo' Squadron was ordered to head towards Vuosalmi on skis once more. The horses stayed behind with their grooms on the bank of the Little Vuoksi.

It was a sunny, frosty day, and the Red Army had just made its first significant gains in the Vuosalmi area: it had occupied the hills of Äyräpää and was thus able to attack Vasikkasaari from the rear. The 'Nurmo' Squadron – together with the 8th Light Cavalry – was given the task of recapturing these hills. Beginning on March 5, the assault developed into a fierce closely-fought battle with heavy casualties on both sides. Yard by yard, the 'Nurmo' men edged forward. The snow-covered slope was ploughed into a muddy sludge by the fighting. Neither side showed any mercy; and the Russians, as well as the Finns, fought courageously,

holding onto their line with grim determination. Entrenched on the dominating Äyräpää hill, they struck back at the Finns relentlessly. Then the Finns ran out of ammunition. The squadron was forced to withdraw, leaving behind 44 dead, among them the commanding officer, Olavi Peltola. In the bitter frosty night of March 6, a band of troopers was to be seen trudging wearily over the Karelian isthmus, by the light of the moon and the enemy star shells. It was the 'Nurmo' Squadron leading its horses from the fighting area.

By March 7, one Finnish soldier in five was either dead, wounded, or missing. All available Finnish reserves had now been brought into the fighting arena and although the little nation was fighting with a courage born of desperation, it was being forced to recognize the superior strength of a giant power and the end was already in sight. Field-Marshal Mannerheim recommended that negotiations should be opened with Moscow, since it was no longer possible to argue that Finland should continue what was now a hopeless struggle.

On March 8, the Finns formed a unit of precisely 30 men from the survivors of the 'Nurmo' Squadron. This depleted group went on over the ice of the Vuoksi on the night of March 9, to take on the defence of a half-kilometre sector of the front. Though they were tired and hungry, they managed to repulse all attackers.

On the evening of March 13, 1940, a group of exhausted and unshaven troopers were sitting by the warmth of a camp-fire on the northern bank of the Vuoksi: the last remnants of the 'Nurmo' Cavalry Squadron. When the troops of the Red Army reached their positions after the cease-fire, none could believe that these few men had managed to hold their own against an entire regiment.

The lull before the storm

By the beginning of March 1940, Major Hubal's 'Special Section' of cavalry partisans had grown considerably, with 312 troopers now on its roll. Preparations were under way for the swearing-in of recruits when on March 13, Colonel Okulicki, overall commander of the ZWZ – then a well-established and sizeable resistance organization – arrived in Galki with orders for the Hubal group to dissolve. 'It is still too early for any sort of partisan action, which, on account of the large number of German military forces in occupation, would undoubtedly lead to severe reprisals against the innocent public.' After the order to demobilize became known, the special section shrank to 70 men. Major Hubal, taken aback by the order, moved these die-hards to new quarters in the village of Hucisko, a few kilometres away, taking 18 machine guns and several crates of grenades. Once again, an envoy was sent from Warsaw with the same order; but this time, the errand nearly cost the messenger his life: the white-horse major was

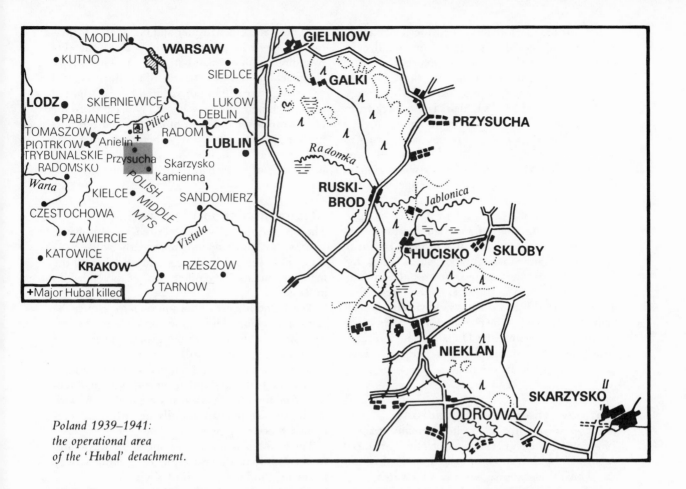

Poland 1939–1941:
the operational area
of the 'Hubal' detachment.

furious and wanted to shoot the man – but then thought better of it and threw him out, telling him to go to hell.

Meanwhile, the Radom Gestapo had not been idle. It had established a tight network of agents and decoys, some of them in Polish uniform – mostly German nationals from the surrounding villages; and it was now preparing for the *coup de grâce* to annihilate the Hubal group. The group celebrated Easter alongside the local inhabitants, unaware that the storm clouds were building up. Father Mucha held Mass on March 24, Easter Sunday, in the big school at Hucisko, and used the occasion to deliver a patriotic sermon. And for the first time, the men were paid – they received 75 *zloty* a head, without distinction of rank, although a few people had been promoted.

While the Hubal group was busy with its traditional Easter festivities, the first SS and police units were moving into nearby Chlewiska. On March 30, came the first clash between the Uhlan irregulars and the Germans.

'A political affair'

The Uhlans, although they were unaware of it, were the subject of sharp differences between the German Wehrmacht and the SS. Needless to say, the SS had got wind of the preparations being made by the German 650th Infantry Regiment for

their action against Major Hubal. On March 12, an SS official appeared before the commanding officer of the 372nd Infantry Division, Major-General Fritz von der Lippe, to demand categorically that the action should be stopped. 'Dealing with the Hubal section is a political affair, and falls within the competence of the top administration of the SS and police departments.' Finally, it was agreed that the Wehrmacht should be given instructions by the SS on what course was to be taken.

On the evening of March 30, the 372nd Infantry Division received the news that the security service had launched a covert operation against the 'Special Section' the day before. The SS had undertaken this without outside support, and had been rebuffed. As a result, the SS was now demanding support both from the Luftwaffe and from the army artillery for its subsequent moves against Hubal and his men. But the Wehrmacht insisted that it could provide such facilities only if it was allowed to run the operation itself. On March 31, therefore, the SS went ahead with a big offensive using its own resources. Those involved were the 12th Motorized SS units, an SS cavalry group from the *Totenkopf* ('Death's head') sections, two police battalions and motorized gendarmerie units with four armoured cars. The cavalry was under the command of Hermann Fegelein, the renowned show-jumper who later became an SS general and Himmler's personal representative in the Führer's headquarters.

This formidable force launched a series of separate frontal assaults, all of which collapsed under the Uhlans' fire. Tereska, the only woman of the Hubal group, was there among the fighters, pistol in hand. While the SS engaged one part of the group, another troop of Hubal's Uhlans, riding back from a patrol some distance away, came upon a parked convoy of trucks which had been used to bring in the SS troops. The Uhlans took the Germans completely by surprise, and the trucks were soon in flames. The SS soldiers could not cope with the desperate courage of the Poles.

On the night of April 1/2, Hubal's men charged the surrounding ring of German forces at full gallop, led personally by the major on his favourite horse, the English thoroughbred Dämon. They disappeared into the dense forest. At a rough estimate, the SS lost 15 men in the action. The intelligence officer of the 372nd Infantry Division, Dr H. Schreihage, noted: 'The planning and execution of the operation against the Hubal group indicated clearly that the command and training of the SS units left much to be desired.'

Norway: the Skolee Squadrons

At dawn on April 9, 1940, the Germans attacked Norway and Denmark. Their troops advanced rapidly along the fjord near Oslo towards the capital, which they captured shortly afterwards.

Before the first scouts of the advancing German forces had even reached the first houses on the outskirts of Oslo, one of Norway's few mounted units, the so-called Skolee Squadrons (from the school for reserve officers), managed to escape from the German encirclement. The small cavalcade, consisting of exactly 52 men, trotted past Ekeberg to the south end of Lake Gjer. On the way to Trondheim, they split up, with 22 horsemen attempting to reach Gardermoen by way of Gjellerasen. They were surprised, however, by a German unit near Böler, on the north side of Gjellerasen, and were taken prisoner. The squadron which had remained behind at Lake Gjer was ordered to march to Lilleström.

'We rode past Ostensjö, and by 10 PM had arrived at Ellingsrud, where we spent the night. The horses and men were quartered in barns and stables, while the officers spent the night in a big farmhouse. We could hear the drone of the German aircraft the whole night long. At three in the morning, we were on our feet again, riding on to Nannestad on the orders of the 2nd Division.'

In the area of Nannestad and Andelva, the squadron acted both as a defence unit and a recce patrol, a tough undertaking for both men and horses, as all the tracks were either deep in snow or covered with a layer of bare ice. When the horses lost shoes there was no chance of replacing them during these exhausting marches, for in the general confusion the squadron blacksmith had been left behind in Oslo.

'At one stage, as we were riding along the open road between Lillehammer and Gausdal, a formation of German planes appeared from the surrounding mountains and attacked us with bombs and machine-gun fire. Nearly all the horses bolted while we were still in our saddles, taking fright at the deafening noise. My horse, Wallach, tore the reins from my hand, and hurtled round the next bend in the road. It was days before we managed to retrieve all the horses. By an amazing stroke of luck, none of them had come to any harm.'

'Regimental shooting practice'

The SS, furious at being defeated in their battle against the Hubal group, burned the villages of Galki and Hucisko to the ground and shot all the male inhabitants. Two other villages also ended up in flames.

The 372nd Infantry Division then took over the campaign against Hubal and his Uhlans. Reconnaissance established that the group had returned to a position near its first winter hide-out after breaking through the SS lines. Two infantry regiments, the 650th and 651st, set out in their direction. And in order to avoid any entanglement with the SS the action was officially described as 'regimental shooting practice'.

The Polish account of the operation was found by accident long afterwards, in 1955, hidden away in the neighbouring town of Kielce:

'On April 29, 1940, the "Hubal Special Section of the Polish Army" was cornered and heavily outnumbered by German troops in the woods near the village of Wolka Kuligowska, in the Opoczno district. The section withdrew under cover of darkness to the Brudzewica forest near the village of Anielin, without having fired a single shot. On the 30th, at 5.30 AM, the Germans launched a surprise attack, our position having been revealed to them by a traitor. Covered by the undergrowth they surrounded us and forced us into an area of only a few square metres. After the first shot from our side, the Germans opened up with great volleys of fire, hitting our leader, Major Henryk Hubal-Dobrzanski, Corporal Rys and Uhlan Koska.'

All this occurred in a small patch of woodland near the farmhouse where the Laskowski family lived.

'All of a sudden four riderless horses, complete with saddle and harness, galloped out of the wood and into the farmyard. They hesitated by the stables for a moment, then turned round and made off in the direction of the village. There was a pause, then German soldiers emerged from the wood, dragging with them a motionless body. Every few steps, they hurled the body to the ground and battered it with their rifle-butts. Then they arrived at the farm. The man with the red beard was still alive and was breathing heavily. His uniform tunic was torn open and covered with blood. It was our major. One of the soldiers took out a camera from his pocket, and the others pulled up the dying major into a standing position and laughed. It reminded me of a group of hunters, posing with the game they had just bagged.'

The next day, May 1, the commanding officer of the central frontier sector, Cavalry General Kurt Freiherr von Gienanth, came to Tomaszów with his staff to pay his last military respects to the dead major in the Blaskowitz barracks. The general paused for a while, deep in thought in front of the open coffin, before laying a pine-twig on Hubal's chest. That evening, the white-horse major was buried secretly somewhere in the surrounding woods, and to this day his grave has not been found.

But at Anielin, a big boulder and the bleached bones of his horse Dämon mark the spot where the commander of the last Uhlan unit of the Polish campaign finally met his end.

The Skolee Squadrons surrender

Three days before their surrender, the Skolee Squadrons of Norway were engaged in heavy fighting with German infantry at Gausdal. It was three weeks after their departure from Oslo that the squadrons and other forces in the Gausdal region laid down their arms, on April 29, 1940. And the next day the '*Weserübung*' – the code-name for the invasion of Norway – reached its conclusion.

From Flanders to the Bay of Biscay

'You mean this isn't the German offensive?'

The skies to the east were pale grey, and wisps of mist drifted along the ground stirred by a light wind: it was daybreak on Friday, May 10, 1940. At battle headquarters of the French Army's 6th Corps, near Luxembourg, the officers were awoken by the dull thud of exploding German bombs. Baron d'Huart of the 3rd Bureau burst into the quarters of the Chief of Staff of the Army Corps, Colonel de Villaret:

'Now, Colonel, is it really serious this time?'

'Oh, no – not yet.'

'You mean this isn't the German offensive?'

'No, we have no orders.'

It was no more than about three hours after the German attack that the French government gave the order to counter-attack. On the southern frontier of Luxembourg, the *3e Division Légère de Cavalerie* (DLC) – a reinforced cavalry unit – was stationed there in preparation. In March 1940, General Petiet, the cavalry officer who had formerly been commandant of the Saumur Cavalry School, had been allotted the task of taking his division through to Luxembourg. Cavalry groups, scout-cars, dragoons, and Spahi regiments were under his command. With these deployed in four columns, a rapid advance along the 40 km wide southern front was possible.

The time lag between the delayed alarm signal and the order to counter-attack, however, was too short and only a few units were ready to move off. The Spahis were outside the city of Luxembourg at around noon. The 1st Spahi Brigade, an outstanding cavalry unit, was formed from the 4th Moroccan and the 6th Algerian regiments. These fierce and courageous horsemen who galloped directly at German troops entrenched in the meadows of Zolver and Sassenheim brought to mind their heroic predecessors of 1914.

A cavalry squadron led by Captain de St Quentin made its way rapidly to Limpach. As it approached the village, the men announced their presence in true Spahi fashion with a volley of shots, and then asked the inhabitants for news of the enemy. A troop of horsemen dismounted and secured the exits from the village; the other two sections headed off in the direction of Bettingen and Reckingen. The momentum of the Spahis' advance was maintained, and their thrust east of Limpach brought them to within 10 km of the city of Luxembourg. On the road to Reckingen, Spahi Hamadi ben Hadj had ridden with his sabre drawn straight at a motor-cycle rider, overturned his machine and taken him prisoner.

The flanks of the wedge-shaped formation of the Algerian and Moroccan troops were constantly threatened by the foremost sections of the Behlendorff Division. The German reports acknowledged that the Spahis fought with both bravery and skill. Towards 11 AM, French cavalry squadrons finally crossed the frontier to occupy the hills on the Luxembourg side. On their appearance, the Germans withdrew from their outposts in the southern part of the steelworks of Düdelingen. Amid scenes of jubilation among the town's inhabitants, the advancing French occupied the place without encountering strong resistance. But the next morning, May 11, the French, together with the Moroccans and Algerians on their Arab ponies, left Düdelingen and went on their way.

German cavalry in Holland

The German 1st Cavalry Division, attached to the 18th Army (under Artillery General von Küchler), had taken up positions along the frontier of western Holland, covering a sector of the front stretching at least 100 km – from Dollart to a point south-west of Lingen. The Division's 1st Mounted Regiment was ordered to break through the Dutch frontier post at Coevorden and proceed to the coast.

For the most part, the terrain made a rapid cavalry advance impossible: there were several big canal systems to cross, and near the coast the polders, partly below sea-level, were interspersed with holes and craters of varying sizes. The first engagements occurred after the Germans had broken through the 20 km deep defence zone, at roads and canal crossings. Many of the bridges had been destroyed, creating additional problems for the mounted units. Trotting along the hard Dutch cobble-stones proved a great strain on the horses; there were no soft bridle paths to make the going easier. Despite these difficulties, the 1st Cavalry Division managed to penetrate a full 3 km into Dutch territory within 20 minutes of launching their assault – they were able to gallop ahead in some parts over ground which would have been totally impassable for motor vehicles. Having broken through the frontier defences, on the evening of May 10 they reached the line set as their target for the day, between Groningen, Assen, Beilen and Meppel. In the first two days of their advance, the cavalry regiments covered an average total of 180 km.

It so happened that on the afternoon of May 11, a map showing the movements of the French Army was being studied by Major Heidkämpers, of Rommel's Panzer Division. It had been found among the papers of an officer who was taken prisoner, together with ten cavalry troopers, at La-Roche-en-Ardenne. The document was revealing. It showed that the two cavalry divisions combined – the *1ère* and *4e Divisions Légères de Cavalerie* – had neither the capacity nor indeed any orders to offer significant resistance on the right bank of the Maas. They were merely to play for time, slow down the German advance and then withdraw to the left bank of the Maas.

The retreat begins

Whit Sunday, May 12. During the morning, the first groups of riders from the 'Chanoine' Division were pouring out of the woods of the Ardennes near Bouillon. They made their way in small sections towards Chiers and the Maas. For the past few hours, the German armoured columns had been approaching Sedan. Shortly before 8.30 PM, the town was shaken by a violent explosion, and, with night falling, the district of Martinage was lit up with a faint glow. A few moments later, the bridge of Turenne was blown sky-high. All the other bridges from Donchéry to Rumilly – whose defence had been assigned to the sappers of the 2nd Army – were also blown apart after the last horsemen of the rearguard of the *5e Division Légère de Cavalerie* (DLC) had crossed over.

Monday, May 13 was a day of fierce battles for the Allies as the defence positions from the Maas to the Dyle were contested. The biggest threat was expected on the Dyle Line, and troops of the French 1st Army were despatched there in force. The Belgian Army regrouped in front of Antwerp and Louvain. The 'Prioux' Cavalry Corps, in conjunction with the 16th Army Corps, found itself involved in heavy clashes between Tirlemont and Huy. The Roucaud group, with the *1ère Division Infanterie Coloniale* (DIC) and the *2e Division Légère de Cavalerie* (DLC) were all positioned at Stonne, where Lieutenant Dalat observed that 'infantry and cavalry were fighting in superb co-ordination. The cavalrymen did not hesitate to sacrifice their own lives to cover the withdrawal of the riflemen. The spontaneous comradeship was marvellous.' Throughout the day (May 13), the Roucaud group defended the hills of Stonne and Mouzon against the German attacks.

The horsemen of the *2e Division Légère de Cavalerie* (DLC) and the colonial soldiers of the *1ère Division Infanterie Coloniale* (DIC) were together carrying out a vital operation to secure the line after the precipitous retreat of the 71st 'Baudet' Division. The tiny village of Morville was the third rendez-vous of the morning for the riders of the 1 DLC. The place had been bombed shortly before by the Germans; dead horses, burned-out trucks and cases of exploded ammunition lay strewn around.

On the left bank of the Maas at Dinant, the shell-fire from the German tank guns mingled with the explosions from the east. Suddenly, shortly before 11 PM, a muffled clatter was to be heard along the Givet road. It was the sound of galloping horses. There was a throng of animals stampeding and colliding with one another. Many of them were dragging their saddles, harness and baggage behind them. Helmets crashed over the asphalt. On the horizon, a massive grey line of German tanks appeared. The horsemen had hurtled off into the forest towards Givet. The first German motor-cycle scouts arrived on the scene. The XV Panzer Corps (under Infantry General Hoth) had crossed the Maas at Dinant...

May 14. Armoured cars of the German 9th Panzer Division were on the outskirts of Rotterdam. Giraud's 7th Army was retreating towards the Belgian–Dutch frontier. During the night, the 'Prioux' Cavalry Corps had withdrawn behind the Wavre–Namur line.

The Queen's Dragoons

The *6e Régiment de Dragons* (La Reine) of Colonel Jacottet was another of the units under General Maillard's control to advance into Luxembourg. It was a regiment which had been founded during the reign of Louis XIV, and originally – from 1675 onwards – its commanding officer had been personally nominated by the Queen. The regiment had fought under Napoleon at Marengo and Austerlitz. '*Le 6e Dragons s'est couvert de gloire,*' said Marshal Bessières in 1806.

During the night of May 13/14, the *6e Régiment de Dragons* – which had suffered rather badly in the retreat – was relieved by an infantry battalion and drawn up again at Anderny behind the

Maginot Line. On the evening of May 15, the dragoons left the peaceful village of Anderny to take over a new sector, on the Somme at Aumale, 550 km further west.

The regiment's nominal strength was 39 officers, 184 NCOs, 832 dragoons, and 1,010 horses. In addition, they had 52 trucks of varying sizes, 25 motor-cycles, some with side-cars, and four anti-tank guns plus another 25 supplementary artillery pieces. The regiment covered the journey to Aumale in 14 stages.

The second regiment of France's 5th Cavalry Brigade – the *4e Régiment de Hussards* – had an equally rich tradition behind it; it was the unit in which Napoleon's Marshal Ney had begun his career as an ordinary hussar.

On June 4, the 5th Cavalry Brigade was informed that it was to relieve two regiments of the 5th DIC. At exactly 3.30 AM on June 5, before the relief operation had been completed, the Germans attacked. The Senegalese, who didn't know the

country and were coming under enemy fire for the first time, were shattered. The Lajeune section of the 'Lévèque' Squadron, which was also in the line of attack, fought back vigorously but was forced to withdraw to Hangest, where Lieutenant Dulac of the 6th Dragoons took over command of the Senegalese company, whose captain had been seriously wounded. The dragoons and the Senegalese defended the village throughout the day. But by 4 PM, there were only 40 survivors huddled in the squadron's battle headquarters. At 5.45, with the German tanks firing from a range of no more than 45 metres, they were forced to give themselves up.

On June 6, Colonel Jacottet, commander of the *6e Régiment de Dragons*, received an order to take over the Cavillon area. The Germans were attacking from both east and west simultaneously. At 6 PM it was decided to pull back the remainder of the 1st and 4th Squadrons to Oissy, which was held by the 3rd Squadron. But before Lieutenant de Balincourt and a part of his squadron were able to

The western front, May 10–15, 1940: the positions of German and French cavalry units in the early stages of the final offensive.

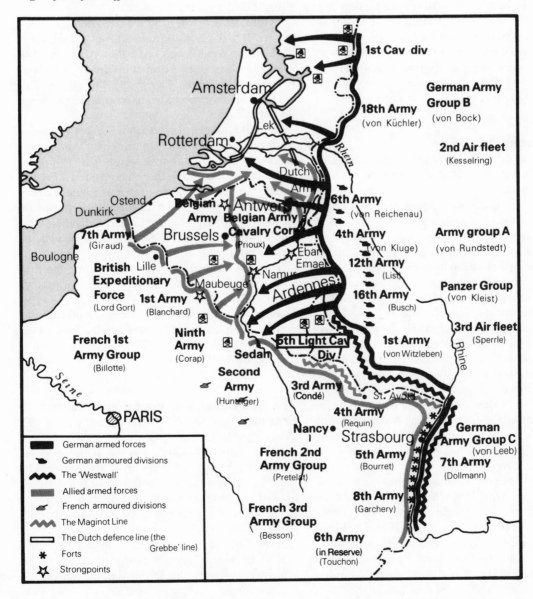

reach the cover of a wood, they were attacked by German aircraft. Half his men and horses were killed or wounded in the attack.

It was nearly 10.15 PM, with the Germans extending their advance to the village of Bougainville, when scouts returned from Mollien with the news that units of the 5th DIC had already relinquished their positions to the German tanks and that the enemy had reached St Aubin. Colonel Jacottet thereupon ordered that the horses should be evacuated by lorry to La Cuillère.

It became suddenly apparent that the *6e Régiment de Dragons* could be in danger of being forced to beat a further retreat – so Colonel Jacottet ordered his squadron commander to move his horses back once more. From then on, the 3rd and 4th Squadrons were cut off from their regiment by the German advance between Poix, Grandviller and Beauvais, and contact could be maintained no longer. All Colonel Jacottet's efforts to link up with his various routed units were in vain. On the evening of June 6, 23 of the regiment's officers, and 510 NCOs and dragoons were missing, with all their equipment. On June 8, at 1 AM, the dragoons were ordered to Rebets. Then on June 9 at 3 AM they proceeded to Pinterville, where two small squadrons were formed from the remnants of the regiment. Finally, General Maillard ordered Colonel Jacottet, his dragoons reinforced by the rest of the 4th Hussar Regiment, to halt the Germans at Les Andelys, and 'at all costs to prevent them crossing the Seine'.

First across the Seine

On the same day (June 9) at about noon, the German 6th Infantry received the order to take the bridge over the Seine at Les Andelys, by surprise if possible. The order for the day read as follows: 'Every officer and man of the division must be made aware that it is vital and indeed decisive for our overall control for this goal to be achieved today.' The motorized units in the vanguard under Major Allert, and those in the reinforced reconnaissance group under Major Machholz, were already within 10 km of the Seine by noon.

The cavalry squadron of the reconnaissance section, under Lieutenant Georg von Boeselager, had the task of forming the bridgehead. The day was oppressively hot and the field-service tunics and riding breeches with their tough leather trimmings clung to the riders' sweat-soaked bodies. The squadron heard the crackle of fire. A short skirmish flared up, then the air was rent with a thunderous explosion: the French had blown up the bridge.

Lieutenant von Boeselager went ahead with two scouts to spy out the French positions on the bank of the Seine. Around the bridge, they could see newly-dug trenches, poorly-camouflaged machine gun nests and two artillery pieces of fairly old design. Surprisingly, a stretch of bank about 100 m to the north appeared to be entirely unoccupied by the enemy. Twelve of the lieutenant's best riders

offered to swim across the Seine.

As a precaution, the rest of the squadron were drawn up on the slope of the river bank to give covering fire to their comrades. The swimmers loaded their rifles, held a clip of five bullets in their mouths, and carried their rifles on their backs. The machine-gunners packed their weapon in a roll of tent canvas. Von Boeselager held the magazine of his sub-machine gun between his teeth.

When the horses could no longer touch bottom on the shelving bed of the Seine, the riders quickly dismounted, holding the horses' manes with their right hand and the reins with the left. The river was fast-flowing and deep at this point, and the water was cold. Then the current slowed down, the water became shallower, and sandbanks appeared, though the other bank was still a good way away. The French sentries appeared to have spotted something, and single rifle-shots whipped over the water. From the other bank of the Seine, the squadron responded with a burst of fire to distract the enemy's attention. The horses were swimming well, and the moment they found a foothold, their riders remounted. Three men of the machine-gun squad failed to reach the bank.

'Right, men, up the bank we go!' cried von Boeselager. It was a critical moment, but on the river bank, there was no sign of further enemy movement. The horsemen stormed up the slope in line. It was exactly 2.30 PM, June 9, 1940, when the German cavalrymen succeeded in crossing to the other side of the Seine.

A small bridgehead was formed, and while more troops crossed over in rubber dinghies, von Boeselager capitalized on his surprise attack by riding on to Villers with his men; there he captured a French battery and took a horse-drawn artillery column and its crew prisoner. Alas for the dragoons of Colonel Jacottet, charged with defending the bridge at Les Andelys; fortune had played an underhand trick.

Thus the 6th Infantry Division became the first and only German unit to cross the Seine on June 9, north of Paris. As a result the French, taken totally unawares, were prevented from establishing a defence line along this strategically important river – and by the same token were prevented from holding on to Paris itself.

The 1st Cavalry Division arrives in France

When the Flanders campaign had ended, the German 1st Cavalry Division was put at the disposal of the 4th Army, and transferred to France. On June 7, at 10 AM, the forward units of the division crossed the Somme north-west of Amiens. Next day, the division's 1st Mounted Regiment had its first encounter with the enemy in France. The 1st Cavalry Division was now fighting as part of the XXXVIII Army Corps; its role was to protect the left flank and carry out reconnaissance duties.

Corporal Hauptvogel of the 1st Cavalry Division describes his experiences:

'We had been riding for a few days behind the retreating enemy. The puttees and steel helmets of the French, and the red turbans of the Congolese and Senegalese were strewn everywhere, along with discarded machine guns and ammunition. We were worn out when we and the 5th Squadron finally reached a big farmhouse. Both the animals and the men badly needed rest, but we were allowed only four or five hours. I was just giving my horse a drink when there was a shout: "Corporal H. to report to troop commander!" My orders were brief: "You will ride on with four men on scouting patrol."

'It was past midnight when we rode out into the darkness. The horses' hooves sounded hollow along the pavement, a few dogs barked at us, but apart from that it was as quiet as the grave. We reached our destination, Jou-sur-Thelles, without any problem. We trotted through the village, dismounted at a barn and looked around in all directions. We rode on towards a wood and were about 400 m from it when the rider nearest to me said: "Corporal – there's some people asleep under the trees on the right." I looked, and sure enough, there were two Frenchmen, snoring away just as if they hadn't been at war. "*Guten Morgen*," I said in German and was astonished to hear one of them reply in the same language. He was from Lorraine and told me they were part of an outpost sent to defend the troops resting in the wood.'

Thirty kilometres from Paris

In the afternoon of June 10, a detachment from the reconnaissance battalion of the 1st Cavalry Division went out on patrol.

'Near to me, the captain was riding along on his big chestnut horse from the Trakehner royal stud in East Prussia. There was no artillery or rifle fire to be heard anywhere in the neighbourhood. Even so, our nerves were on edge. We were acting here as the advanced spearhead of the 1st Cavalry Division barely 30 km from Paris. There were still enemy stragglers dotted around. Our target was Meulan on the Seine. We were on the lookout for three cavalrymen who had failed to return from a patrol the day before. But we had little hope of finding them still alive. The outriders galloped in rapid darting movements from hill to hill to see the position from the best vantage points.

'The last village before Meulan was ahead of us. The streets were dead, except for a few mangy dogs still hanging about the houses. The clatter of hooves rang out as we galloped over the paving. Meulan was already in sight ahead of us. On a road parallel to ours, to our left on the high bank of the Seine, we could now make out an endless procession of horse-drawn carts and motor-cars stretching as far as Meulan: a vast caravan of refugees whose progress had been halted since yesterday by the dynamiting of the bridge over the Seine.

'"Dismount and prepare for battle!" ordered the captain. The horses were led away to find cover. Sub-machine guns and rifles were held at the ready along the entire length of the village street.'

Mines around Meulan

The 1st Cavalry Division was still engaged in protecting the left flank of the XXXVIII Army Corps on June 11. The Meulan road was entirely jammed by the stream of refugees, stuck there because the

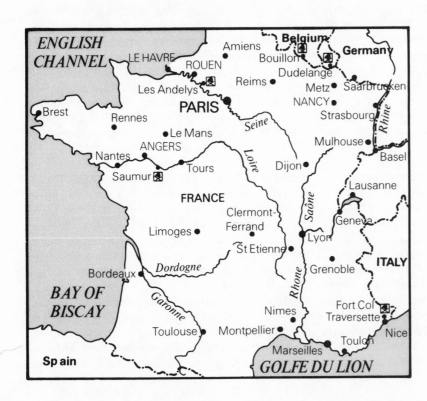

France, May–June 1940: the battles of the French cavalry.   31

bridge was impassable. The scouting patrol proceeded from there to Mézy, over the hills to the west of the road going northwards. Large numbers of French tanks had pushed through to Meulan and so the divisional sappers mined the eastern approaches to the town. The French, however, obviously got wind of this and during the morning sent out several riderless horses into the minefield.

'The field canteen had just arrived with breakfast coffee, when the crash of exploding mines resounded from the town, mingling with the blood-curdling cries of the wounded animals. Dozens of horses, driven frantic with pain and terror, were racing madly hither and thither through the minefield, till one after another they were blown to pieces. Moments later, the entire field was carpeted with a bloody, seething mass of horses' bodies. We found we'd lost our appetites for breakfast!'

On June 15, the French 6th Dragoons were ordered to cross the river at Mayenne, and to reach the woods in the region of Noircoup, where the *2e Division Légère de Cavalerie* (DLC) was to be freshly assembled. It was an 80 km journey, during which the regiment had to run the gauntlet of continual air attacks, with the German tanks ever present in the background. The cavalrymen were in the dark about the overall situation, for they had merely received the order to change positions and had had no opportunity to reconnoitre. Each man fit for combat had to lead several horses. The regiment finally joined the rest of the brigade on June 20 in the woods near La Guerche. Soon, the whole district was surrounded by German troops.

The honour of France

After a forced march of about 200 km, closely pursuing the retreating French, the vanguard of the German 1st Cavalry Division reached the Saumur area at 3 AM on June 19, with the object of crossing the Loire as quickly as possible.

An attempt to take the bridge south-west of Boureuil by surprise was foiled; at the very moment that the scouting patrol stepped onto the bridge, it was blown sky-high and the German patrol with it.

The bridges in Saumur had likewise been destroyed. The German cavalry encountered unexpected resistance, and were prevented from reaching the left bank of the Loire from there to Tours. Among the toughest pockets of resistance was Saumur itself, where the Germans found themselves involved in two whole days of bitter fighting. It was here, at Saumur on the Loire, that the famous cavalry school founded in 1768 had its home. Many distinguished figures from France's recent history have been trained at this august establishment – de Gaulle, Leclerc, de Lattre de Tassigny, and the United States General Patton. It is hardly surprising that the cadets of Saumur wanted to save the honour of France precisely there, in the hot June days of 1940.

Under the leadership of Colonel Michon, the 2,200 young men had marched off to defend the bridges of the Loire from Montsoreau to Gennes, along a 25 km front. Their only equipment consisted of their training weapons: four vintage Hotchkiss tanks, three armoured cars with machine guns, four 75 mm cannon from World War I, ten 25 mm guns, a few light mortars and their small-arms. As well as the Saumur cadets, there were also three North African battalions, parts of the 3rd Armoured Division, and the cadets of the academies of Saint-Maixent, Poitiers and Fontainebleau involved in the battle.

On June 18 at 8 PM, the enemy was sighted 20 km away. Iron rations were handed out and a patrol sent to investigate. At 9 PM, there was an excited phone call from the station master at Château-sur-Loire announcing that strong German units were moving up, some of them towards Saumur. It was the German 1st Cavalry Division advancing. At 20 past midnight, the first of the Saumur bridges was blown: the Pont Napoléon first, followed by the Pont Montsoreau and finally the railway bridge.

Saumur

'But it's certain death, Lieutenant!'

'Look on it as an honour, monsieur,' answered Lieutenant de Galbert to the appeal of one of the Saumur cadets during the battle to defend the Loire. All the cavalry school cadets were from the younger age-groups and none of them had been under fire before. They were divided into 28 brigades each of 25 to 30 men, commanded by an officer-instructor. Their weapons – often of antediluvian design – were daubed in fantastic camouflage colours, and the most important buildings in the town were transformed into strongholds; one brigade took up position in front of the theatre, another in a hotel, and a machine gun was placed on a war memorial for the dead of the 1914–18 War.

Near the breach in the Pont Napoléon, a vehicle appeared out of the darkness, flying a white flag and carrying one German and one French officer. They brought a demand for the town's surrender. The cadets, now faced with a real live target for the first time in their lives, either misunderstood or failed to notice the white flag. A burst of machine-gun fire and an artillery shell killed both passengers and destroyed the car. A German ambulance drove up to recover the bodies. After it had left, the German artillery started a heavy bombardment, and in the afternoon Stukas appeared over the town. The cadets responded with what little means they had at their disposal.

However, the attack was not limited to Saumur. On the bridges of Gennes, defended by Lieutenant Desplat's brigade and a group of marksmen, the course of the battle took a dramatic turn. Lieutenant Desplat urged on his cadets, telling them that 'a soldier must be ready to sacrifice his life'. At midnight, the second bridge, to the south, had been blown up as ordered. This meant that the Desplat brigade was cut off. It had no escape route and its soldiers would die rather than surrender.

For two days, June 19 and 20, they fought with all the bitterness of youth, in a desperate effort to hold the banks of the Loire against the Germans. Desplat's brigade and the scattered snipers were finally subdued only after hand-to-hand fighting.

At 4 PM on June 20, General Pichon ordered Colonel Michon to retreat towards Vienne, as he put it, 'to prevent the young cavalry élite being massacred'. At 9 PM, they received the order to ground arms, and the Germans crossed the Loire.

The end – in France...
In the western Alps, the Italian army group under Crown Prince Umberto crossed the French frontier on June 21 and attacked the weak French alpine army led by General Olry. Two Italian cavalry units – the *Nizza Cavalleria* and the *Cavalleggeri di Monferrato* – took part in the offensive. The Italians captured the fort at Col de la Traversette

and advanced towards Menton.

Forward units of the German 1st Cavalry Division reached La Rochelle and Royan early on June 23. That night they were given the news of the armistice. The horses and their riders had, on average, covered 2,000 km from their first battles in northern Holland through to the Bay of Biscay, to say nothing of their achievements in battle.

... and in Kielce
Scattered between Kielce, Radom and Warsaw, those troops of the Hubal Special Section who had survived the clearing operation by the Germans gradually re-assembled. On June 25, 1940, about 40 Uhlans appeared for inspection at a forest house near Kielce. The captain, whom they had hoped would now take on the command, pulled a document from his pocket and read out their final order. The Special Section was, at last, to disband, as demanded by the supreme command of the resistance movement. The Special Section had been fighting on in the hope of French victory; and the French had capitulated three days before.

In the mountains

The ride to Kassala
The war in East Africa began at the start of August 1940, with the conquest of British Somaliland by the Italians, who thus strengthened their control over the southern access to the Red Sea. Another target of the Italian operation was the provincial capital of Kassala in the Sudan. Founded in 1840 by the Egyptians as a frontier stronghold to protect the border with Abyssinia, it was also an important trading centre on the railway from Khartoum to Port Sudan and on the Upper Nile waterway. Among the groups which advanced on Kassala were the colourful mounted troops of the *Raggruppamento di Cavalleria per l'Africa orientale Italiana* – consisting of the *Cavalleria Coloniale* and the *Cavalleria di Neghelli*. Corporal Francesco Stella of the *Cavalleria Coloniale* takes up the story:

'We halted at midday at a place which looked like a garden run wild, where our horses enjoyed themselves for an hour. In the afternoon the sky became overcast and the heat grew more intense. It was oppressively sultry. Suddenly the wind changed. It came at us in strong gusts, whipping up crackling grains of sand and clouds of dust in great whirls. We turned our horses as a protection against the storm. Bushes and great tufts of grass swept over our heads. The storm vanished as quickly as it had appeared. We were still shrouded in a yellowish layer of dust, covering our uniforms and horses from head to toe, when the rain came down in torrents and left us caked in mud.'

On June 27, 1940, English armoured cars exchanged fire for the first time with the Italian cavalry. A detachment from the Italian 2nd Squadron, riding towards Kassala at dawn to reconnoitre, came under a sudden hail of machine-gun fire from armoured vehicles as it was crossing an oasis. The horsemen, undaunted, galloped off to form a firing line and returned the shots. The 3rd Squadron of the XV Group heard the firing, mounted and joined in the battle. When the English saw more and more Italian cavalry appearing, they withdrew rapidly towards Kassala, firing at random.

'At sunset we continued towards Kassala. Though it was a clear night, it was very dark, for the black rock on the ground swallowed up the moonlight. Our band of cavalry crept along a winding track in two long rows, almost without sound. There wasn't even the creak of a saddle, nor the rattle of equipment to be heard. The quiet made the darkness seem even more sinister.

Under air attack
'The next morning, there was a continuous downpour. We were glad to be able to replenish our water supplies. Then we rode on down the valley in the cooler air. The bed of the valley was formed from fine quartz grit and white sand. We were dazzled by its sparkle, and the whole ground seemed to dance as the spikes of grass were shaken by the wind. The bare rock on either side of the

track threw out heat, making us dizzy and head-achy. We continued for another four miles before pitching camp in a dense thorn thicket. From where they were tethered in the shadow of the trees, we could hear the horses stamping and snorting, tormented by flies. Suddenly, three horsemen rushed up at full gallop with news that the English troops were advancing. Shortly afterwards, a plane flew over us and dropped bombs – one, two, three, all close by. The fourth landed right among us. Two men fell, their horses writhing in a bloody mass on the ground. Two more bombs, then a great reverberation which sent my horse whirling round, throwing me half out of the saddle.'

On July 4, the Italians attacked Kassala. The cavalry group advanced, its units widely separated in three waves, and with scouts sent on ahead.

The Monte Mocram Pass

At 8.15 AM, the advance guard, which had reached the Monte Mocram Pass, came under heavy machine-gun fire and was forced to dismount.

'We took cover immediately and returned the fire. Our hands were burned by the rifle barrels which were scorchingly hot from the sun and the firing; but despite that, we had to aim carefully and steadily to save ammunition. The searing heat of the rock where we lay stretched out in our firing positions burned our chests and arms, so that our skin peeled off later in great swathes. Our only consolation was the thought that it was even hotter for the enemy out there on the open hills.'

The Italians, convinced that the English were only putting up such tough opposition as a means of winning time until reinforcements arrived, decided to take Kassala by storm, whatever the cost. Speed was essential, and so the cavalry was entrusted with the operation. The colourful squadrons of the *Cavalleria Coloniale* formed up in stages, their officers at the head of the formations. The battle cry 'Savoia' resounded through the steep pass. The squadrons rode off at full speed, cloaks waving in the air. A hail of shots rained down on the attackers from the mountains round Kassala as the charge gathered momentum.

Cavalry attack Fort Kassala

'We spurred our horses on in a mad gallop down the slope. It was so steep that each of us ran the risk of toppling over his horse in the crazy stampede. We took the English by surprise, bursting through their flank into their advanced positions. There's no stopping a charge by a cavalry troop hurtling forward at 30 km an hour. That's not to say that the English didn't put up a heavy barrage of fire, but it's not easy to hit a horse at full gallop. I fired my revolver, then suddenly my horse lurched as though struck by an axe. I was thrown through the air in a great arc, landing on the ground with a crash which nearly knocked me out of my senses. I thought about what my squashed remains would look like if the whole mass of horses trampled over me.'

About 500 m from Fort Kassala, the cavalry charge collapsed under the fire of the English. But at the very same moment, the 2nd Squadron sud-

East Africa, 1940/41: the action against the Italian cavalry.

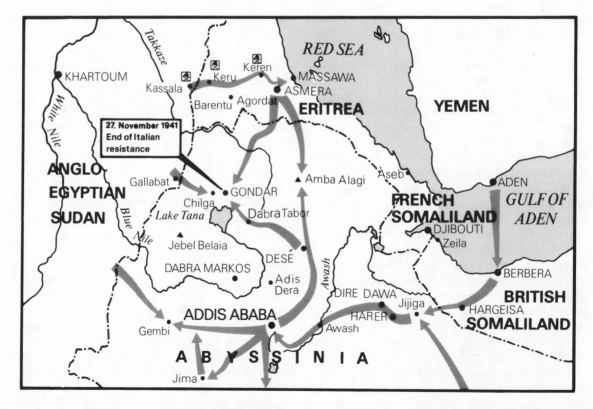

denly appeared from the north, and its troopers launched a determined attack on the fort, some on horseback and some on foot. After a while, a group of cavalrymen succeeded in forcing their way into the fort; and at 11 AM, the Italian flag was raised over the ramparts – a signal victory for the courageous troopers.

The Red Cavalry of Mao Tse-tung

In the middle of 1940, the Japanese had a strong cavalry force in China, as well as 35 infantry divisions and their air-force units. The Japanese controlled the lines of communication and the river crossings in the territory they occupied. They split up the main bases of the National Revolutionary 8th Army into a large number of smaller strong points. In the north, the Japanese gave up their attempts to advance into Shensi province, so Mao Tse-tung remained undisturbed in his north-west frontier region, the so-called special district, with Yen-an as its capital. With enormous foresight, Mao established partisan bases in the mountainous regions between the lines held by the Japanese. The partisans were under the control of the regular troops; and the tightly-knit communist organization began to prepare for action.

By summer 1940, Mao's troops were ready for battle. He was determined to establish the reputation of his Red Army once and for all, and started what came to be known as his 'Hundred Regiments Campaign' – the only serious strategic offensive carried out by the Communists against the Japanese in the Second World War. The Hundred Regiments mounted a series of frenzied attacks against Japanese bases and lines of communication in northern China.

The Red cavalry units had an important role to play in the campaign. They combed virtually impassable trackless districts, harrying the Japanese with their pin-prick tactics. They often rode for weeks on end on their small, shaggy horses to reach their objectives.

'The weather was dry, and every mounted unit, indeed every single horseman, kicked up great clouds of dust as they moved. Behind us and around us there were mules, horsemen, ankle-deep yellow dust and camels. The mountains looked as if they had been cut out by a giant with a great knife. The desolate peaks were lashed by the wind and the slopes were covered in stones and dense undergrowth, a favourite haunt of snakes. Gusty winds blew in from the Gobi desert and the sun shone dimly. When the wind dropped, the heat became oppressive. We wore gas-masks against the dust. All credit should go to our horses, which carried us carefully over the dangerous slopes. In places the track was so dangerous that we had to lead the horses by their reins.'

The 'Hundred Regiments Campaign' was hailed by Mao as a great success, but it was victory bought at great cost.

Crisis in the Pindhos Oros mountains

In August 1940, Mussolini demanded that Greece should renounce the independence guarantee given by Britain. The Greeks refused, whereupon he accused them of breaking their neutrality, and proceeded to gather a force of 162,000 men on the Albanian–Greek border. On August 17, Ribbentrop was still advising the Italian ambassador against a military action in Greece; but nevertheless, at 5 PM on October 28, 1940, half an hour before Mussolini's ultimatum was due to expire, Italian troops crossed into Greece.

On October 30, the Greek Cavalry Brigade was placed under the command of the West Macedonia Army and, together with a light cavalry squadron of the motorized cavalry regiment and a battery of Skoda guns, set out for Konitsa. On the night of October 31, the brigade was attached to the 3rd Army Corps operating in the Pindhos Oros mountains. The 1st Cavalry Regiment and the 2nd Reconnaissance Group were placed at the disposal of the Cavalry Brigade.

On October 28, the cavalry units *Lancieri di Aosta*, *Lancieri di Milano* and *Cavelleggeri Guide*, under the Italian High Command in Albania, crossed the frontier and advanced to the river Kalamas, which, however, proved to be unfordable. It was only after bridge-building materials had been brought in that they were able to traverse the fast-flowing torrent.

The Greek Cavalry Division was ordered to move as quickly as possible to the Métsovon district with an infantry regiment and an artillery battery. The Cavalry Division was ordered to secure the line between Yannina and Kalambaka and thus to provide a link between the 8th Division and the II Army Corps, to back up the attack on Koritsa. After the position at Distraton had been cleared, the Cavalry Division was to join the 'Aoos' battle group, which was covering the right flank of the 88th Division around Vryssochori. On November 2, the first sections of the 1st Cavalry Regiment arrived by truck and promptly rode on to Skourtza. The area had been shrouded in thick fog since early morning, with visibility practically nil. Then it started to rain. Raindrops fell from every leaf and twig, running over the horses' manes and down the necks of the troopers, making their uniforms wet and clinging and generally creating a mood of depression. In the heavy grey skies, the flicker of lightning was visible in the distance, but so far away that the thunder could not be heard. Slowly the skies cleared. The troopers rode on without encountering any sign of the enemy. The light motorized company, alone, was involved in a brief skirmish around 3.30 PM – as a result of which it captured Samarina and took 11 prisoners from the 8th Alpini Regiment. Later a large number of machine guns and four radio sets came into its possession. At the same time, the 3rd Reconnaissance Battalion and the 1st Cavalry Regiment arrived at Wousion, where advanced units of the 1st Cavalry Regiment were already in position. 35

November 1940:
Greek cavalry actions
against the Italian Army.

Map labels: Durazzo, Tiranë, Italian 9th Army, YUGOSLAVIA, Elbasan, Lake Ohrid, Monastir, Lake Prespa, Pogradec, Berat, Florina, ALBANIA, Valona, Meskopolis, Koritsa, MACEDONIA, Kastoria, Italian 11th Army, Klisura, Erseke, Aliakmon, Tepelenë, Vijosë, Dhrin, Himarë, Konitsa, Argyrokastron, Pindhos Mts, Metsovon, Sarandë, Corfu, Yannina, Trikkala, Paramithia, EPIRUS, GREECE, ADRIATIC SEA

Legend:
- Italian offensives
- Greek counter-offensives
- Land over 1000m

Meanwhile the Italians attacked with their 3rd Alpini Division – the 'Julia' – in the valley of the upper Aoos and advanced towards Métsovon, surrounding the Greek Army in Epirus. On November 2, they captured Distraton and a day later took Vovousa.

On November 3, the II/4 Battalion continued its march towards Vovousa on foot. Because of the heavy rain, darkness and the inexperience of its officers, most of the battalion failed to reach its allotted positions in time. The recce squadron of the B-Reconnaissance Battalion was the first to arrive to support the troops in the Pindhos Oros mountains.

Meanwhile, the Italians' 8th Alpini Regiment was moving out of Distraton towards the village of Vovousa. Here they were engaged in heavy fighting with an infantry company of the Pindhos Division, until the arrival of the II/4 Battalion. It was a fierce struggle. At 4.30 PM, the defenders came under direct fire at extremely close range.

On the same day, the first troops of the motorized cavalry regiment arrived in the district of Métsovon.

In the early morning of November 4, the Greek reconnaissance battalion won back the Romios area and took a large number of prisoners. The capture of the Romios district and of Samarina enabled the Greeks to sever entirely the Italian lines of communication. This was the day that the Greeks won the upper hand and forced the Italians to retreat. Vovousa was the southernmost point the 'Julia' Division was able to reach in the Pindhos hills, where the Italians had made their largest in-

cursion into Greek territory. These battles amidst the mountain crests were a great success for the Greeks, and here it was that they inflicted a heavy defeat on the greatly superior Italian forces. The cavalry acquitted itself superbly in this unfamiliar battleground, amid prolonged rain and snow falls.

From the afternoon of November 4 onwards, the Greek Cavalry Division formed part of the combined front as the Greek Army advanced. Between November 5 and 8, the Greek Cavalry Brigade attacked Distraton, cutting the Italians' last line of retreat to Armata–Pades. Fierce skirmishing took place on the strategically-important Smiliani hills, until the 1st Cavalry Regiment, in a courageous counter-attack, was finally able to capture and hold the position. On November 9, the Mounted X Reconnaissance Battalion repulsed strong enemy attacks in the mountains of Smolika. The Italians failed to break down the Greek defences, were forced to beat a hasty retreat by the increasing cold of the early morning, and left their heavy equipment behind them.

On November 16, Konitsa was recaptured by a combined attack of the left wing of the II Army Corps in the north, and the Cavalry Division in the east – in spite of enemy resistance. Then the cavalry continued its advance, managed to repel a thrust by the Italian 47th 'Bari' Infantry Division, newly arrived from Italy, and was able to occupy Premet on December 3, 1940, and to push on further north.

On December 28, Italy asked for German support in its war against Greece. Hitler considered sending in a mountain division but finally decided against the plan.

36

Still a vital role for the cavalry

A salute from the British

'The broad valley radiated peace and stillness, as I rode through it on a reconnaissance exercise with my soldiers,' wrote Lieutenant Francesco Stella of the Italian cavalry in East Africa. 'I was just about to light a cigarette when I caught the distant sound of an engine which was quiet at first but rapidly became louder. A Hawker fighter biplane appeared on the horizon. It was not hard to spot us in the flat, barren valley and moments later, the Englishman was able to use us for target practice. Our only means of escape was to gallop directly at the Hawker and then, at the very moment when we could expect to be raked by a burst of machine-gun fire, to wheel away suddenly out of the firing line. At last the Englishman gave up, circled overhead by way of salute, waved, and disappeared as quickly as he had come.'

This Hawker with its sportsmanlike pilot was the first sign of the force led by General Sir William Platt, the British commanding officer in the Sudan, who was preparing to drive the Italians out of his area and also Abyssinia. The British stirred up sedition among the mountain tribesmen, attacked isolated strongholds, spread a feeling of insecurity throughout the Italian-occupied territories, and announced the return of Emperor Haile Selassie. Mussolini himself was under no great illusions about the situation. By saying that the fate of Italian Africa would be decided in Europe, he had, in fact, given the commander of the Italian troops, the Duke of Aosta, a free hand to do as he saw fit.

On January 19, 1941, the two Italian divisions and cavalry units evacuated Kassala after an air bombardment. The British followed up their attack, pursuing the Italians who put up no significant resistance. General Platt's troops marched to Keru in Italian Eritrea, and the English long-range motorized artillery made life particularly unpleasant for the Italians, who had nothing similar to match up to it. Once again, the job was given to the cavalry: a detachment of the *Gruppo Bande Amara* under Lieutenant Togni was sent out from Keru against the British artillery column. Togni, with his hundred troopers, lost no time. Reaching a small wood through which the British artillerymen were expected to pass, the Italians dismounted and lay in wait for the arrival of the column. The unsuspecting British gunners took up position there and prepared to open fire on Fort Keru. Choosing their moment so as to make the maximum use of surprise, the Italian cavalry then launched their attack, galloping headlong at the enemy position and hurling hand grenades into their ranks. Lieutenant Togni was killed in the act of climbing on to a British tank, and several of his men also lost their lives.

The British did, in fact, retreat – but they reappeared near Fort Keru shortly afterwards. The dismounted cavalry put up a spirited resistance, and the men of Major Segreto's third squadron threw themselves into the struggle with sabres drawn, but nevertheless, the fortress was eventually captured.

Before the fall of Keren

The Italians were now faced not only by the British and native guerrilla forces, but also by the French Foreign Legion, South Africans, and even a Belgian unit under General Gilliaert – which had made the difficult journey across Africa from the Congo.

At the beginning of February, General Platt reached the mountain stronghold of Keren. Here both enemy divisions put up strong resistance. As his initial attacks were unsuccessful, General Platt decided to bide his time and prepare thoroughly before finally storming the position. Meanwhile, attempts to stir up the insurrection in Abyssinia were taken a stage further.

The man in command at Keren was the dynamic General Carnimeo, who had ordered that the 30 km long defence line should be held 'until the last drop of blood had been shed'. In the middle of March 1941, the *XX Grupo* under Captain Zana rode out late one afternoon from Keren in the direction of Agordat. It had orders to find out whether the enemy would, in fact, try to cross the Aful pass. The road to the pass led through a deep gorge, shaped like the barrel of a gun. There was no question of trying to protect the flanks; only an advance guard could be used – II Squadron was chosen – and it picked its way cautiously through the stony terrain. After four hours, at dusk, when the exhausted riders had reached a spot where they planned to pitch camp for the night, their forward patrol suddenly came under heavy fire from a South African unit which had been lying in wait for them. The horsemen immediately took cover. A fierce struggle followed, ending in hand-to-hand combat. The cavalry, which had to avoid the risk of being surrounded, pulled out rapidly. Captain Zana himself, badly wounded, was carried on a

37

stretcher for more than 25 km by the lóyal Askari, and they were able to regain their base once more.

Keren was staunchly defended. Churchill noted that the battle was a fierce one, with the enemy launching counter-attacks again and again and showing no immediate sign of weakening. The cavalry had not yet been sent into the battle in conjunction with the infantry. Nevertheless the horses suffered heavy losses, for the animals – there were about 400 of them – had to be taken twice daily to be watered at a spring 1 km away, which was directly in the line of fire of the British artillery.

Early on March 16, at 5 AM, the troopers were again able to prove their fighting qualities: the XV *Grupo* broke out of Fort Dologorodoc and succeeded in flushing out the enemy forces which had penetrated its defences.

The massed attack on Keren was resumed on March 25. Two days later, the Italian defence collapsed and Keren finally fell on March 27. The pursuit was swift; the remains of the Italian Eritrean Army and its cavalry withdrew about 370 km southwards through the mountains, to take up fixed positions at Amba Alaji, but General Platt's men were hard on their heels, chasing them all the way through the rocky terrain.

In the Balkans

The Germans began their assault on Yugoslavia and Greece on April 6, 1941, with no formal declaration of war.

In the Greek campaign, one part of the German forces was faced with tough resistance at Vranje and on the upper Ibar, which was not subdued until the end of the operation. The three German divisions which attacked the Greek 'Nestos' Brigade were brought to an abrupt halt. In the narrow pass at Rupel, the 5th Mountain Division suffered heavy losses and the 6th was able to make only slow progress along the ridges west of the Struma. For three days, heavy land and air attacks were launched to no avail on the Metaxas Line. A massive German force was sent in to Greece to try to overcome the weak Greek Army which had already been engaging 24 Italian divisions since October 1940. The Greeks were helped by a British tank brigade and two infantry divisions; Lieutenant-General Sir Henry Maitland Wilson, known as 'Jumbo', was in command of this small expeditionary force.

At the time of the invasion on April 6, 1941, the Yugoslav Army was being mobilized secretly. Only 11 divisions were anywhere near their assigned alert positions, however, and none of these

The Balkans, April 1941: the actions of the Yugoslav and Greek cavalry.

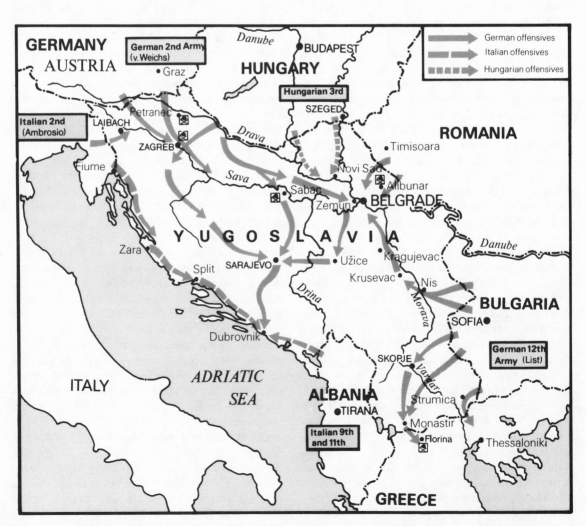

were complete. They came under attack from 30 German, 14 Italian and about five Hungarian divisions. The frontier guard units, for their part, put up a tough defence, but under the onslaught of the German armoured columns they began to collapse and the cavalry was powerless.

The Yugoslav 7th Mounted Regiment, formed from the remains of the 2nd Division in Skopje, was engaged in the fighting as early as April 7. But because of heavy air attacks, it could not stop the enemy advance, and German tanks were already entering Skopje by 5 PM on the same day. On April 8, as the collapse of the Yugoslav armed forces became apparent, the Greek Cavalry Division was attached to the West Macedonia Army. It was ordered to march into the Varnoù and Vernon area to defend the mountain ranges nearby. The cavalry division was then to make contact with the British troops operating on its right wing; with their assistance, it was to secure the railway junction of Florina, of vital importance for supplies to the Greek forces in Albania.

Meanwhile, back in Yugoslavia, the units of the Yugoslav 1st Cavalry Division fought from April 7–10 north of Zagreb. The 2nd and 81st Mounted Regiments led repeated counter-attacks on open ground in the valley of the river Drava, despite heavy enemy artillery fire and air raids. The cavalry spent the night of April 8/9 in the village of Petranec, where they met up with the other troops. These two horse regiments, left on their own without support, fought the whole day of April 9 against a vastly superior German force.

The so-called 'Marmor' mounted division was hastily formed in the Nisa region from elements of the Yugoslav 1st and 61st Mounted Regiments. Partly as a result of the destruction of the bridge over the Morava river, and partly because of the strong defence put up by the cavalry, the German advance was held up here for a full ten hours on April 9. The Yugoslav 3rd Cavalry Division moved out of Backa and away from the Banat without meeting enemy opposition. They then moved back towards Srem. On the night of April 10/11 they crossed the Sava river at Sremska Mitrovica. The 66th Cavalry Regiment joined the 3rd Cavalry Division, and took part in the battle at Samac. A counter-attack by the horsemen of the 3rd Cavalry Brigade collapsed in the face of the German firing, and they suffered heavy casualties. The German 41st Motorized Corps, advancing from Romania, met fierce resistance from the Yugoslavs at the town of Alibunara in the province of Banat. The Yugoslav 5th Mounted Regiment was positioned there.

Cavalry battle at Florina

Visibility on April 10 was poor, with thick mist, rain, and intermittent snow showers. A reconnaissance troop of the Greek 3rd Cavalry Regiment was involved in an exchange of fire with a German motorized unit in the afternoon. From then on, the invaders' motorized troops made repeated attempts to cut the road between Pisoderion and Florina, but they were thrown back by the 3rd Cavalry Regiment. Starting at 9.45 PM, the Germans launched a night attack, with artillery, mortar and machine-gun support. But after a three-hour battle they were forced to pull back to their original positions.

The German XXXX Armoured Corps (General Georg Stumme), whose left wing had come in from the Monastir area, was engaged by Greek cavalry and a British armoured brigade; heavy fighting lasted three days. During April 11, the German attacks against the positions held by the Greek cavalry intensified. But in spite of the heavy artillery fire and close-range fighting, the cavalrymen managed to extend their positions. The 3rd Cavalry Regiment warded off all attacks on the Pisoderion Pass, and contributed to considerable losses on the German side. On April 12, two strong German armoured units broke through the line between Kiru and Derven, but the Cavalry Division held out and fought on undeterred. The 1st Cavalry Regiment was ordered to attack with support from a machine-gun company, in order to cut off the advancing German troops.

At midnight on April 12 the High Command in Athens announced: 'Our troops are engaged in a fierce battle in the area of Florina and Vevi, defending their positions against the Germans.' These few terse words hid one of the most dramatic developments of the Balkan campaign: the battle between the Greek cavalry and the German XXXX Armoured Corps. The Greek cavalrymen – who, like the Poles in the earlier stages of the war, had no motorized support – hurled themselves against the artillery of the German élite troops, showing immense courage as they faced their enemy on horseback, armed only with sabres and rifles. The effect of shrapnel was horrific, mowing down the horses and tearing their riders to shreds in their saddles. Here and there, horses, with their entrails pouring from their mangled bodies, wandered crazily around, trotting towards the surrounding hills. The entire valley was strewn with horses' carcases. The cries of the dying animals sent shivers down one's spine. Horses rolled on top of each other in agony, or lay on their mutilated hindquarters, beating madly in the air with their forelegs.

Despite the enormous losses of both men and beasts, the action was successful in stopping the German advance along the Florina–Pisoderion road for long enough to allow the Greek and British forces to get their breath back and to evacuate the essentials from the crowded supplies depot at Florina. Florina itself fell, and so the Greek Army was finally cut off from the most important supply route in the northern sector of the Albanian front.

Throughout the day of April 16, the remains of the Cavalry Division gathered in the mountain ravines of Skalochori. All the division's equipment, and those vehicles which could not be brought with them, had been destroyed. In the narrow defile, among what remained of the cavalry, was a miserable army nag, emaciated and unharnessed, at the end of its strength – a broken, pitiful creature. He was motionless. He stood there like a symbol of collapse, and was avoided by everyone. During the retreat, the Greek Cavalry Division was to form the east wing, protecting the other troops. They were now out of contact with the staff of the West Macedonia Army which was re-designated Army Corps 'C'; thus it was only at midday on April 20 that the cavalrymen learned of the capitulation negotiations which had already been under way for some time.

The war in the Balkans had been lost and won in 11 days. The Wehrmacht had won its cheapest victory in Yugoslavia, having suffered no more, than 151 dead, 15 men missing and 392 others wounded. It was not long, however, before entire German divisions were to re-pay this blood debt in full. The remains of the Yugoslav Army, men who had avoided imprisonment, kept their weapons and gone into hiding, now formed themselves into innumerable partisan groups. For years they were able to inflict severe losses on the occupying forces in the mountains of Yugoslavia.

Meanwhile when Haile Selassie, the emperor of Abyssinia, came down from the hills on horseback on May 5, 1941, and appeared in Addis Ababa to 'repossess his capital', the extended British campaign in East Africa was by no means ended. Duke Amadeo of Aosta led his remaining forces, including a few decimated cavalry squadrons, into the inaccessible mountains around Gondar and Amba Alagi and put up a significant resistance operation there for several months.

France's *Groupement Collet*

After the capitulation of France in June 1940, the mandated territories of Syria and Lebanon presented a threat to the British which had to be taken seriously. In the hands of the Vichy troops whose relations with the Germans were undefined, they could at any time provide Hitler with a springboard towards the rich oilfields of the Middle East. So when Luftwaffe aircraft appeared in Iran and Syria, the British decided that the time had come, and prepared to end Vichy control of the mandated territories.

A French cavalry officer, Colonel Collet, also learnt of the presence of German aircraft on the runways of Rayak and Damascus. His cavalry, the *Groupement Collet*, was a squadron of Circassians – the best riders and marksmen of a Caucasian mountain race, who had formerly dealt with disturbances in the Levant. They were brought up from an early age to be at home with their thoroughbred horses, and were a unit to which only the pen of a Tolstoy could give a just description. As the frontier strips were now their home territory, it was not too difficult for Colonel Collet to send them over the mountain paths of Syria into British-occupied Palestine.

Colonel Collet and his wife arrived in their turn in the most peaceful and relaxed manner imaginable: one night their sleek heavy limousine, with Madame at the wheel, arrived at the frontier post with headlights blazing and a great deal of hooting. The sentry lifted the barrier and saluted the pair as they passed.

The British welcomed this reinforcement and arranged a military camp for the Circassians in Galilee, where they were newly equipped and organized. At night-time, the Circassians left their tents and reconnoitred the villages on the other side of the frontier – a useful preparation for the incursion which was to follow.

That operation – the invasion of Syria – was the last occasion on which the British cavalry, whose traditions went back for centuries, played a notable part in a military action.

Operation 'Gamble'

There was no hope of the French putting up a mere token resistance: Marshal Pétain's troops were loyal and were fighting as fiercely as ever against the British and indeed against their own countrymen. The British force included the 7th Australian Division, a group of Indian brigades, a tank regiment and various shock troops, as well as the Cheshire Yeomanry cavalry regiment. In the advance into Syria, the Cheshire Yeomanry was attached to the 21st Australian Brigade, though its B-Squadron was attached to the 25th Australian Brigade. The entire operation was given the codename 'Gamble'. At first, the mood of the cavalrymen was rather like that of a group of picnickers. Each rider had rations for himself and his horse packed in his saddle-bag. Tension grew, however, as the order was given to blacken sabres, stirrups, cap-badges, buttons and anything which might glint in the dark. The front riders were equipped with three flags to cover all eventualities – a Union Jack, a white flag, and the flag of the Free French.

The regiment started out at midnight on June 8. By daybreak, they had crossed the frontier. Because of the danger of air attacks they marched in a loose column nearly 10 km long. Captain Verdin of the B-Squadron tied a white shirt to his sabre, and shortly before 4 AM, they reached the first Syrian border village. The captain held his sabre and shirt over his head, Lieutenant Dawson carried a Union Jack, while the interpreter, Baadi, waved the banner of the Free French. They tripped past a night sentry who was fast asleep and didn't even stir. Baadi wanted to cut his throat there and then, and he was restrained only with difficulty.

After reaching the village, Baadi shouted loudly to the enemy to give themselves up. Thereupon all hell broke loose, with firing from several directions, forcing the flag-bearers to take rapid cover.

The group under Lieutenant W. J. Cunningham, realizing the flag-bearers were being fired upon, went into action unhesitatingly. The lieutenant ordered the anti-tank guns to be moved up and to direct their fire at the house from where he thought the shooting had come. A few moments later, a sleepy French officer, who later turned out to be the *Commandant*, appeared in front of the lieutenant, who promptly levelled his revolver at him and fired until the magazine was empty. In the heat of the moment, however, he missed. At the same time, the whole squadron opened fire, inadvertently setting fire to a haystack with tracer bullets.

Tedious and protracted surrender negotiations then followed, in the course of which the *Commandant*, still furious that Lieutenant Cunningham had wanted to dispatch him to the happy hunting grounds, declared that he would only be prepared to surrender if he was allowed to keep his weapons. It was finally agreed that the French troops should be allowed to take their weapons with them, though without ammunition.

At the Litani river

At Adeisse, the first goal of B-Squadron, an attempt was made to contact Brigade headquarters. Unfortunately, however, they were out of range of the antiquated radio equipment carried by the pack-horses. Then, a short way from Kafr Kila, shells suddenly started exploding ahead of the squadron. As they were coming from their right flank, the cavalrymen guessed correctly that the shells were being fired by the Australians. The squadron reached the Syrian village of Alma Chaab, and a troop of horsemen was sent ahead to cut telephone wires. Meanwhile the headquarters squadron also came under fire from the Australians, who in these early days were showing themselves to be more dangerous than the enemy! Shortly afterwards, B-Squadron was brought to a halt by machine-gun fire from French Spahis.

Next morning, two scouting patrols were sent out to explore the possibility of crossing the Litani. This fast-flowing river passed through a narrow gorge; its steep northern bank was more than 350 m high, and provided a real obstacle. With the help of a native guide, Lieutenant Rogers found a bridge which was still intact but as he rode onto it, sudden bursts of machine-gun fire rang out from the hill. A moment before, Trooper F. E. Mellors had already crossed over the bridge, and Lieutenant Rogers was himself nearly across. Rogers and Mellors found themselves alone on the other side of the Litani, but were then joined by Corporal Spencer. When the rest of the group tried to turn back, the horses collided with each other, and presented a sitting target to the enemy. It was lucky that no more than six horses were killed.

The regiment had to be informed immediately that the bridge over the river was now covered by the enemy. As Lieutenant Rogers was no longer in contact with his men, who had taken cover on the other side of the river. Trooper Mellors acted as messenger. Protected by the hillside he worked his way along the river until he was out of range of the enemy machine-gunners. Then Lieutenant Rogers began to doubt whether Mellors would be able to find his way without a map, as it had been vital earlier to use a native guide. So he decided to send Corporal Spencer off with his map and an additional message.

Spencer thought it would be safer to swim across the river – and he rode his horse, a mare called 'Little Nell', into the raging torrent. In the middle of the Litani he lost his horse. Actually, Little Nell reached the other side quicker than Spencer, but in the process had lost not only the saddle, rifle and sabre but also – even worse – the map. Spencer at last managed to scramble out of the water, mounted Little Nell, who was shivering with cold, and the war journal describes how he managed to rejoin his regiment no more than an hour later, after riding bareback and soaked to the skin. As a result of this splendid achievement, he made newspaper headlines and was honoured with a military decoration.

A duel with aircraft

The second day's march in Syria achieved little, it took 11 hours to get from Srifa to Kakiet ej Jisr, a distance of only 8 km as the crow flies. The regiment delayed its departure on the morning of June 10 because it had lost contact with the Brigade once again. The regiment was then ordered to advance against the left flank of the Vichy forces.

After arriving at Adchite, Lieutenant Shaw posted his machine-gun section on a piece of high ground overlooking the village, and ordered the rifle section to march into Adchite. The village had been declared clear of the enemy; but just as the horseman approached with this news, shots suddenly rang out, striking the ground exactly midway between him and the lieutenant. The machine-gunners promptly went into action. As it was their first chance since the beginning of the operation, no-one wanted to miss the opportunity to fire off at least a few rounds each, and the men crowded behind the machine guns to the envy of the horse-handlers, who had no chance to join in the fun. One or two minutes later, some Spahis were seen galloping off in a cloud of dust, helped on their way by the cavalry's shooting.

Generally, a cavalry regiment is too large a unit to be able to operate effectively in mountains. In this case, however, its size turned out to be an advantage. Spread over a wide area, it appeared to the enemy spotter planes as a powerful force. And indeed, it was discovered later from prisoners that the arrival of the Yeomanry at the Litani river had been a decisive factor in the retreat of the Vichy troops.

On June 11, when the Yeomanry reached the Mediterranean coast, an excited liaison officer

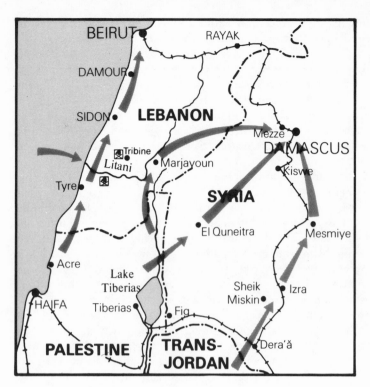

stormed into the regimental headquarters to announce that enemy cavalry was approaching from the north-east. The machine-gun troop marched out instantly – only to find that the 'cavalry' consisted of a herd of grazing cows. Later, an Australian machine gun opened fire on the unit. There was one more adventure that day: an aircraft flew so low over the squadron that it was assumed that it must be British. The soldiers waved to the pilot – and it was only when the plane curved round that they realized that it was, in fact, an enemy machine.

There were several enemy air raids on June 12. There was most excitement for the 4th troop of B-Squadron, who were first attacked by a single aircraft. The cavalrymen were on a mountain track at the time, with a high cliff on one side and a precipice on the other. Corporal E. Laycock took the only possible course of action open to him – he rapidly led the advance section right up close to the cliff wall. This decisive move saved both men and horses, for the pilot was unable to go near the cliff. The horsemen then galloped down the mountain track and were able to find cover before the aircraft could return.

One hour later, B-Squadron was again attacked. Two Vichy planes flew low over them, opening up with machine-gun fire at every available target. The cavalry fired back with their rifles, holding their horses in position. The planes circled overhead, but did not dare to renew their attack.

On June 14, 1941, the Manchester *Evening Chronicle* reported what it described as one of the most unusual battles of modern warfare – a duel in Syria between fighter planes and cavalry. As the newspaper put it, it was the cavalry who won.

Colonel Collet and his *Groupement Collet* were ordered to protect the flanks of forces led by another Vichy deserter, General Le Gentilhomme, during their advance towards Damascus; a tough operation in which many horses were lost. But on Saturday, June 21, at 2 PM, the *Groupement Collet* rode through Bab Tuma into Damascus. On June 23, the Yeomanry too were entrusted with a dangerous mission. Tension grew dramatically when it was learned that only single men were to be sent on a patrol to establish whether motorized Vichy troops were using the roads from Damour to Beit ed Dine.

Lieutenant Shaw set out with some cavalry at 1.15 the next morning, and it was still dark when they reached the point overlooking the road. Some 400 m away, they spotted a section of the Foreign Legion with a tank, blissfully unaware of the enemy presence nearby. So the patrol returned the way it had come. On July 1, the regiment discovered that Germany had already been at war with the Soviet Union for a whole week. Two days later, they made a vain attempt to advance over the mountains instead of along the coastal plain.

On July 11, C-Squadron was ordered to advance to Kafr Houn. On the very first evening, they came under heavy artillery fire, but the terrain gave the cavalry good protection. Lieutenant Paterson rode cautiously round the flank. Barely 2 km away was a Vichy mountain-gun emplacement. The lie of the land was ideally suited for a cavalry charge, so the squadron was promptly ordered to capture the battery. Shortly before midnight, however, just as the men were saddling up to prepare for the attack, a dispatch rider galloped up with the news that the campaign was over. Thus the squadron lost its chance to make what would have been the last charge in the history of the British cavalry.

Cavalry on the road to Moscow

'Tanks ahead!'

Sunday, June 22, 1941. Shortly before dawn, Hitler's Germany attacked the Soviet Union. 3,000,000 men, 600,000 vehicles, 3,580 tanks and 7,184 artillery pieces moved over the frontier, supported by 1,830 aircraft. In addition, 750,000 horses were used by the Germans – though these, it's true, were employed mostly for hauling artillery or as pack animals. Only a small proportion belonged to mounted units. The Führer's contempt for cavalry was to have disastrous consequences.

At 3.15 AM, the 1st and 2nd Brigades of General Feldt's 1st Cavalry Division, the only formation of its kind in the German Army, crossed the River Bug. The day's target destination was reached, and the cavalrymen were already on the edge of the wood east of Rogalzna by midnight. On the morning of Monday, June 23, the 1st Mounted Regiment received the first 'tank alert' of the war in Russia, near Nowosiolki, on the eastern bank of the Bug. Around 8 AM, the noise of fighting in the east could be heard growing louder and louder. Soon afterwards, motor vehicles of the divisional staff and other units were racing by at full speed amid clouds of dust. A series of violet smoke flares burst in the sky, the warning signal for a tank attack. A troop of bridleless horses, many of them without saddles or trailing their saddles, stampeded in fright towards the river. Between the riderless horses were isolated riders shouting 'Tanks ahead!' But this time they were wrong. It was a false alarm. The next day, the Cavalry Division was under orders to capture Horodel, and then to move on towards Pinsk. That meant a ride of at least 70 km. A short distance beyond Mokrany, Soviet aircraft attacked the horsemen and horse-drawn artillery for the first time.

The planes roared in over the rear of the long column, flying low and firing with all their guns. Terrified groups of horses – ammunition pack animals, and six-horse gun-carriage teams – went head over heels in panic, sending one cavalry column after another crashing into each other. There was no cover on the treeless road, which ran through the middle of a marsh. Riders fell from the stampeding horses, and others were torn from their saddles as the animals swept past.

Painfully and with great difficulty, the head of the column reached some cover in the wood, and eventually the horses were subdued. But on the road, before order could be restored, the aircraft appeared once more, chasing the riderless horses towards Mocrany and back.

Only one day after the German invasion, on June 23, the command of the Soviet western front (General Pavlov) ordered the VI Cavalry Corps (Major-General Nikitin) and two mechanized units to mount a counter-attack south of Grodno. Even as it was setting out from the Volkovysk area, the Soviet 36th Cavalry Division was attacked by the Luftwaffe and virtually wiped out. An army group under Lieutenant-General I. N. Boldin, withdrawing from the Grodno sector, covered the 6th Cossack Division led by General Mikhail Petrovich Konstantinov. The Cossacks of the Don who were superb riders fought desperately to escape from the encircling Germans. Their cavalry charges, however, collapsed one after another in the face of the machine-gun fire of a motor-cycle gunner battalion. On June 29, their General Konstantinov was badly wounded near the village of Ross, in the Volkovysk district. Only at the last minute could his men get him away from the front.

The first cavalry raid

In July 1941, the Soviet High Command, or *Stavka*, sent cavalry to carry out operations behind the German front; they were ordered to move up behind the Germans' central army group and to harry its movements.

The 50th and 53rd Cavalry Divisions, which had hitherto been operating on the right wing of the Russian western front, were to penetrate the German-occupied hinterland and to spend several weeks operating in the Yartsevo area. General Lev Mikhailovich Dovator was put in command of these cavalry units.

In the dense and seemingly endless forests between Rzhev and Velikiye-Luki, the cavalry regiments assembled for their first big raid of the war behind enemy lines. The 50th Cavalry Division (General Pliev) began to disembark and unload on July 18, at the small railway station of Staraya Toropa, in the middle of the heath. One train after another moved in. Long columns of horses were led by the Cossacks, bearing saddles, arms, and equipment of all description. The whinnying of horses could be heard from the nearby forests, while between the dark green of the pine trees one saw the occasional flash of red from the trimmings of the lamb-skin headgear and the woollen capes of the Cossacks. Squadrons were forming up and disappearing into the heath. Dusk was already falling when the last transport arrived at Staraya Toropa. The division was complete and marched off immediately so as to lose no time.

The vanguard was formed by the 37th Cavalry Regiment under Colonel Vasily Golovsky. At first they followed forest paths, and then, led by a guide from the local forest Kolkhoz, the cavalry picked its way through the middle of a peat bog alongside Lake Verezuni. From time to time a horse snorted and the clink of a sabre or the crackle of branches beneath the horses' hooves could be heard. Then, far ahead, came what sounded like the call of a night-bird – in fact, the scouts announcing that the coast was clear. By sunrise, the division had reached the ford over the river Meza near the village of Zabiedovo, then, continuing on the north bank, the cavalry paused for a rest in a big clearing. Local people reported the presence of German vehicles along the highroad. During the night of July 22, two Cossack squadrons under Captain Batlyk and Lieutenant Lyushenko went along the south bank of the Meza and reached Troyitskoye by secret paths and byways. Several scouts rode out from a pine-wood, hidden from the Germans who were only 1 km away. They were to ferret out information about the enemy positions and to take prisoners, if this were possible without making any noise. Cossack Georgi Krivorotko laid an ingenious trap using leather straps stretched across the road – and soon, a motor-cycle dispatch rider fell into it. Before the German had time to come to his senses, the Cossacks had dragged him off on their horses and were riding back to their squadron with their victim.

'There, we've brought this for you, Comrade Captain,' declared Krivorotko. The prisoner was taken to headquarters, and an order for the 6th Infantry Division to take up a new position on the south bank of the Meza was found in his dispatch case. For two weeks, Dovator and his riders disrupted the communications of the German 9th Army, keeping behind the German front.

The German horsemen

On July 29, General Kamkov's cavalry succeeded in halting the advance of the German armoured columns of General von Kleist at the crossing of the river Bug; at Smolensk, the Russians wheeled round in a fierce bid not only to escape the German encirclement, but also to win back the city of Smolensk. On the Dnepr, Timoshenko planned to hem Guderian in. But Timoshenko's strategy failed.

It was largely due to the horsemen of the German 1st Cavalry Division, under General Feldt, that Timoshenko's attacks were warded off. Together with the 10th Motorized Infantry Division and parts of the 4th Armoured Division, the cavalry covered the flank of Guderian's tank group. The Russian troops fought bravely throughout, but they lacked the manœuvrability and tactical experience of the German army units.

On the evening of August 12, the German 1st Mounted Regiment, attached to the 2nd Cavalry Brigade, resumed its march eastwards.

'We rode along a narrow forest track past shaggy spruce trees and groups of ancient birches, their silvery trunks shining in the moonlight. Soon after midnight, though, the fun was over. The old and all too familiar drill started up again: "Halt! – Dismount! – Mount! – March! – Halt! – Dismount! – Unload!" Then, just as the machine-gunners had finished unloading and were lying down, came the order: "Load up! Make ready!" We all got up, but still there was no order for us to march off. One man after another sank down onto the damp grass,

huddling together because of the cold. Then, maybe, we would have to march or lead the horses another 200 or 400 m and halt for another hour or two. We were freezing as if it were winter. Finally we were given the long-awaited order: "Great-coats on!" Seldom was an order carried out with such enthusiasm.'

Italy's 3rd Light Division

In the second half of July 1941, several long military transport trains steamed out of Verona in Italy, making their way east. They were carrying two mounted regiments, the *Savoia Cavalleria* and the *Lancieri di Novara*, which were to fight against the Red Army, joining the Italian expeditionary force in Russia (the *Corpo di Spedizione* or CSIR) as part of the 3rd Light Division *Principe Amadeo duca d'Aosta*, commanded by General Marazzani.

The 3rd Light Division reached the battlefront on the Dnepr in August, after a gruelling journey of nearly 1,000 km in scorching heat. Here they took over the defence of a sector of the front stretching over about 120 km. The front line was a gently undulating plain of corn, maize and sunflower fields. A large proportion of the field artillery, ammunition columns and supply convoys were horse-drawn; and the exertions took an inevitable toll of the horses.

At the end of September, the division joined the Bersaglieri in the attack on the Dnepr front. Shortly afterwards the cavalry crossed the river and was ordered to pursue the retreating enemy.

The Hussars

On June 27, Hungary had declared war on the Soviet Union. Its Light Army Corps, consisting of two motorized brigades and a cavalry brigade, began to advance. On July 9, both hussar regiments of the 1st Cavalry Brigade crossed the Zbruch river at Skala, which formed the frontier between Russia and Poland. Here, however, the activities of Hungary's Carpathian Army Group came to an end. It was disbanded the same day. The Hungarian Light Army Corps, and with it, the 1st Cavalry Brigade, continued its advance as part of the German 17th Army (under General Stülpnagel).

The motorized brigades made poor headway on the muddy roads of the Ukraine, which had been damaged by rainy weather. So in order to pursue the enemy more effectively, the 1st Cavalry Brigade was sent on ahead. The hussars proceeded with the dash and verve for which they were traditionally renowned, advancing towards Zvanczyk.

At dawn on August 6, at Golovanevsk (in the Ukraine) some units of the Red Army broke out of their encirclement at Uman, and threatened the headquarters of the German Army Corps. On his own initiative, the commander of the Hungarian Cavalry Group led his horsemen in a spirited attack north of Molodovka, closing up the encircling blockade once more. Those elements of the 4th Hussar Regiment which had been held in reserve took part in the recapture of Golovanevsk.

After the battle at Uman, the Light Corps was attached to the armoured group of General von Kleist, and on August 10 it began its advance towards the Black Sea port of Nikolayev along a 45 km front. The Red Army launched heavy defensive attacks and several German units were saved from destruction only by the swift action of the 1st Cavalry Brigade, which sent its hussars into a counter-charge.

Bryansk

On September 3, the German cavalry suffered a disconcerting setback: it began to rain, and it was immediately apparent that this was a very different downpour to what they were accustomed to at home. The rain came in torrents, and there was absolutely no sun to dry out the layers of mud. The dense, sticky mire made riding a miserable undertaking. It was, however, a mere foretaste of what was to come in the real muddy season. Losses were especially high among the teams of draught-horses, for the German animals found it hard to cope with the conditions they met in Russia. Moreover, the number of horses captured from the enemy didn't begin to approach the losses on the German side.

On September 29, the 175th Reconnaissance Battalion was ordered to ride east towards Romny.

'The road to Romny was sandy, and it seemed that the fertile area of the Ukraine was already behind us. Considering that a horse has to carry a load of about 115 kg, counting the rider and equipment, you can imagine the strain Comrade Horse has to put up with. From Romny, we rode north-eastwards, and the first snow fell as early as October 6 – a big surprise for us. The snow was followed by rain, transforming the roads into a morass. The muddy season had begun with a vengeance. What's more, the wind was so cold that there wasn't one of us now who wasn't cursing the whole war. When we dismounted, we would sink right up to our calves in muck.'

On the morning of October 8, the German 1st Cavalry Division began an operation to clear the encirclement of Bryansk. Scouts were sent out in all directions. Corporal Hopp wrote:

'Slowly we penetrated the forest, which was like a tract of virgin jungle, as yet unspoilt by humans. It was unbelievably quiet, which meant that each sound made by horses or riders sounded much louder. The track had an uneven surface and was lined with thin branches, while low overhanging trees formed a sort of roof overhead. For long stretches it was in half-darkness. We were half-way along when suddenly both scouts started into a trot on a sharp curve to the right. We followed them, and were suddenly confronted by six Russian soldiers and two officers. In those first moments we must have looked a pretty wild bunch. The long

Russian bayonets stretched up to our nostrils and we could see right down the barrels of their guns from where we stood. Both officers seemed to be rather confused by the situation. They grasped hold of our horses by the stirrups, not taking their eyes off us for a moment, and keeping one hand in the pockets of their long greatcoats. Trooper Haddas told the Russians that our regiment was advancing this way and scarcely had he got the words out when the rest of our recce section came round the corner and saved the situation. The two officers exchanged a few words and then spoke to their men, who propped their rifles up against a tree and stood there watching every move we made like hawks. The men were disarmed first, and then the two officers. Two men took the prisoners back to the squadron, and the rest of the patrol continued on its way as ordered.'

Late autumn

The muddy season had well and truly arrived. Persistent rainfall, interspersed by snow, had begun in the middle of October. Rivers overflowed their banks and on the roads vehicles sank to their axles. Exhausted from the fighting, the horses of the mounted formations of the Hungarian 1st Cavalry Brigade also suffered a great deal from the cold weather. Many of them had anyway been overridden to such an extent that they were no longer fit to march; so a large proportion of the hussars now had to attend to the led horses and thus were not involved in the fighting. Accordingly the Hussar regiments were detached from the Light Army Corps on October 12 and began to make their way back to Hungary. During this period, the Italian 3rd Light Division, including the cavalry regiments *Savoia Cavalleria* and *Lancieri di Novara*, was starting its advance on Stalino (the city known today as Donetsk), which was the most important armaments centre of the Donets sector, the main industrial region of the Soviet Union. The division formed the spearhead of the German Mountain Corps, charged with the task of capturing this area; but, as over the entire eastern front, operations were brought to a standstill by the autumn rains. Vehicles remained stationary, and even the light tanks of the 'San Girogio' group got stuck in the mud. It was only then that the true value of the cavalry and horse-drawn artillery batteries was appreciated. They took over the tasks of the 3rd Light Division. Protected in front and on both flanks, the Bersaglieri forged their way forward in spite of the weather. On October 17, the *Savoia Cavalleria* forced enemy units back to the river Sukyie Yali. In the course of this action, a section of the 1st Squadron of the *Savoia* under Lieutenant Franco Vannetti Donnini launched a surprise flanking attack on some Russian infantry entrenched on the other side of the river. On the same day, the dismounted horsemen of the *Lancieri di Novara* recaptured Uspenovka in a battle against

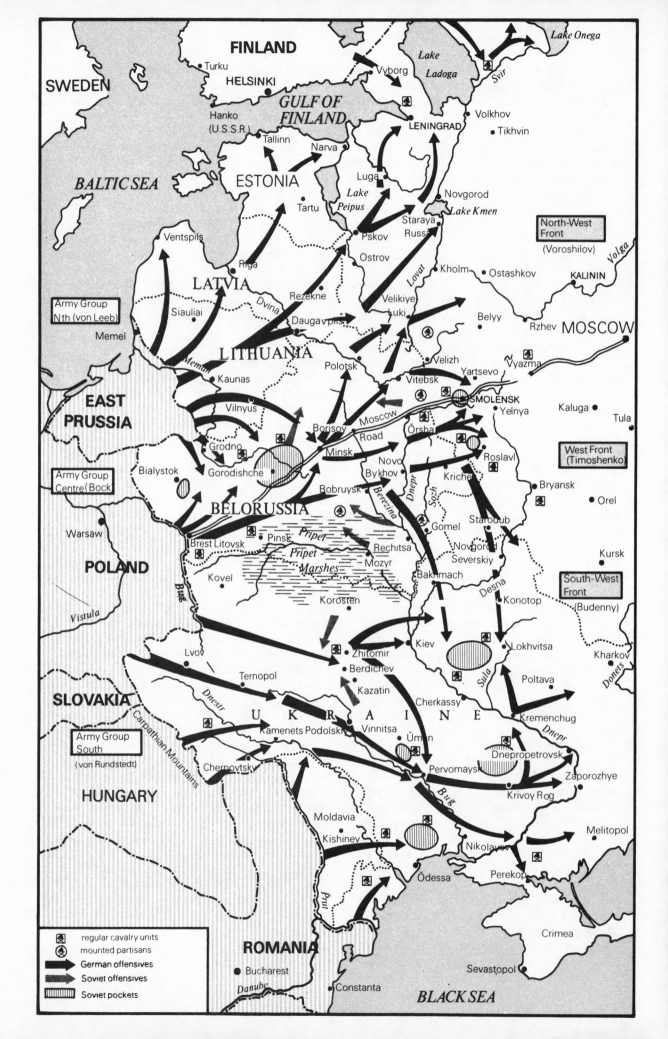

SWEDEN

FINLAND
• Turku
HELSINKI
Hanko
(U.S.S.R.)
GULF OF FINLAND
• Vyborg
Lake Ladoga
Lake Onega

BALTIC SEA
Tallinn
Narva
ESTONIA
• Tartu
Lake Peipus
Luga
LENINGRAD
• Volkhov
• Tikhvin

Ventspils
Riga
LATVIA
• Siauliai
Rezekne
• Daugavpils
Ostrov
Pskov
Dvina
Novgorod
Lake K'men
Staraya Russa
Lovat
Kholm • Ostashkov
KALININ
Volga

North-West Front
(Voroshilov)

Army Group Nth (von Leeb)
Memel
LITHUANIA
Kaunas
Memel
Vilnyus
Velikiye Luki
Belyy
• Rzhev
MOSCOW

EAST PRUSSIA
Grodno
Gorodishche
Borisov
Moscow Road
Minsk
Polotsk
Velizh
Vitebsk
Yartsevo
Vyazma
SMOLENSK
Yelnya
• Kaluga
Tula

Army Group Centre (Bock
Bialystok
BELORUSSIA
Novo Bykhov
Bobruysk
Berezina
Dnepr
Roslavl
Kriche
Sozh
• Bryansk
• Orel

West Front
(Timoshenko)

Warsaw
POLAND
Brest Litovsk
Pinsk
Pripet
Pripet - Marshes
Rechitsa
• Mozyr
Gomel
Novgorod Severskiy
Starodub
Kursk

South-West Front
(Budenny)

Kovel
Korosten
Bakhmach
Desna
Konotop
Kharkov
Donets

Lvov
Dnestr
Zhitomir
Berdichev
Kazatin
Kiev
Sula
Lokhvitsa
Ternopol

SLOVAKIA
Carpathian Mountains
Kamenets Podolski
Vinnitsa
U K R A I N E
Cherkassy
Poltava
Kremenchug
Dnepr

Army Group South
(von Rundstedt)
Chernovtsky
Bug
Ŭman
Pervomaysk
Dnepropetrovsk
Krivoy Rog
Zaporozhye

HUNGARY
Moldavia
Kishinev
Nikolayev
Melitopol
Perekop

Prut
Ŏdessa
Crimea

ROMANIA
• Bucharest
Danube
Constanta
Sevastopol
BLACK SEA

regular cavalry units
mounted partisans
German offensives
Soviet offensives
Soviet pockets

strong Soviet rearguard forces. Finally, on October 30, the 3rd Light Division, still leading the German 1st Mountain Division, advanced into the outskirts of Stalino. A day later, the Soviet 12th Army withdrew from this major industrial city.

On October 11, General Rokossovsky had received the order to march off to the Volokolamsk area. 'We were to muster all the troops we could find and to organize defences from the Moscow reservoir in the north to Rusa in the south.' Assembly points were hastily set up for the units, or even for isolated soldiers, who had managed to break out through the encircling enemy lines. The first force to arrive in the area north of Volokolamsk was the 3rd Cavalry Corps under General Dovator. It broke through the German blockade and reported to General Rokossovsky on October 13. Despite heavy losses, the 3rd Cavalry Corps was still a force to be reckoned with. Dovator's cavalrymen were attached to the Soviet 16th Army. They included the 50th Cavalry Division (General Issa Aleksandrovich Pliev) and the 52nd Cavalry Division (Brigadier-General Melnik). Dovator – a young, energetic, but prudent officer – thoroughly understood his job. The fact that he had led his corps out of the encirclement and kept it fighting fit bore eloquent witness to his military ability. The *Stavka* could be confident that he could be relied on to defend such a long front line – from north of Volokolamsk to the Volga reservoir.

General Dovator's cavalry was deployed in the area of Novo-Petrovskiy. There, after three months of almost uninterrupted fighting and marching, there was at last an opportunity for the horses to rest and for the men to get their equipment in order. However, as early as October 17, the Dovator corps was attacked north of Volokolamsk and the scouts announced that the Germans were advancing in force on Volokolamsk itself, towards the right of the Soviet 16th Army.

Tragedy on Lake Ladoga

On the Finnish front, Finland's Karelia Army (Lieutenant-General Heinrichs) had by this time recaptured the area between Lake Ladoga and Lake Onega. The Finnish Cavalry Brigade (under General Oionen) and the units assigned to it took Petrozavodsk; the VI Army Corps (Major-General Talvela) and VII Army Corps (Major-General Hägglund) advanced on to the Svir. On the left wing of the Soviet 'Northern Front' Army Group (Lieutenant-General Frotov), the weakened Soviet 23rd Army (Lieutenant-General Pshennikov) was forced to give up territory occupied in 1939/40 and had withdrawn behind the frontier as early as August 1941.

In the district of Vouksen, the wild areas on the edge of the dense forests of Raikkola were over-

The eastern front, June–September 1941: cavalry operations.

flowing with Russian troops from the end of October 1941. Nearly all the Russian horse artillery and horse-drawn baggage trains streamed there from the northern sector of the Karelian isthmus in the hopes of being able to cross Lake Ladoga and so escape from the surrounding Finnish forces. The winter was already promising to set in with its usual severity and the tug-boats, rafts and landing craft which were to bring the artillery pieces and horses to the safety of the far bank had not yet arrived. Meanwhile the Finns were becoming more and more active: their crack ski battalions were attacking the rear and flanks of the encircled army. Two days after reaching the bank of the lake, the Russians were not only surrounded by the Finns – but the forest was on fire as well. And here on Lake Ladoga one of the most agonizing tragedies involving horses in World War II began to develop.

The Finns closed off numerous escape routes and started shooting in the direction of the wall of fire with whatever weapons they could muster. The blaze spread rapidly, fanned by the north wind, and thousands of horses, driven wild with pain, raced towards it, ignoring the rapid fire of the machine-gun batteries. Many of them galloped to and fro like giant torches, bellowing and shrieking in agony until they finally burned to death. Another few thousand raced in terror from the raging flames and hurtled towards the lake.

A great tide of horses poured out of the forest and plunged into the waters of Lake Ladoga. Moments later, a small, shallow bay was seething with animals scared out of their wits and seeking shelter from the blazing shore and the untold depths of the lake in these shallows. Soon, a cloud of mist swept over the swarm of hemmed-in animals, covering them with a coating of ice as the evening frost rapidly descended over their shivering mass.

The first Finnish scouts who made their way next morning through the burned forest and reached the shore of the bay were astonished by what they saw. 'The lake was like an endless sheet of marble on which someone had placed hundreds and hundreds of horses' heads. They looked as if they had been disembodied by the sharp blow of an executioner's axe. Only the heads were visible, staring towards the bank. One could still see horror in their eyes. Near the bank was a confused mass of horses trying to rear out of their icy prison.'

The German cavalry is disbanded

On November 4, the German 1st Cavalry Regiment reached the region of Rogi, about 20 km north of Gomel. By this time some squadrons had only a third of their full complement of horses. And while the Russian cavalry was constantly and increasingly demonstrating its value, it seemed that time was slipping away for the German mounted units. But it was neither the enemy nor the severity of the weather which was eventually to bring about 47 their end: the decisive blow came from the distant headquarters of the High Command, in an edict from the Führer himself.

At 2.30 PM on November 5, 1941, the amalgamated squadrons of the 1st Cavalry Division made their way in exemplary order across a snow-covered stubble-field a few kilometres west of the town of Gomel. Under the melancholy grey skies of the Russian autumn, the last great parade of the German cavalry took place. The divisional commander, General Feldt, rode down the silent ranks as the trumpeter corps on their white steeds sounded the Last Post. The regiments then rode off at a trot, to the beat of the Finnish cavalry march.

The highly-trained cavalry horses – surely as good as any in the world – included the pick of those looted from Czechoslovakia, Poland and France, but they were now transferred to the lowly duties of drawing waggons and carts; the more fortunate were later incorporated into the German Cossack units. The 1st Cavalry Division, which had acquitted itself so well on the battlefield, was converted into the 24th Armoured Division. But because the armoured units had to wait so long for their desperately-needed equipment, it was to be months before the horsemen became fully-fledged armoured troops.

At the same time as the disbanded German cavalry, without its horses, was being carried home in long military transport trains, cavalry units were emerging as part of Tito's Liberation Army in the mountains of Yugoslavia. A squadron of cavalry, in fact, took part in the parade marking the anniversary of the Bolshevik revolution, on November 7, 1941, in the town of Uzicka Pozega in liberated territory in West Serbia. By autumn, 1941, the partisan groups of Uzicka Pozega and Cacansk could boast a cavalry squadron apiece. These first troopers of the Liberation Army were used mainly for scouting operations or as couriers.

'How great are the casualties?'

The Cossacks were among those fighting to defend Moscow, the Soviet capital: in the north, a Cossack cavalry division attached to the 2nd Corps of Cavalry Guards under Major-General L. M. Dovator; and in the south, the Cavalry Corps of General Belov, a popular cavalry leader respected even by Stalin. He commanded two Cossack cavalry divisions.

Operation Typhoon, described as 'the last battle of the year aimed at crushing the enemy and capturing Moscow', started on November 15. At dawn on November 16, Germany's III and IV Tank Groups penetrated the sector defended by Dovator's cavalry corps. At 8 AM, swarms of Junkers 87s swooped down over the cavalrymen. When Dovator telephoned Lieutenant-Colonel Smirnov, commander of the 43rd Cavalry Regiment, to ask how things looked, he received the reply: 'It looks good, Comrade General, I am just counting the black-birds coming towards us – there are at least 35!' The

cavalry's anti-aircraft guns brought down two Stukas. Then, after artillery preparation, the Germans stormed the villages of Morozkovo and Ivanovo, both defended by the Dovator cavalry regiments. After heavy fighting, the cavalry was forced to withdraw from the burning village of Ivanovo. On the right flank, the 43rd Cavalry Regiment managed to hold on to the ruined village of Morozkovo for another half an hour. As soon as Dovator heard about the evacuation of the two villages, he summoned the commanders and commissars of the two yielding regiments. As they approached the corps battle headquarters he galloped towards them from a distance on his brown gelding 'Kazbek'. How great are the casualties?' he shouted before he reached them. The officers, who were used to Dovator's quick temper, were prepared for anything. 'Up to ten per cent in the mounted squadrons, Comrade General,' announced Smirnov. 'Our country has ordered us to keep the Germans away from Moscow at all costs, even at the cost of our lives, and we have no right, comrades, to yield even two burned-out villages so lightly. Give the soldiers their supper,' Dovator said to Pliev, 'and get them to retake the positions tonight. Report to me by three in the morning at the very latest on the execution of this order!'

In this crucial phase of the battle for Moscow, the 16th Army was boosted by new cavalry units from the 17th, 20th and 44th Divisions, each 3,000 men strong, from outer Mongolia. 'Unfortunately the cavalry was scarcely mobile,' General Rokossovsky noted, 'as the horses had not been shod for winter, although the ground around Moscow was already frozen and covered with ice in marshy areas.'

Cavalry charge at Mussino

Near Mussino, between Volokolamsk and Klin, the mists lifted after the foggy morning of November 17 to reveal the edge of a forest stretching as far as the eye could see. Ahead of the B-position of the German 3rd Battery of the 107th Artillery Regiment in the 106th Infantry Division, were snow-covered fields dotted with small, bare bushes. To the right were rows of straw-thatched hovels.

Suddenly, four Russian tanks appeared from nowhere, halting at the huts where the 3rd Battery was quartered. The anti-tank gunners opened fire. Then in a flash, mounted cavalrymen hurtled out of the woods, at first singly and then in vast numbers, forming up in the twinkling of an eye. Stirrup to stirrup, bent low over their horses' manes and brandishing their glittering sabres, the cavalry regiment raced over the fields in a full gallop. The 3rd Battery fired from its open position.

The first shots whistled past into the charging ranks of the cavalry, and the shells of the anti-tank guns exploded in great red flashes. From the village, too, there came heavy firing. A wall of billowing smoke from the exploding shells hovered over the

Continued on page 209.

Operational briefing. The *Rittmeister* (captain) in peaked cap issues his order. The *Oberleutnant* (lieutenant) on the right and the three NCOs are wearing steel helmets of 1935 design with chin-straps. All the horses carry saddle-blankets. A good example of the regulation sitting position at the halt, reins held with one or both hands. 'The correct sitting position must be combined with a good military posture. The upper part of the body should be aligned vertically from the hips. The sole of the foot should have its whole width in contact with the stirrup. The entire breadth of the buttocks should rest on the horse's back with muscles relaxed. The inner side of the calves should maintain sensitive contact with the horse.' From the *Ausbildungsvorschrift für die Kavallerie*, Berlin 1939 (a cavalry training manual).

Above: Daybreak on September 1, 1939. German cavalry invades Poland: 'The column is to advance in double file covering both sides of the road.' To the rear of each file are two pack-horses with grooms.

Below: A patrol. *Below right:* On a country lane in Poland, men of the German 1st Mounted Regiment.

Overleaf: A rest for the cavalry. An acting corporal (*Gefreiter*) is holding the snaffle reins; he is wearing a 1935–model steel helmet, combat tunic, and riding breeches, and is carrying a canister with a gas-mask and bayonet. *Overleaf above left:* A scout. *Overleaf above right:* The vanguard.

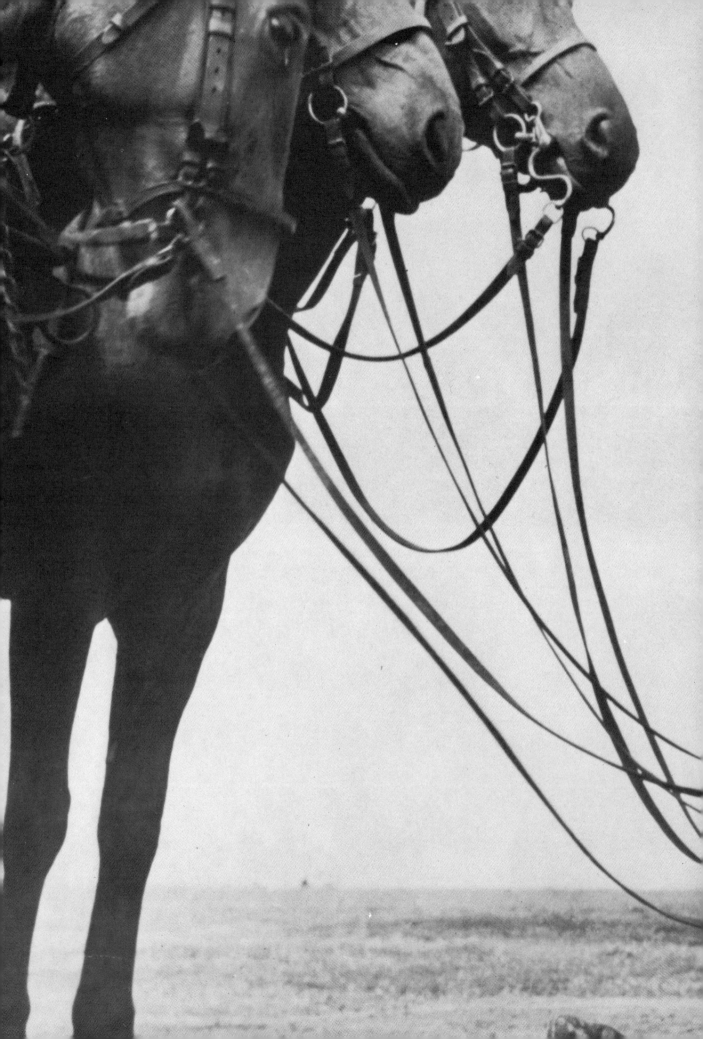

Previous page: Polish cavalry attacking German armoured scout-cars (Sd 232s). (A scene from the Nazi propaganda film *Kampfgeschwader Lützow*, directed by H. Bertram, in 1941.)

Above left: The reconnaissance battalion of a German infantry division in action.

Below left: Polish mounted troops halt in the Campinos forest; in the foreground is a group of officers wearing the well-known Polish-style riding boot.

Above: Polish cavalry. A force without a rational combat doctrine.

Below: Polish cavalry and horse artillery move forward.

Above left: Horsemen of a scouting patrol conferring with motor-cycle gunners.

Centre left: 'Take cover!' The groom brings the animals to safety, after unharnessing them for speed of movement.

Below left: Shortly before the signal to mount. The German cavalrymen are dressed in 1935-style helmets, military service uniforms on the 1936 model (combat tunic and riding breeches) and riding boots with spurs. They are armed with 98k carbines and bayonets and are carrying gas-masks and haversacks. The horse on the right is an East Prussian with typical lop-ears.

Above right: After the Polish cavalry battle on the Bzura; towards the Vistula.

Below right: Kutno, September 9, 1939. The end of a horse-drawn gun battery.

With lance and sabre: a Polish cavalry charge.

Right: Poland, September 1939. A horse amidst the inferno.

Below left: Sochaczew, 60 km west of Warsaw.

Below right: A German cavalry troop in the burning town of Vegrov.

The end in Poland: German troops enter Warsaw. The officers ride past the commanding officer of an army corps and his staff. The setting is the well-known Poniatowski bridge in Warsaw.

The Soviet cavalry enters Vilna.

Left: Warsaw. Kettle-drummers of the band of an SS Death's Head cavalry unit (The *Totenkopf Reiterstandarte* I). A Lippizaner horse with typical ceremonial headgear, neckharness drawn through an ornamental breast-link, and reins fastened to the mounting-stirrup.

Below: The Janov Podlaski stud. Witez, one of the many Arab thoroughbreds captured by the Germans in Poland.

Right: The kettle-drummer of a German artillery regiment. Another example of the ceremonial head harness, this time in a mounted unit of the army.

Below: The band of the 1st Mounted Regiment.

Above left: Winter 1939/40 on the lower Rhine: a horseman of the mounted artillery.

Centre left: A cavalry squadron halts in the market place of a small town. The front saddle-pack worn on the horse's left flank is clearly visible. This would contain an ammunition pack of 15 cartridges; two front horse-shoes with nails, horse-shoe screw calk, and one tethering ring in the horse-shoe pouch; 500 gm of rusks, 200 gm of preserved meat or mess-tins; one pack of tools, a sewing kit with scissors, spoon, mirror and comb, toothbrush, soap, razor, shaving-brush, one clothes-brush, one horse-cleaning kit, field-cap, song-book and one halter-chain. The other left-hand pack contained a pair of underpants, a pair of socks and the rifle in its holster.

Below: Manœuvres in the countryside.

Right: Norway, autumn 1939. Pictures of a cavalry regiment on manœuvres.

Above: Finland, autumn 1939. Cavalry advancing. The riders wear German helmets of 1918 style, and carry Mossim-Nagat 91/27 rifles.

Left: A dragoon regiment from Uusima in East Karelia.

Right: A troop of Finnish cavalry. Their tough, intelligent Haflinger horses from the lower Alps are somewhat unusual in appearance, having an Arabian profile and beautifully rounded form but clumsy hindquarters. They are said to be 'kings in front, but peasants behind'.

Above far left: Poland, January 1940, at Fryszerka, near Kamienna. On the left is Tereska (Maria Cel) and in the centre, wearing a scarf, is Major Hubal.

Above near left: At Fryszerka, January 1940. On the left Captain J. Walicki (Walbach) with Captain R. Rodziewicz (Roman).

Below left: The road to Kamienna, March 1940. A German mounted patrol searching for members of the Hubal group.

Right: Anielin, April 30, 1940. The body of Major Hubal with the soldiers of the German 650th Infantry Regiment.

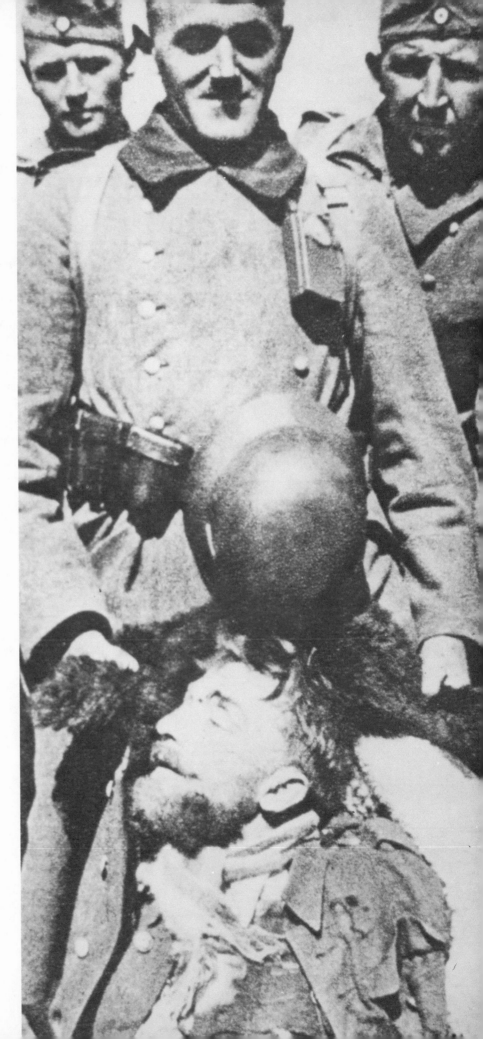

Above left: Before the prize-giving ceremony after an army riding competition – horses of the 2nd Mounted Regiment in close formation. 'The horses should stand with all four legs perpendicular to the ground, and should be held by the reins with shoulders parallel to the ground.' The horses are pure East Prussians.

Centre left: A tricky exercise – the horse has to get up from the ground with the rider in the saddle.

Below left: A mountain climb. 'The rein hand must not move backwards. Right hand grips the mane, the bit is free, knees gripping tightly, feet pointing forward through the stirrups.'

Above right: Balancing exercises on horseback.

Below right: A group outing with jumping exercises. 'Crouch down and follow the movement of the horse. Knees tight, feet well in the stirrups. Hands forward, but not losing contact with the horse's mouth, curb-rein loose.' The horsemen were originally armed with 98k carbines and sabres, but in 1940 the sabres and rifle holsters were phased out for the cavalry squadrons. The rifles were from then on carried on their backs.

Above: Japanese horsemen: sabre-fighting exercises on horseback.
Below left: The colours borne by the Japanese 3rd Cavalry Regiment.
Below centre: Japan's 25th Cavalry Regiment in China.

Above: Training new horses in Numaengo. On the right, Lieutenant Asamosuke Matsui.
Below right: Front rank of the 1st Cavalry Regiment in Manchuria.

Above: May 10, 1940, French campaign. Into action at full gallop – a horse-drawn double machine gun.

Below: The *coup de grâce* for a wounded horse.

Far right: A rest from the battlefield, and a time to renew old friendships. There are four East Prussians with a Hanoverian in the centre. The Hanoverians were an old German breed. At the beginning of the 18th century, when the house of Hanover acceded to the English throne, the existing stock was strengthened by crossing with English thoroughbreds.

May 15, 1940, in France, near Sedan: a mounted reconnaissance group. The horsemen's left-hand saddle-packs are clearly visible.

Right: A dispatch rider racing through the forest – note the long rein and light saddle.

Below: The mounted reconnaissance section of an infantry division advancing in the Ardennes.

Above: March past by a troop of Cuirassiers with sabres drawn.

Below: German horse-drawn artillery advancing. The front horse is a Trakehner with typical slightly drooping ears. It is a noble animal with an Arab-like head, splendidly curving neck and long, high withers.

Above: A French army waggon team in the retreat.
Below: A French cavalry unit.

Above: The road near Laon (Aisne), June 1940. A French cavalry patrol after an exchange of fire with the German cavalry.

Below: Horse and rider share the same fate.

Above: In a small town somewhere near Paris, a German mounted battalion moves ahead.

Below: ... in the market place: what remained of a French battery after a German attack.

Above: Paris, June 14, 1940. A victory parade.

Left: ... along the Atlantic coast.

Right: A German cavalry troop in Paris, Place du Palais Royal. A midday break for the horses with girths loosened and stirrups raised.

Above: Late summer on the French coast – some relaxation for the draught horses.

Below: Operation Sea-Lion, the landing in England, in a practice exercise.

Right: A German horseman under the Arc de Triomphe.

Above: Along the demarcation line in early 1941. The preparations for the attack on the Soviet Union.

Centre: A scout-car with a machine gun mounted on the chassis of the Adler Standard six. It belongs to the Reconnaissance Battalion of the 3rd Cavalry Regiment.

Below: Grooms bring their horses under cover.

Above and below: On the way from France to Poland – what do the horses and men think of it?

Above: Early June 1941, hidden in the forests somewhere along the Soviet frontier. The field-smiths of the 1st Mounted Regiment.

Above right: The saddler of the 4th Squadron repairing harnesses.

Centre right: A vital operation, attending to the horse's hooves. Here the German Army's No. 32 shoe of hardened steel is being used (it came in 12 different sizes).

Below right: Working with a light field forge.

Above: Sunday morning, June 22, 1941; crossing the frontier. The horseman is wearing a 1935-style helmet, haversack straps for fixing camouflage material, and a gas-mask canister and dispatch bag on his back. His rear pack includes a great-coat with a collar on top and an opening in front (a third of its breadth to be over the cantle), binoculars in a leather container, a strap, a stable-halter and a sleeping blanket.

Above right: A horse-drawn artillery battery moves forward through the dust of the Russian summer.

Below right: Softer going along a river.

Above and below left: Horses – dumb witnesses to a tragedy.

Above: June 1941, at Grenoble. A horse and rider of the *2e Régiment d'Artillerie de Montagne* (Vichy troops) during a rest period.

Left-hand page, above: Fun for horses and their riders – bath time for all.

Left-hand page, below: A river in Russia: the riders cross by rubber dinghy while the horses swim. On the extreme right is a Trakehner.

Above left: At a crossroads in the east – a German cavalry unit's operational signposts. The fish sign shows the way to the 35th Infantry Division.

Above right: A short pause at a Russian aerodrome.

Below right: An obstacle easily surmounted by the dispatch rider.

Above left: The supply columns toil on for days on end through the dust and heat.

Below left: A cavalry troop rides its thoroughbreds through a collective-farming village. In the foreground is a Soviet anti-aircraft gun.

Above: East of Smolensk. The last few kilometres shortly before reaching their destination. On the right is a Haflinger horse.

Right: A dispatch rider in difficult country.

Above: A reconnaissance unit fording a river.

Right: Horsemen work their way towards the enemy.

Far right: At full gallop with an important dispatch. As protection against the weather, the rider is wearing a triangular waterproof ground-sheet. With his head through its centre, it provides an adequate cape. The 62 buttons and buttonholes were so arranged that the ground-sheet could be worn in various ways, protecting the rider and yet allowing him freedom of movement. The rider here is armed with a 98k carbine and stick grenades attached to his front pack. The horse, a Hanoverian, wears a nosebag round his neck.

Above and below left: A time for the horses to relax. They are fine examples of Hanoverian breeding.

Above: Summer 1941. A field camp captured from the Soviet cavalry.

Below right: The emergency veterinary hospital of the German 1st Mounted Regiment. The veterinary surgeon has a whole range of varied equipment – but his patients cannot tell him where it hurts most.

Above: Summer 1941, northern sector of the eastern front (Lapland). Supplies for the forward positions. The horse in front is a fine Haflinger, packed with muscle; he has a long back and an unusually developed croup. His hindquarters are powerful, he has a long, low-set tail, and a broad chest. The Haflinger was a natural mountain-climber.

Below: A short breather for the pack-horses.

Right: A horse carrying a light mountain-gun. The heavy load – a good 150 kg – is strapped on with additional rear harness.

Above left: A few minutes' respite from the war in the Ukraine in the middle of fields in full flower.

Bottom left: The eastern front. A quick bite of grass before the action.

Above: Przemyśl, autumn 1941. Crossing the bridge over the San.

Above left: Imphal, April 1942. Troops of the Indian mountain cavalry.

Bottom left: Horsemen of the Indian 1st Punjab Regiment with their saddles.

Above: Imphal, April 1942. Indian mountain cavalry on field exercises.

Right: The Indian Naik Farman of Rawalpindi with a thoroughbred.

Left: Beirut, summer 1941. Two of the British mounted Military Police.

Below: Palestine, May 1941. A British mounted unit. The horses are getting a thorough grooming.

Above: Syria, summer, 1941. A troop of the Trans-jordanian Frontier Force Cavalry Regiment in difficult country.

Above: The Near East, summer 1941. A detachment of the British mounted Military Police. The second horse from the right is an Andalusian, highly regarded for its obedience and elegance, and also for its *paso de andatura* – a strong, smart movement somewhere between a walk and a trot. The Andalusian is an expressive animal, with big, fiery eyes, small ears, a curving well-positioned neck, and a compact body with beautifully rounded ribs and low withers. Its tail is set rather low, its croup is round, its legs very slim, and its coat fine and long.

Below left: Syria, June 16, 1941. A patrol of Yeomanry cavalry on the bank of the Litani.

Above right: Syria, summer 1941. Three horses and riders of the Transjordanian Frontier Force Cavalry Regiment.

Below: Palestine – Galilee. 1941, A troop of the Transjordanian Frontier Force Cavalry Regiment waters its horses in the Jordan.

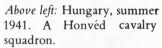

Above left: Hungary, summer 1941. A Honvéd cavalry squadron.

Centre left: Eastern front, near Pervomaysk, August 1941. A Honvéd trooper and horse.

Below left: The Hungarian Light Corps. Saddle check before the morning ride.

Above right: Eastern front near Winniza, September 1941. A cavalry patrol by the Hungarian occupation forces. The officer's horse, even at first sight, is clearly a temperamental animal of fine breeding.

Below right: Ukraine, autumn 1941. German riders resting; the horses are wearing the so-called French curb.

Below far right: Berdichev, autumn 1941. An airy stable for the Honvéd horses.

Above left: Cossack Taras W. Samodurev, a veteran of World War I, serving as a volunteer in the Soviet Kuban Regiment.

Above centre: The Bashkir Cossacks of the Red Army. From the left, M. Zakirov and M. Minigaleyev wearing a *purka*–a stiff cape of pressed camel hair which protects both horse and rider.

Below left: A forward party of the Don Cossacks.

Above right: Soviet Union, south-western front. The Commander of a Red Army Cossack regiment on a finely-bred stallion with some Trakehner blood.

Below right: A Red Army cavalry regiment.

Above left: Soviet Union, summer 1941. A collective-farm horse troop.

Above right: Soviet Union, summer 1941. A military crash course for collective farmers.

Below left: A real steam-horse! The mounted field canteen of a Red Army mountain troop.

Below centre: Taking over new supplies of horses, summer 1941, at a Red Army cavalry centre. Leg and girth measurements are being taken.

Below right: Summer 1941. One of the many cavalry reserve schools of the Red Army. The commanding officer in front is mounted on a superb Arab thoroughbred. The Cossacks carried out their combat activities in self-contained groups of 150 to 250 men each. Each of these squadrons would be provided with enough rations and ammunition for eight days; they were given no precise orders, and it was left to them to decide when and where they would attack the enemy columns or harry the rear lines of the enemy.

Above: Eastern front, summer 1942. Forward under the sign of the death's head for the cause of Cossack liberation.

Below: German Cossacks (*left*) at a briefing session and (*right*), an escorting troop.

Above: Cossacks – a race skilled not only in fighting, but also in dancing.

Below: On the left, one of the Cossacks serving under the notorious SS brigade commander, Mieczyslav Kaminsky.

Above and below: Don Cossacks in the German Army wearing Tsarist uniform.

February 1943, somewhere between the Dnepr and Donets rivers: a Cossack squadron is organized.

Above left: Colour party of the Cossacks of the Don.

Below left: Taking the oath, with '*Heil Hitler*', swastika flag and priests of the Orthodox Church.

Above: The first riding expedition of the new squadron.

Right: The *Starchisna* – the senior officers of the new squadron.

Transported from the Crimea to distant Croatia: Cossacks in the Balkans summer 1944.

Above left: The leading ranks of a Don Cossack regiment.

Centre: Saddlers at work.

Below left: A Cossack woman acts as vet. The horse appears to be bleeding from its nostrils and it has saddle-sores on its back.

Above and below right: Whether night or day, there was always plenty of entertainment.

The men who exchanged the Red Star for the Swastika: Hitler's Russian horsemen.

Above right: This rider (an NCO) has a PPSH (M-41) 7·62 mm sub-machine gun (the most popular Russian model) around his neck. At his side is a Red Army officer's map and dispatch case.

Below right: Dispatch rider of a Cossack regiment.

Below far right: A picturesque rider of the Calmuck Cavalry Corps in winter gear. He is wearing a wolfskin cap with ear flaps, a German army greatcoat and belt, and a machine-gun ammunition belt slung across his chest.

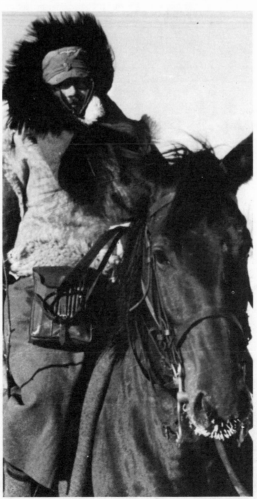

Above: The Channel coast, summer 1940. Exercises on the beach with a really obstinate thoroughbred as part of the team pulling a light field howitzer.

Below: England, Dartmoor, August 1940. A mounted Women's Patrol training for action to meet the expected German invasion.

Above: Boulogne-sur-Mer, summer 1940. Practising for the invasion of England.

Below left: England, summer 1940. A pack-horse of the mountain troops with a complete 3-inch mortar.

Below right: England, winter 1940. Gas alarm for horse and rider alike. The horse, an Arab thoroughbred, is wearing its own gas-mask.

Above left: England, December 1941. Pack-horses of Northern Command loaded with ammunition cases.

Above right: Wales. A mounted signals operator of the mountain artillery.

Below: Training for a Scots cavalry regiment.

Above: Channel coast, summer 1940: cavalry parade.

Below: Summer 1940. In the sand-dunes of the Channel coast with a two-horse team.

Above left: Yan'an district, northern China, 1942. Mao's cavalry by the Great Wall of China near Yang-Kao, in the north of the Heng-Shan mountains.

Below left: A warm reception for a mounted patrol near Mizhi.

Below centre: A night ride through the Hu-t'o-Ho river in the Shan massif.

Above right: Morning parade for a cavalry regiment in Yangchang. The small, mouse-coloured Mongolian horses in the foreground had an all-purpose role in Mao's army.

Below right: With skill and cunning – a mounted scouting party.

Above: On the Don front, summer 1942. A squadron of the Italian cavalry regiment *Savoia Cavalleria* in action.

Below: Italian East Africa, New Year's Day, 1941. Riders of a Savaris squadron with their Arab thorough-breds. Note the graceful neck, the strong hocks, silky 'pheasant's tail', rather high-set, sinewy limbs, exceptionally robust bone-structure, and small, round, hard haunches.

Above: Northern Italy, early 1944. A Slovak cavalry regiment being used against partisans.
Below: Albania, early 1941. Greek cavalry on the advance.

Right: Greece, April 1941. The mounted rifle squadron of a mountain unit.

Below left: Yugolsavia, March 1941. A cavalry regiment on manœuvres.

Below centre: Hungary, early 1941. A hussar with his splendid Arab thoroughbred. Its lips, jaw, and the fine broad and mobile nostrils form a triangle; its forehead is arched like a shield, the big, tender and expressive gazelle eyes are almost round, and its eyelids are edged in black with long, thick lashes. The horse is wearing a curb without a snaffle-bit, known as a pelham.

Below right: Ethiopia (Abyssinia), February 22, 1941. Negus Haile Selassie on an inspection ride in the liberated part of the country.

Syria, Palmyre, early 1941. Native Mehari riders engaged in manœuvres on their Arab thoroughbreds.

Left: Damascus, June 25, 1941. The *Groupement Collet* of the Free French Circassians enter the city. In the limousine is Colonel Collet with his wife.

Below: Beirut, July 18, 1941. General Sir Henry Maitland Wilson inspects the Yeomanry Cavalry Regiment.

Above and below right: Syrian campaign, June 1941. Mehari riders.

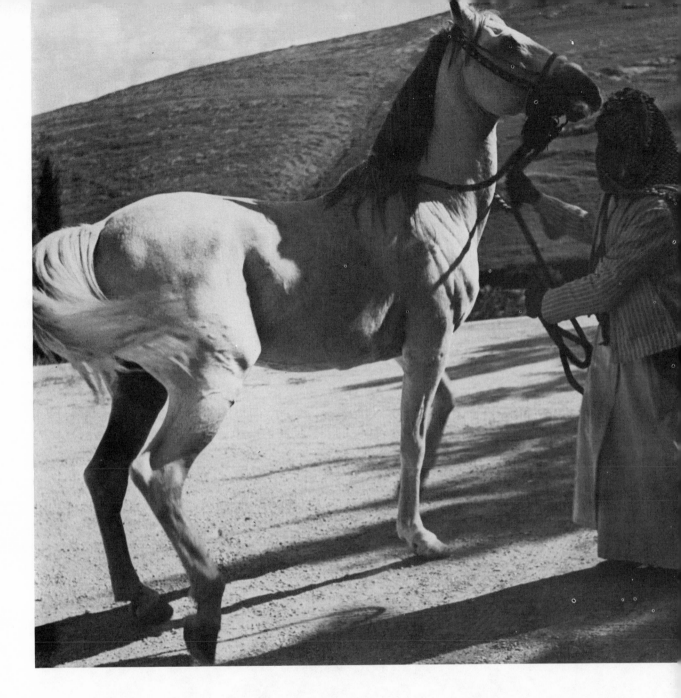

Above left: In the Jordan valley, September 1940. An Arab trooper of the Palestine Police with his Barb, distinguishable from an Arab by its longer and less sinuous head. This breed has a rather flat upper neck, slanting shoulders, high withers and a short back. Other characteristics are its strong, round haunches, angular but powerful croup, deeply-set tail and powerful legs with strong hocks and tendons. Its forelegs are short, its shanks long, and its hooves small and hard. The Barb in this picture has a strong English thoroughbred strain.

Above centre: Horsemen of the Palestine Police with Camargue ponies, a breed from the Rhône delta. Because of their capacity to move without difficulty on either rock-hard or marshy ground, they played an important role in the building of the Suez Canal. Camargue ponies have large, fiery eyes, strong jaws, short, slanting shoulders, long haunches, a divided croup, and long forelegs and shanks. Their limbs are powerful, their hooves hard and their manes luxuriant.

Below left: Summer 1941. These thoroughbreds belong to the bodyguard of King Abdullah of Trans-jordan. The *Areef* (corporal) is wearing the traditional Circassian uniform of the Tsarist army.

Above: This splendid example of a true, élite Arab horse – the extremely rare Asil – belonged to King Abdallah.

Above: Summer 1941. An inspection of the Palestine Police. The horsemen are wearing an Arab shemagh as headdress together with British Army issue battle-dress, and are armed with Mk III Lee-Enfield rifles.

Below: Parade exercise in the training camp of the Arab legion in Abdali.

Above right: A detachment of the Palestine Police crosses the Jordan.

Below right: Arab thoroughbreds of the Arab Legion, a force of the Transjordanian king's household organized by British officers.

Below left and right: The leading ranks of a Mehari squadron.

Left: Nigerian mounted levies. Battalion leader Mallan Amadu Dangi on his high-spirited horse.

Below: Palestine, early 1941. British cavalry at a field watering-trough of sail-cloth.

Right above and below: Nigerian mounted levies, early 1941. The mounted troops of the British colonial force on a patrol in the north of the country.

Above: Cairo, 1942. The stirring sight of the bandsmen and kettle-drummers of the Egyptian royal guard.

Below left: North Africa, 1941. The Spahis, one of the most colourful cavalry units of the Free French forces. This venerable desert warrior, armed with lance and rifle, rides a Barb with blinkers and a polished bit.

Right: A picturesque group of Spahis on their pure-bred Arab horses.

Overleaf: Eastern front, 1942. While an observer keeps watch for the enemy, the baggage train (*above right*) takes a breather near a wood. *Above left:* typical draught harness, without shafts, for pulling heavy loads.

Above: Eastern front, autumn 1941. An endless crocodile of humans and animals crawls along the dusty road.

Left: The scouting patrol, which acts as the forward feeler of the reconnaissance battalion. Scouting patrols used existing tracks as far as possible, riding on from vantage point to vantage point.

Above: On the advance. Supply convoys follow the fighting troops.

Right: In enemy country. A drink of water for horses and riders.

Above left: Eastern front, 1941. Sentry duty; horse, rider and a heavy field howitzer.

Below left: A dispatch rider and his horse. The rider is wearing his ground-sheet as a rain-coat.

Above right: Behind the front line in Russia. Re-inforcements come in at full speed. On the left are two Haflingers with their fine heads adorned with a white blaze, and broad jowls. Their nostrils and lips are narrow and mobile like those of Arab horses; they have small diminutive ears, power-ful necks curved almost like those of a deer, shal-low slanting withers, and their legs are short and dependable. They are typical examples of the breed.

Below right: Waggons of the 1st Cavalry Division on a pontoon bridge.

Overleaf: A scene from the Wild West. While the baggage column stretches away into the distance, the regiment's vanguard has already reached its destination (top right).

Left: No obstacle could stop them – the reconnaissance group of a Soviet cavalry brigade.

Above: Eastern front, autumn 1941. The first muddy period sets in.

Right: Orscha, winter 1941/42. Captured saddles bear witness to the defeat of a Soviet cavalry unit.

Above left: Russia, November 1941, central sector. First signs of winter as a cavalry troop crosses by a temporary bridge.

Below left: First things first – keeping the horses warm.

Above right: The machine gun troop of a German cavalry squadron.

Below right: Paced riding on a reconnaissance patrol. The standard speed was 275 steps per minute at the trot. One kilometre took about 1330 steps. 'A horse with all its equipment should not be expected to cover one kilometre in under six minutes at a normal pace.'

Above: Gomel, November 5, 1941. The final parade of the 1st Cavalry Division: the last appearance of a great cavalry formation in the history of the German Army.

Above and centre right: While the German cavalry was being dissolved, the mounted units of the Red Army increased in size. Here, the Soviet cavalry are charging.

Below right: Siberian cavalry patrol in winter camouflage coats. The men are riding small Mongolian ponies, renowned for their endurance and tough constitution. These horses were so sure-footed that they were ideal as pack-horses or saddle-horses in mountainous country. The animal has a broad forehead, thick neck, shaggy mane and dark protective hair. Often there is no forelock. They have strong quarters, hard, resistant hooves and a thick, long coat. Height at the withers is 122–142 cm.

Above: Eastern front, winter 1941/42. A thirst quencher . . . a short pause for reflection for men and horses.

Below: Horses of a German cavalry unit drinking in a Russian village.

Above right: Forward at the trot.

Below right: 45 degrees below zero in Russia – no complaints from the horse, although his nostrils are coated with ice.

Left: How to climb down a cliff: the US Cavalry in a breakneck field exercise.

Right: Philippines, December 10, 1941. The road to Pozorrubio: one of the squadrons of the US 26th Cavalry on its way into action. On the left, a Stuart M.3 light tank.

Below: US Cavalry on a river-crossing exercise.

Above: Volchov, early 1942. The horses struggle on with their heavy loads.

Below: Yugoslavia, early 1942. A baggage column of the German mounted riflemen.

Above right: Eastern front northern sector, early 1942. Horses get through where motor vehicles will not venture.

Below right: Spring is here. A German scouting party in enemy territory.

Above: Eastern front, summer 1942. The first section of the cavalry squadron of the 26th Reconnaissance Battalion. In front is an East Prussian with typical lop ears.

Below: A horse-drawn double-barrelled machine gun crossing a stream. The two-horse team is equipped with single rear harness and swingle tree, so as to increase haulage power and ease braking.

Above: Where a short time ago all was slush and mud, the baggage horses now stir up a thick cloud of dust.

Below: A mounted signals troop in action.

Above left and right: Russia, central sector, summer 1942. Underground stables act as protection against bombs and shell splinters.

Left: Horses were given special steam-baths to rid them of all kinds of troublesome insects.

Right: A narrow-gauge
railway brings fodder for
the animals.

Left: Eastern front, autumn 1942 – a long-suffering dental patient.

Left: A chance to use modern apparatus to examine a horse; here his fetlock is being examined by X-ray.

Right: A badly-wounded animal is hung in a sling to ease its legs.

Centre: Inmates of a military horse hospital.

Right: A clean, light operating theatre.

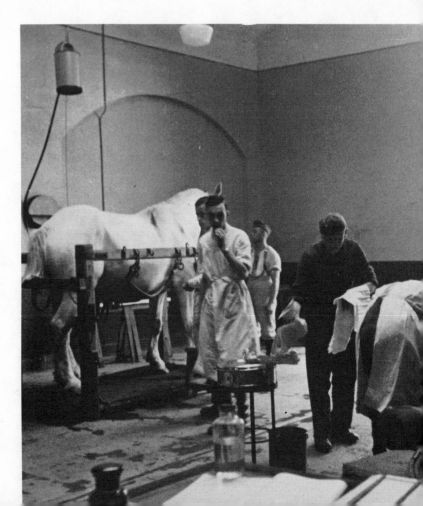

Above left: Manchuria, autumn 1942. Manchurian cavalry trained in the Japanese style.

Bottom left: Tatishev near Saratov, December 13, 1941. Cavalry of the Polish 5th Division (General Boruta Spiechowicz) of General Anders' army.

Right: Palestine, summer 1941. Cavalry practice with a dummy victim: the soldier is in the Polish Brigade, which had been evacuated to Syria.

Below: A cavalry troop of the *Brygada Karpacka.*

Above left and right: Finely-bred horses in the Slovak cavalry.

Below left and right: The Romanian cavalry. On the left are two Calarasi troopers; on the right pack-horses of a mountain rifle squadron carrying a heavy machine gun.

Some rare pictures: the cavalry of the Russian Defence Corps in Serbia, the RSS. Commanded by General Staifon, this force of about 15,000 men (in 5 regiments) was mainly composed of former Tsarist officers or their sons. These White Russians had reached Serbia via Turkey before the 1917 Revolution. The corps was set up in Serbia in 1942 to fight against Tito's People's Liberation Army.

Above left: A white-horse squadron of the Russian Defence Corps in Serbia.

Bottom left: Officers of the RSS.

Above right: A former captain of the Tsarist Guards.

Above left and below right: Northern Greece, summer 1941. A Bulgarian cavalry troop takes up position.

Below left and above right: Southern Serbia, 1942. Guerrillas collaborating with the Germans: the so-called Chétniks of the Pécanac who fought against Tito's partisans. Below left – one of the Pécanac horsemen.

Russia, Don Front, July 1942.

Above left: A charge by the *Savoia Cavalleria*.

Above right: A horse is used as a gun-rest and shield by the *Savoia* cavalry during field exercises.

Bottom left: Mounted *Carabinieri*, in southern France in 1942.

Bottom right: Colour party of an Italian cavalry regiment.

Above: The *Armée de l'Armistice* of the Vichy government, May 1942: a squadron of the *3e Régiment de Hussards*.

Below left: Camp de la Courtine, May 1942. Field exercises with the *2e Régiment de Dragons*.

Below centre: Cadets of the *Ecole d'Application de la Cavalerie* at Saumur in a cross-country race.

Right: Aix-en-Provence, February 1942. Cavalry cadets of the *Ecole Spéciale Militaire de Saint-Cyr*.

Russia, behind the German front line, summer 1943. Partisan movements.

Above: Disguised as harmless peasants – a partisan scouting party.

Below left and right: Forest streams – much favoured as riding routes by the mounted partisans.

Above left and right: Russian front, central sector, summer 1942. Unconventional methods used by a German cavalry troop in the fight against the partisans.

Below left: Late autumn 1943. A Soviet baggage-waggon comes to grief in icy cold water.

Below right: At a well on a collective farm. The horses are wearing an extra ring on their breast-collar harness, and chains instead of leather traces.

Above: Russia, winter 1943/44. A scene reminiscent of the retreat of Napoleon's *Grande Armée* in 1812.

Below left: Eastern front, winter 1943/44. A baggage-convoy.

Below right: Yugoslavia, winter 1943/44. A horse-drawn German battery in a snowstorm in the mountains.

Above: Russian front central sector, 1943. An orderly delivers orders to a 'Rhinoceros' self-propelled gun.

Below: Russian front, central sector, 1943. Sergeant Rohde of the German 25th Grenadier Regiment and a task force defending a railway line.

Right: On the salient of the front around Kursk, July 5, 1943. The end of a Soviet horse-drawn gun battery; in the background is a German half-track.

Above: Cavalry units of the Red Army: a regiment of cavalry guards.

Below and top right: Moscow, Stalingrad or Kharkov – the cavalry of the Red Army was always there.

Below: In the forests of Karelia. Mounted Red Army patrols.

Above left: Serbia, 1944. A cavalry troop of the Yugoslav People's Liberation Army works its weary way uphill.

Centre: Yugoslavia, 1944. The western allies' war correspondents with a mounted unit of the People's Liberation Army. On the left is Jara Ribnikar, wife of the Minister of Information.

Below left: Greece, summer 1944. Two riders of the ELAS Cavalry Brigade.

Above right: 'Warning – wet paint!' Camouflage for horses in Yugoslavia, early 1944.

Below right: In the Vilna district, early 1944. A mounted patrol of the Polish Home Army (AK).

Above: Soviet summer offensive, 1944. 'Two brigades from each armoured corps were to advance through the breach, in wedge-shaped formation.'

Above right: Scorched earth – the trademark of war. In the foreground are artillery draught-horses.

Below right: The retreat on the eastern front – the trek westwards.

Overleaf

Above left: Early 1945. The end: a horse, the soldier's loyal comrade in good times and in bad.

Above right: Cossacks of the Red Army water their horses on the Elbe near Magdeburg.

Below: Klagenfurt area, late May 1945. Disarmed by the British, and wrongfully handed over to Stalin: the Cossacks of General Pannwitz.

Map legend:
- regular cavalry units
- mounted partisans
- Soviet front line December 5/6, 1941
- Soviet offensives
- German counter-offs

Kalinin-Front

Russian 29th Army

Russian 39th Army   KALININ   *Volga Reservoir*
Russian 31st Army

•Oreshki

• Staritsa   Russian 30th Army

Lotoshino   Klin   • Dmitrov   Aleksandrov
Vysokovsk   Yakhroma
Solnechnogorsk   Russian 1st Shock-Army

Shakhovskaya   • Volokolamsk   Russian 20th Army

Russian 60th Army

Istra   Russian 16th Army   *Kljasma*

Ruza •   *Moskva*   MOSCOW

Gzhatsk   Russian 5th Army

Mozhaysk   Naro-   • Podolsk   West Front
Fominsk
• Borovsk   Russian 33rd Army

Russian 43rd Army

Medyn •   Maloyaroslavets   *Oka*
Ugra   Serpukhov

---

cavalry as they continued their headlong charge. Yet not even this concentrated fire seemed to stop them, though the bursting shells tore great holes in their ranks. Then, as if directed by a magic wand, the massive body of cavalry wheeled round towards the village in a single movement. The artillery had meanwhile found its most effective range. Mangled horses' bodies flew through the air to come crashing to the ground, riders whirled round in a vast throng of men and animals. Isolated groups of riderless horses rushed in all directions.

In the middle of this inferno, the 2nd Regiment broke out of the forest in a further charge. Of the 3,000 men of the 44th Mongolian Cavalry Division, however, only about 30, led by an officer holding his sabre aloft, managed to reach the village. And once there, they were still subjected to machine-gun fire. The snow-covered fields, which only half an hour earlier had been undisturbed, were now red with blood. The exhausted little Cossack horses trotted towards the village with tongues hanging out and their saddles empty.

Winter around Moscow

Meanwhile Radio Moscow announced that General Belov's Cavalry Corps was to be renamed the 1st Corps of Cavalry Guards – an honour granted to only a few units. In addition, General Blinov's 5th Cavalry Division, which reached Kaschira the same day to join the Belov cavalrymen, was now to be called the 1st Division of Cavalry Guards.

On November 26, the German 3rd Armoured Division succeeded in forcing back Soviet troops and cutting the main route to Moscow north of Tula. However, the 1st Corps of Cavalry Guards under General P. A. Belov, together with the Russian 112th Armoured Division, brought the Germans to a halt in this sector. The Russian winter here was of a severity previously unknown to the Germans. The night lasted from three in the afternoon until ten in the morning. Temperatures fell to −20 degrees regularly; and soon, from November 27, temperatures of −30 and even −40 degrees were recorded. The German Army was unable to cope with such weather. Tanks, automatic weapons and radio sets failed to function because of inadequate frost protection. There was a high casualty toll among the men because of frostbite or exposure; and the horses suffered from the cold no less than their riders. Supplies of oats had long run out, and the frozen straw from the roofs of the hovels failed to ease their hunger, indeed it made them ill. Horses collapsed and died in droves.

Early in December, not far from Istra, the German 35th Infantry Division took Matuschkino and at a crossroads there found a signpost saying: 'Moscow 22 km.' A reconnaissance group of the 258th Infantry Division of the 4th Army even reached a tramway terminus in a Moscow suburb, and through the smoke of battle caught sight of the towers of the Kremlin.

The Russian counter-offensive began on December 5/6 along the entire 800 km front from 209

Kalinin in the north to Yelez in the south. One in every three soldiers of the Red Army deployed there had come directly from Siberia. They were excellently equipped for the winter war, with felt boots, fur caps and white snow-camouflaged greatcoats. The small, tough, shaggy horses of their numerous cavalry regiments also had a high capacity for survival and phenomenal reserves of strength, even when they were given nothing to eat except rotting roof-straw or conifer twigs. And whereas the German communications were paralysed because of radio breakdowns in the cold, or because motor-cycle dispatch riders got stuck in the snow, the Russians were still able to send out mounted patrols and their mounted dispatch riders saw to the delivery of orders.

Death of the general

After the breakthrough, the Cossack regiments gathered at various strongpoints, formed up into battle groups and launched surprise attacks on German headquarters and supply depots around the countryside. They blocked roads, disrupted communications, blew up bridges and repeatedly ambushed baggage trains. Around midday on December 19, General Dovator reached the highway between Rusa and Volokolamsk. Following the principle of 'leading from the front', Dovator always rode his faithful horse Kasbek at the head of the column with his staff squadron. A peasant boy from a village in White Russia, he had worked his way up the ranks in the Soviet Army from private soldier to become a great leader of cavalry.

About 12 km north of Rusa, between the villages of Tolbusino and Palashkino, Dovator's men caught up with the German 252nd Infantry Regiment, which they had been pursuing for days, and exchanged fire across the river Rusa. The Germans were only poorly protected by the frozen river, but put up a bitter resistance. The horsemen of the 1st Squadron launched a charge and came under machine-gun fire, whereupon Dovator ordered Lieutenant-Colonel M. P. Tavliev, the commander of the 20th Division, to attack on the other side of the river and to cut off the German column beyond Palashkino as they made their way along the road.

Both cavalry regiments, the 22nd and the 103rd, attempted to gallop towards the snow-covered river bank, but were forced to dismount by machine-gun fire. Then, dismounted, they stormed on to the river, only to be halted on its icy surface. Dovator yelled to his staff: 'We must get our lads out of there!' Brandishing his revolver, he ran to the river bank, followed by Lieutenant-Colonel Tavliev, Adjutant Teichmann and Commissar Karasov. When they were only a few yards from the front riflemen, they were all mown down by a burst of machine-gun fire.

By the end of December, the Russians had managed to drive two wedges into the German lines in the north and south ends of the central sector of the front: the German position was now critical.

In South Asia

... like foam on the crest of a wave

In the first week of December, while the Russian cavalry was making life difficult for the German troops in the deep snow and severe frost outside Moscow, a convoy of ships was ploughing through the waves of the Pacific Ocean 10,000 km to the east. Crammed into the hold of one of the vessels were the horsemen of the Japanese cavalry, huddled together on the way to their distant destination.

The 5th Mounted Reconnaissance Regiment had been formed from the reorganized 5th Cavalry Regiment (Lieutenant-General Takuro Matsui). Its commander, Colonel Shizuo Saeki, had distinguished himself in the Chinese campaigns as commanding officer of the 40th Cavalry Regiment. Saeki's new regiment included two motorized and two armoured companies, a machine-gun company and a number of quick-firing field-guns. At the beginning of October 1941, the reconnaissance regiment, attached to the 5th Division, was posted to the Shanghai region where it was prepared for jungle warfare.

While these training manœuvres were going on, the commanders of some other units questioned whether Colonel Saeki's regiment would achieve the same successes in the Malayan jungle as it did in sand-table exercises. Saeki boiled with indignation. Gritting his teeth and folding his arms over his chest, he answered that the ridiculing of his combat ability would spur on his cavalry to great self-sacrifice.

At the beginning of November, the 5th Reconnaissance Regiment left Shanghai harbour one misty night and sailed southwards. On the way, on the island of Hai-Nan Tao, the last preparations for their mission were completed, using the practical experience of the research centre for tropical war. The cavalrymen suffered uncomplainingly the ordeal of a sea crossing deep in the ship's hold, with three men crowded onto two square metres of straw matting at times, and with food rations limited to a bucket of rice or barley a day per section. Their horses fared little better.

It was only when they were well under way that Colonel Saeki was allowed to open the sealed envelope containing his secret orders: 'The 5th Regiment, minus its armoured company, will land in southern Thailand at the harbour of Singora and will proceed to the railway junction of Hat Yai.' Strictly speaking, the Malayan operation was beginning a few hours before the attack on Pearl Harbor. The first Japanese landing took place on December 8 at 3 AM local time. Surprise was complete and the troops landed like foam from the crest of a wave.

A rough sea created difficulties for the unloading of tanks and trucks, but nevertheless the 5th Reconnaissance Regiment advanced immediately. Soon after, it ran into heavy fire from Thai forces based in the mountains west of Singora, but Colonel Saeki continued his advance towards Hat Yai. A Thai company which barred their way was beaten back, and the Japanese approached the town of Tonri unchecked. As the enemy had 2,000 men entrenched in the mountains east of Tonri, the Japanese gave them the offer of capitulating. When this was refused, the Japanese went into the attack and unexpectedly met with only minor resistance.

Colonel Saeki's raid

Various trucks and motor vehicles were captured by the Japanese in the barracks at Tonri and with these they reached the Hat Yai railway junction, which they occupied without difficulty. The mounted reconnaissance regiment had managed to carry out its advance as planned; and it then took up positions in the Hat Yai area to protect the advance of the main Japanese force. That evening, the army headquarters staff arrived at Hat Yai with the remaining sections of the 5th Reconnaissance Regiment, a company of field artillery and some tanks. Here the staff learnt that strong British motorized units had just crossed the Thai–Malay border and occupied Sadao. The mounted reconnaissance sections were then ordered to spy out the Sadao area and explore the situation on the frontier.

Despite darkness and heavy rain, the reconnaissance troops headed into the jungle. After a forced march of nearly 30 km, they came under fire from all sides a short distance from the town. The Japanese immediately went over into the attack and forced the enemy back, and by midnight on December 8, the cavalry was at the frontier after a journey of around 70 km. On December 9, the divisional staff followed during the day. The

mounted reconnaissance troops then investigated the frontier, discovering that several bridges to the west of Sadao had been blown up. That morning, as a precaution, a unit of sappers was brought in, but they could not tell how long the repair works would take.

That evening, while the tanks and motorized units waited for the bridges to be repaired, the reconnaissance regiment advanced further west and later that night, its leading group reached a customs post about 500 m from the frontier. A base was hastily established there for the reconnaissance troops. The road on the Malayan side had been badly damaged and was bristling with obstacles. Immediately behind the customs house the Japanese were met by strong enemy fire and suffered some casualties.

Colonel Saeki sent a dispatch rider to the divisional staff with the message: 'The regiment has reached the frontier and is proceeding to reconnoitre. So far, it has found nothing of significance for the division's mission. It has not been possible to carry out the order to find out the fighting strength of the enemy. The roads have been entirely destroyed. By proceeding through the jungle and rubber plantations it will be possible to continue reconnaissance and to disengage from the enemy. The regiment is continuing its scouting operation.' Late in the evening of December 10, the third day after the landing, the regiment resumed its advance, supported by two infantry companies. The discovery of a post marking the border with Malaya was a great encouragement to the troops.

The successes of the regiment and its commanding officer were rewarded with a special commendation at divisional level, and Colonel Saeki was recommended for double promotion. In Japan, the 5th Reconnaissance Regiment's raid was celebrated as one of the greatest achievements of the imperial cavalry. After the frontier positions had been taken, the regiment contributed to the defeat of the British 1st Armoured Regiment near Anson, and in a courageous surprise attack further south it took the fortified positions around Jitra. The defenders were demoralized by torrential rains which held up their reinforcements but did not even slow down the Japanese advance. By Christmas, all northern Malaya was in Japanese hands.

South Thailand, December 8–10, 1941: The movements of the Japanese 5th Reconnaissance Regiment.

The last horsemen of the United States cavalry

From July 1941, the forces in the Philippines were placed under the command of the United States and the defence of the archipelago became the responsibility of one of the most striking personalities of the war – General Douglas MacArthur. At the time he was also Commander-in-Chief of the American troops in the Far East (USAFFE). MacArthur had at his disposal more than ten divisions of 19,000 American soldiers and 160,000 Filipinos, with about 200 aircraft, but most of these troops were poorly trained and ill-equipped. The 26th Cavalry, the Philippine Scout Regiment (the only mounted unit in the United States Army), was based at Fort Stotsenburg, Pampanga, about 100 km north of Manila. It was under the command of the energetic Colonel Clinton A. Pierce, and was the only effective combat unit in the area. On December 9, immediately after the announcement of the air attack on Pearl Harbor, the 26th Cavalry was dispatched to the nearby forests.

At first light on December 10, 1941, a Japanese invasion force reached the coast of the Philippines. Their landing was hindered by a strong north-easterly wind and rough seas, but they advanced in force along the Damortis Rosario road, threatening to crush Colonel Pierce's cavalry. The armoured company supporting the 26th Cavalry started to retreat at 8 PM and as the last of its armoured cars disappeared, the rearguard of the 26th Cavalry came under fire from the Japanese tanks. On December 12, the second wave of the Japanese force landed near the small village of Apari on the northern tip of Luzon, and close to Legaspi, on the south-eastern coast of the Bicol peninsula.

The 26th marched to Damortis and opened fire on the Japanese as they landed, using all the firepower at their disposal. For a while it seemed as if they had managed to beat off the Japanese invasion in this sector, but enemy aircraft attacked the cavalry again and again, and their losses included a number of their best horses. As planned, however, the 26th Cavalry succeeded in luring the Japanese eastwards to Rosario, by engaging them in skirmishes as they advanced.

At 10.30 on the morning of December 12, Japanese bombers launched a surprise air raid on the headquarters and barracks of the 26th Cavalry at Fort Stotsenburg. One soldier and nearly 40 horses were killed. The losses would probably have been greater if the indefatigable regimental commander, Colonel Pierce, had not ensured that part of the regiment should stay behind in the forests. For all that, the regiment was finally evacuated to a camp near Pampanga 24 hours later, to avoid further losses – in the nick of time as it turned out, for that day there were no fewer than seven air raid alarms at Fort Stotsenburg.

These first Japanese landings were cautious and exploratory. The real invasion did not begin until December 21, when the 48th Division landed on the shores of the Bay of Lingayen. The same day, the 26th Cavalry, weakened by heavy casualties, was ordered to march off to Pozorrubio, where it was to be drawn up afresh. Meanwhile the Japanese had extended their bridgehead to Vigan and forced back the Filipino troops in the district. General Wainwright planned a rapid attack on this narrow coastal plain and directed the 26th Cavalry to take up a position north of Rosario.

The night at Rosario

Japanese aircraft attacked the regiment as it was marching off to take up its new position. The aircraft were followed shortly by tanks, supported by naval artillery. At 8 PM, in pitch darkness, Japanese tanks suddenly appeared in the middle of the highway. Attempts to get the regiment off the road failed; there were barbed-wire fences on the left and steep escarpments on the right. Panic broke out as some troopers rushed to and fro awaiting orders, crashing into the others. The horses were driven wild by the shouting, and many of them bolted. Colonel Vance and his staff tried to stay in position amidst the chaos, but then the enemy tanks opened fire. The only way of saving the regiment was by retreating towards Rosario, and so the troopers raced back along the road in complete disarray, with many of the horses riderless. Some horsemen were hit by the hail of fire from the Japanese tanks, while others were trampled to death by the terrified horses as they broke loose and ran amok in the darkness.

Only the decisive action of two officers – Major Thomas J. H. Trapnell, commander of the 2nd Squadron, and Colonel Vance, who formed the rearguard with him – saved the regiment from total destruction. About 3 km from Rosario, with the Japanese tanks at their heels and in the face of heavy machine-gun fire, they pushed a lorry onto a wooden bridge they had just crossed, and set it alight. The Japanese advance was halted, and the regiment continued its retreat without further loss.

The retreat

On the morning of December 24, the 26th Cavalry was ordered to retreat to Bataan. Colonel Pierce's horsemen were at the time engaged in a furious battle with the advance guard of the main Japanese force, covering the retreat of the 71st Division to the river Agno. The 26th had been reduced to a mere 450 men, but Colonel Pierce held the position at Binagonan until the afternoon of December 24 despite the obviously superior strength of the Japanese. In the course of the fighting, the cavalry attacked the Japanese vanguard again and again, engaging them in battle 'such as would make any cavalryman's heart beat faster', as General Wainwright put it when he later promoted Colonel Pierce to Brigadier-General.

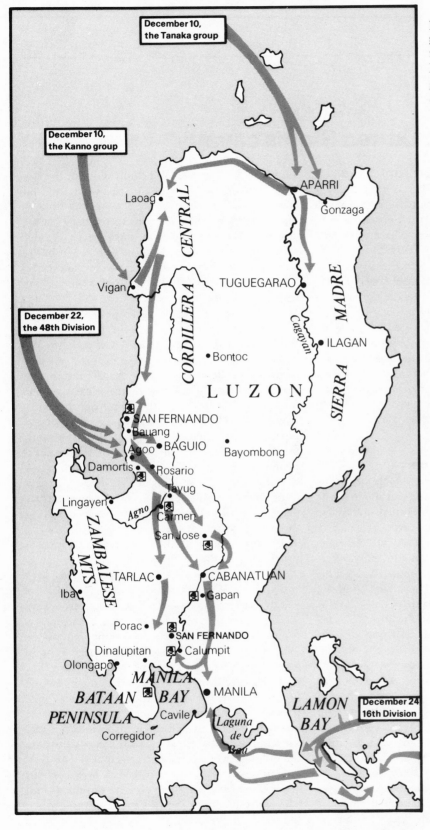

December 10,
the Tanaka group

December 10,
the Kanno group

December 22,
the 48th Division

APARRI

Laoag

Gonzaga

Vigan

TUGUEGARAO

CORDILLERA CENTRAL

Casayan

ILAGAN

SIERRA MADRE

• Bontoc

L U Z O N

SAN FERNANDO
Bauang
Agoo • BAGUIO
Damortis
Rosario

Bayombong

Agno

Tayug

Lingayen

Carmen

San Jose •

ZAMBALESE MTS

TARLAC •

CABANATUAN

Iba •

• Gapan

Porac •

SAN FERNANDO

Dinalupitan

Calumpit

Olongapo

MANILA BAY

BATAAN PENINSULA

Cavite

MANILA

LAMON BAY

Corregidor

Laguna de Bay

December 24
16th Division

*The Philippines,
December 1941–February 1942:
the actions of the US 26th Cavalry (P.S.)
against the Japanese.*

While the Japanese were preparing to attack Binagonan, the 26th Regiment formed up on the highway; B troop acted as the rearguard. Then suddenly two enemy tanks emerged from a bamboo thicket. Lieutenant Seymor of B troop and an officer of the regimental staff waited in hiding until the first tank had driven past, then they simultaneously threw a series of hand grenades. The tank was undamaged, but it halted and the regiment was able to make good its escape.

Shortly after noon on December 25, a Japanese advanced detachment of Lieutenant-Colonel Kuro Kitamura's 28th Reconnaissance Regiment, moving eastwards from Binagonan, encountered scouts of the 26th Cavalry on the river bank outside Tayug. At around 7 PM, Kitamura's troops forced the horsemen back to the Agno. The 2nd Squadron then established a bridgehead on the opposite river bank and because of the deep mud of the Agno, the Japanese tanks were forced to halt there. The battle continued late into the night, and when the Japanese crossed the river at 2 AM the next morning, the cavalry retreated. The Japanese occupied Tayug at 4 AM. There was no longer any point in remaining there, so Colonel Pierce moved off to Umingan. On the way his cavalrymen blew up eight bridges between Tayug and San Quintin and finally, severely depleted, reached the American lines. On December 27, MacArthur declared Manila an open city. Two days later, the regiment discovered it was to march to take up new positions at Porac. That was the final blow – men and animals alike were thoroughly exhausted and their equipment was in a dreadful condition after the battles and marches of the last weeks.

213

The end of the United States cavalry

... As if led on by a phantom hand

Moscow area, early January. The German 6th Infantry Division had ringed the town of Sychevka with extensive minefields, and the Germans within imagined they were in safety. The first Soviet attacks were all failures; then General Gorin of the Cavalry Corps was despatched to this sector.

'It was pitch dark. and one could see so little that I felt virtually blind. So we gave the horses a free rein and let them simply walk on. As if led on by a phantom hand, they managed to avoid all obstacles. Then, having evaded the mine barriers, our cavalry regiment stormed into the town and we had captured Sychevka before the Germans had recovered from their surprise. How the horses managed to detect the mines under a knee-deep layer of snow remains a mystery to me.'

'The vanishing cavalry corps'

During the renewed offensive which began on January 9, 1942, considerable use was made of the Soviet cavalry. Some of the mounted units were spectacularly successful. The Corps of Cavalry Guards led by General Belov, for example, attacked the flank of the German 4th Army, overran its main supply-line, the Smolensk–Vyazma railway, and linked up with partisans south of Yukhnov. By the end of January, six cavalry divisions were operating behind the lines of the 4th Army, which lacked any body of troops mobile enough to engage the cavalry in battle.

Major-General A. F. Bychkovsky, the commander of the 6th Cavalry Corps, was less fortunate. His corps, consisting of the 26th, 28th and 49th Divisions, reached the Alexeyevka area on January 23. It remained inactive there for four days. Meanwhile, however, the Germans were bringing in reserves from Kharkov. As a result, the corps was prevented from advancing to Balakleya and was instead involved in a series of punishing assaults in various villages. Bychkovsky launched three of his cavalry divisions in frontal attacks against infantry entrenched in the villages. In the course of this the horsemen suffered severely from air attack.

Marshal Timoshenko put General Kyril Moskalenko in charge of finding out why the 6th Cavalry Corps had been so singularly unsuccessful.

'The Po-2 which flew me into the area where the 6th Corps was now operating landed on the edge of a village. But clearly the pilot was not happy about this landing site. We climbed out of the aircraft, but he was careful not to switch off the engine. And sure enough, we saw a group of German soldiers running towards us over the snow-covered field. Quickly, we climbed back in, sent off with a whole fireworks show of flares from the Germans. Luckily everything went smoothly. Soon afterwards we landed again, this time in our own cavalrymen's positions.'

On February 12, while the corps was still under scrutiny, an order was issued for Major-General Bychovsky to be recalled, and General Moskalenko was appointed to succeed him as commander of the corps. 'It was only then that I fully understood why I had been sent there.' Next day, the 6th Cavalry Corps was withdrawn from the front. It was to be refurbished and re-equipped as soon as possible. All soldiers and staff officers were mobilized, and enormous help was given by the local people: they cleared the roads, helped with transport and provided stabling for the horses. Everything had to be done at night, since German spotter planes were flying over the entire district during the day in search of the vanishing cavalry corps. Then on February 18, the 6th Cavalry Corps was ordered to capture the town of Losovaya.

'The success of our operation depended on speed and surprise. We moved only at night, and paid all possible attention to camouflage.' At dusk, troops would be sent on ahead to prepare hiding places for the corps. By dawn, everything had to be lodged in the huts of the collective farms, or in schools or clubs, and kept under camouflage. The result was astonishing: 'The surprise attack resulted in the cavalry division cutting the railway line between Dnepropetrovsk and Stalino.' But the Germans hastily brought their forces into this sector and the Luftwaffe attacked the corps for days on end: 'As we had neither air support nor anti-aircraft defences, we were forced to break off our advance on March 1.' The clashes continued with varying results until the first days of April, when the front stabilized.

In the mountains of Bataan

On January 2, the Japanese marched into Manila and advanced as far as the Porac line defending the Bataan peninsula; they took the line almost at once in a surprise raid. Despite the surprise, however, the attackers came under heavy artillery fire.

Around 3.30 AM on January 6, the 26th Cavalry reached the new line, which ran to the south of Layac junction. The newly-formed Filipino Army, the Philippine Scouts, and the US Army garrison all withdrew onto the Bataan peninsula and Corregidor island. As long as these positions held out, the Japanese could not advance into Manila Bay and were unable to use Manila harbour.

The 26th was transferred to Abucay Hacienda, in the mountains of the Bataan peninsula. The track leading there was broken by deep ravines. There was no more fodder for the horses, but the men found heaps of highland rice-straw left over from the last harvest so the beasts had at least something to eat.

On January 9, 1942, Major Fleeger set out with a mountain guide to find a way of crossing the largest gorge. Finally, with considerable difficulty, he managed to reach the other side. It took the whole of the next day to get all the horses over the gorge. The cavalry had to take meandering, zig-zag paths up the steep slopes, cutting down the undergrowth with machetes, and on several occasions the animals had to be pulled over the most inaccessible parts with ropes. A number of them fell almost to the bottom, but luckily they were caught by the bushes which covered both sides of the ravine. In the end, every man, beast, and piece of equipment, including the radio sets, managed to reach the plateau, where almost the whole unit collapsed with exhaustion after the exertions of the crossing.

From January 10 to 15, the regiment remained in its new quarters, about 1 km north of Bagac. There, they had a chance to rest and to shoe the horses, while the scouting patrols set about familiarizing themselves with the district. There were about 80,000 soldiers and 26,000 civilians in the area; the Japanese made a frontal assault after heavy artillery preparation. But the position was strong enough to hold against this attack.

'... with curry and rice'

After the first few weeks, the supply situation on Bataan became so serious that the search for food took on more importance than enemy action. Rations were cut down to 200 gm of rice a day per man, and despite this scarcity, everyone had to carry on fighting. Meanwhile on March 12, MacArthur was flown out and Lieutenant-General Wainwright took over the command. Shortly afterwards Wainwright decided that the 26th Cavalry, now a part of the Luzon Force Reserve, should encamp at Bobo Point. Incessant hunger, the torrid heat, malaria and dysentery (for which medicines were scarce), as well as the agonized cries of wounded men, all contributed to make life unbearable – the more so when it became known that the Japanese were advancing yet again. Moreover, all the rice-straw to be found on Bataan had been eaten up by the horses.

March 15, 1942, became a notable day in the annals of the United States cavalry. For it was on this day that its last horses met their end – in the stew cauldron. The 250 horses of the 26th Cavalry, plus 48 baggage mules, were slaughtered and eaten. 'Their tough flesh tasted good with curry and rice.'

Great Britain's last cavalry charge

Late in the afternoon of March 18, 1942, three British officers were riding along a jungle track in Burma towards Toungoo, 250 km from Rangoon, with 100 soldiers of the Burmese Frontier Forces (F. F. 2). They had been on the move for weeks, making their way from the distant Chinese frontier. The riders and their small but sturdy Burmese horses were at the limit of their endurance.

There had in fact been no British cavalry as such since the Syrian campaign in 1941; the only mounted British troops still in being were the Burmese Frontier Forces, recruited from the various Burmese tribes and commanded by British officers

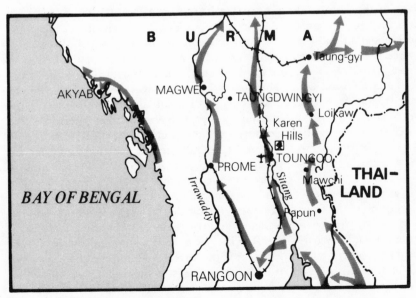

Burma, March 1942: the last cavalry charge of the British Army.

215

seconded from the Indian cavalry. When the Japanese approached Burma at the end of 1941, the Burmese Army was reinforced and the mounted troops of the frontier guard were converted into a reconnaissance unit. The frontier forces, which operated independently of each other, were divided into columns of 100 men, each group being led by two or three British officers.

The 2nd Frontier Forces column (F. F. 2) was attached to the Chinese formations under General Stilwell, and given reconnaissance duties. Half of the unit was destroyed by the Japanese while making its way to central Burma; the remainder, commanded by Captain Arthur Sandeman of the Central India Horse, were ordered to move eastwards from Toungoo to the river Sittang, where they were to observe the movements of the Japanese. A Chinese regiment some 25 km to the south, had as yet made no contact with the enemy.

Captain Sandeman's column rode past an airstrip and reached the plateau below. After two or three miles, two scouts reported several soldiers digging trenches and setting up machine-gun positions. As this was inside the British front line, Sandeman assumed that they must be Chinese troops. He examined the situation through his field-glasses but saw nothing suspicious (especially as the uniforms of the Chinese and Japanese were nearly identical). The column rode on and was already within range of the machine-gunners when Captain Sandeman halted his men, rode forward alone and called out in English and Burmese: 'We are a British patrol!'

The machine-gunners opened fire from two sides at once; the patrol had fallen into an ambush. Captain Sandeman instantly drew his sabre, ordered the bugler to give the signal for attack, and galloped towards the enemy. This was to be the last cavalry charge in the history of the British cavalry. With the battle cry 'Sat Sri Akal!' his riders followed. But neither the captain nor any of his men reached the Japanese positions. Captain Sandeman died in a hail of bullets, sabre in hand.

The end on Bataan

In the Philippines, the American and Filipino troops went to pieces during the last days of the defence of Bataan peninsula. Radio links broke down and headquarters often had no knowledge of what was happening. Many units disappeared into the jungle and were never heard of again. But about 2,000 men and women managed to escape from Bataan in small motor-boats on the night of April 8/9, 1942. Among these, together with 300 US infantrymen, a number of soldiers from the Filipino Army and a few marines, were three or four survivors from the 26th Cavalry.

Between the Dnepr and the Volga

The advance on Chebotarevsky

On July 11, 1942, the Italian expeditionary corps in Russia (CSIR) began to advance towards the Don. The mounted units *Savoia Cavalleria* and *Lancieri di Novara* were sent to carry out mopping-up operations in the Krasny Luch area, and a few days later made contact with the Italian 3rd Light Division. In formation with the Italian 8th Army they reached the central sector of the Don in a forced march of 31 days. Here they took over a defence line between the 2nd Hungarian and the 6th German Army. Just one week later, they were attacked by strong Soviet forces.

By August 21, 1942, the 3rd Light Division was in a critical situation. The cavalry regiments *Savoia* and *Novara* had been sent into the area between Yagodny and Chebotarevsky to halt the enemy advance, and on August 23 they were ordered to attack the Russians, who were preparing to advance on Chebotarevsky.

At dawn on August 24, news arrived of a strong enemy formation, created during the night from newly-arrived detachments, which was trying to isolate the road threatened by the *Savoia*; three battalions of the Soviet 812th Infantry Regiment, with artillery and mortar support, were only a few hundred metres away from the Italian lines.

Colonel Bettoni immediately returned the enemy fire, and the Italians observed the Soviet infantry withdrawing from their furthest advanced positions. Taking advantage of the confusion, Bettoni ordered his 2nd Squadron under Captain De Leone to counter-attack. A *'carica di cavalleria'* – a perfect Italian-style cavalry attack – then followed.

Cavalry charge, Italian style

'2nd Squadron – mount!' In a second, the horsemen were ready to move off. Captain de Leone was given his orders by Major Conforti; he was 'to attack the enemy's left flank with all possible force'. The enemy front line was clearly visible in the dawn light because of the muzzle-flashes of the machine guns. A few moments later, the 2nd Squadron galloped out in close formation 'as if on the parade ground', moving out from the village and passing through a broad arc as if to head back in a circle to their original position. Suddenly, they wheeled round on the spot, and the attack started in earnest; the cavalry 'as if launched by a catapult' hurled its full weight against the flanks and rear of the Russian lines. At this moment, Major Dario Manusardi, the former leader of the 2nd Squadron, was unable to resist temptation, and rushed in behind the squadron, followed by his batman. 'So our old captain's back again!' shouted Leone. 'Evviva, Manusardi!' cheered the squadron. 'One more sabre at your service' was Manusardi's courteous reply, though he forgot that he hadn't brought his sabre with him and was armed only with a riding whip. The cry of 'Savoiaaa!' resounded triumphantly through the Italian ranks.

Fire from the Italian machine guns and the cannon of the horse-drawn artillery raked the Soviet positions. The entire enemy front was crushed by the thunderous barrage of fire and the shocked enemy troops tried to creep back into their trenches. Captain de Leone's horse, his beloved 'fiery Ziguni', was hit by a burst of machine-gun bullets and collapsed on the field. His quick-witted batman offered him his own mount – but it bolted before the captain, winded from his fall, was able to remount. Meanwhile, Major Manusardi took over command, his resonant voice, easily audible over the din of the battle, crying 'Savoia!'.

'The cavalry sabres bore furiously down on the enemy infantry, horses' hooves crashed into the machine guns, cartridge belts and ammunition cases. A few troopers, having lost their horses, were fighting on foot like lions and took some prisoners.'

Captain de Leone, who like his batman was now forced to fight on foot, obviously had other problems as he fired his carbine. 'First we use up all our ammunition, then we kill ourselves rather than surrender, is that clear?' 'Very good, Captain,' his batman replied.

Meanwhile, the rest of the squadron was in the process of cutting through the Soviet line from the rear. Under incessant fire, Manusardi led the way and the squadron carried out a rapid manoeuvre, returning to the thick of the battle and recklessly passing through the enemy line a second time – but this time in the reverse direction. 'Where the horsemen couldn't reach the Russians in the trenches with their sabres, they threw in hand grenades.' Several individual horsemen accomplished feats of amazing heroism. 'For example, Corporal Valsecchi saw another NCO lying wounded, with his horse killed under him. In the turmoil, the corporal climbed out of his saddle and offered the NCO his horse. Then he fought his way through with his fists and managed to take several prisoners.' Corporal Dirti, who fell with his horse in the middle of the Russian positions, was no less lucky. 'He lay with one leg under the animal, and although he was unarmed, he managed to intimidate three enemy soldiers so much that they lifted him to his feet and eventually allowed him to take them prisoner.'

... like a rocket

The squadron had shrunk to half its original size. Riderless horses trotted round dripping with blood and whinnying with pain. Since the Russians were apparently not allowing themselves to be influenced by what had happened, and, as reported, 'the enemy once more tried to attack the regiment', Colonel Bettoni ordered the 4th Squadron under Captain Abba to follow up the first attacks, this time with a frontal assault on foot.

'Abba, at the head of the squadron, sub-machine gun in hand, spread death and destruction among the enemy ranks ...' But the Russian machine-gunners, it seemed, were undeterred, and when Colonel Bettoni realized this he sent in Captain Marchio with the 3rd Squadron and, as a precaution, also launched the dismounted 1st Squadron of Captain Aragona into the battle.

'The 3rd Squadron shot off like a rocket.' Major Litta, seeing the squadrons moving off one after the other, could bear it no longer. 'He leapt into the saddle and galloped off behind them,' followed, rather to the major's disapproval, by his adjutant and his batman. He tried in vain to send them back half-way. Meanwhile all the squadrons had already reached the enemy. 'The hand-to-hand struggle was vicious and bloody', and this must have struck a nerve in Captain Abba's artistic temperament. For, although he was a fearless cavalryman, now that he was on foot in the midst of the raging battle, he pulled out his camera, and knelt down to take a few snapshots – only to fall dead a moment later,

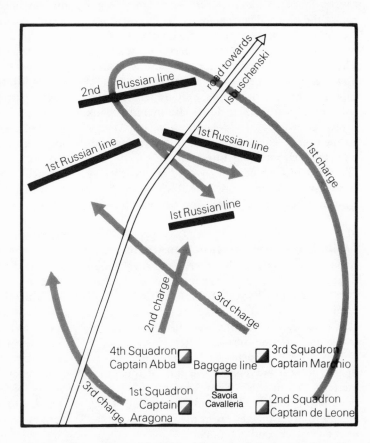

The Don front August 24, 1942: the attack of the Savoia Cavalry. 217

riddled with machine-gun bullets. At the very same moment, Major Litta, an old show-rider, fell while storming a machine-gun battery, brandishing his sabre 'like a grand seigneur at full gallop.'

Italian casualties on August 24, 1942, were three officers and 36 men dead, another 74 troopers seriously wounded, 170 horses unfit for combat. When the battle was over, Colonel Bettoni gave the order to mount, and the remaining cavalrymen who had escaped injury rode for a time with sabres lowered as a mark of respect 'for all those who fell on the field of victory'.

According to the Italian report, all that remained of the enemy force were a few groups of stragglers seeking to escape. On the battlefield lay 150 dead and 300 wounded. The number of prisoners ran to nearly 600. Among arms captured by the Italians were four field-guns, 10 mortars, 50 machine guns and automatic rifles and many other weapons.

Day in and day out

During the Russian campaign, the cavalry squadrons of the German reconnaissance battalions (A.A.) attached to every infantry division had their hands full. Day in and day out, three combat-ready scouting patrols from the A.A. squadrons were in action, each comprising at least two sections and each with one mounted radio squad. The middle patrol covered the division's main line of advance, while the other two protected the flanks over a radius of about 10 km. The greater part of the cavalry squadron was, therefore, on the move right round the clock. The remainder, at the most one section per column, and the machine-gun squadron, were, if possible, not used on combat missions. The divisional reconnaissance battalions would, however, often be consulted about the rapid capture of important bridges, hills, or defiles on the route of advance. Their duties also included flank protection for the division or sealing off enemy escape routes. The scouting patrols generally rode off in the early morning, often returning to the battalion as late as 11 PM. They would frequently stay out the whole night so as to be able to ride off the next morning on a new mission radioed to them.

'Valuable reconnaissance material'

Around the middle of 1942, there were cavalrymen fighting on the eastern front who had exchanged the red star of the Soviet Union for the swastika of Nazi Germany. They were regarded as second-class citizens, who 'might well die with the Germans, but in the meantime remained without rights'. They were shamelessly abused but, nevertheless, fought bravely on the side of their new masters. Among the million Russian soldiers who went into battle for Hitler and the German Reich were a number of men from the equestrian tribes of the Cossacks and Calmucks.

In autumn 1942, the deeper the 'A' and 'B' Army

Groups advanced between Stalingrad and the Caucasus, the broader became the gap between the spearheads of their columns in the steppes of the Calmucks. A single German division—the 16th Motorized Division under General Graf von Schwerin—was finally left to cover this entire region. Poltermann, the divisional officer responsible for reconnaissance, decided to take advantage of anti-Soviet feelings among the Calmucks to set up groups of Calmuck horsemen to protect the division's open flanks.

The people of the steppes led a nomadic life which was frowned on under Stalin. The Calmucks were Buddhists and spoke Tibetan. And it was not without significance that their priests identified the swastika as an old Buddhist sacred sign. Poltermann was given the assistance of the interpreter Dr Otto Doll, who was said to have had experience among the Calmucks. 'Dr Otto Doll' was the pseudonym of the counter-intelligence officer Rudolf Vrba, who came from the Sudetenland and had already been at work in the southern military command in the Ukraine.

The mysterious Dr Doll, who it seems had been a Soviet NKVD (secret police) agent, now organized squadrons of Calmucks, for whom he provided German uniforms and procured looted weapons.

The 1st and 2nd Calmuck Squadrons—later to be known as the Calmuck Legion—were sent into action in the steppes. These masters of small-scale cavalry warfare soon proved themselves to be of inestimable value with their cavalry raids and reconnaissance expeditions into the Soviet interior. They covered the otherwise unprotected flanks and rear of the German troops concentrated at Justa, on both sides of the Elista–Astrakhan road, at Utta and at Chalkhuta; moreover they fought well against Soviet patrols and proved their worth as advance sentries.

Soon, seven freely-enlisted squadrons were operating under their yellow national flag. By the end of 1942, a squadron of Calmucks had knocked out half a battalion of partisans near Ulan Tug south of Utta. Though the Calmucks were totally without discipline in the western sense, they launched themselves passionately into their work. Indeed, they set about wiping out groups of Russians in the steppes with such ardour that the German Army at times had to intervene to prevent atrocities. General Graf von Schwerin said that the duties taken on by his division would have been entirely impossible without the reliable information provided by the Calmucks' reconnaissance. From the activities of the Calmucks, the German leadership gained 'enormously valuable reconnaissance material about the disposition of the enemy in the regions of Astrakhan and the Volga Delta'. In fact, the Calmucks' intelligence operations provided early reports of the preparations for the Soviet winter offensive, which was to lead to the annihilation of the 6th Army at Stalingrad.

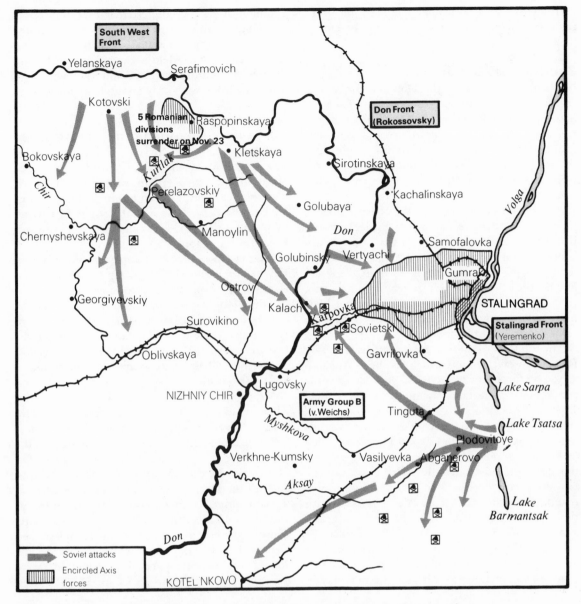

Between the Don and the Volga, November 1942: Soviet cavalry trap the German 6th Army.

Partisans on foot and on horseback

Starting only a few weeks after Hitler's invasion of the Soviet Union, the Russians themselves had in fact been carrying out operations similar to those that the Calmucks were now organizing behind the lines of the Red Army in autumn, 1942. In his first speech after the outbreak of war, Stalin demanded that 'partisan groups should operate both on foot and on horseback in the enemy-occupied territories'. And in due course, hunting on horseback for 'Fascist invaders' developed into a regular national sport in many regions of White Russia and the Ukraine. Sizeable partisan groups emerged, linked with Moscow by radio, and, due to the inadequacy of the Nazi occupation methods, they flourished. They were renowned for their cavalry raids hundreds of kilometres behind the German front lines. The exploits of their commanders, such as Kovpak, Saburov, Rudniev and Vershchihora, now belong to the established repertoire of the history of the Russians' great patriotic war.

At a conference of partisan leaders in September 1942 in Moscow, Stalin assigned Saburov and Kovpak the task of carrying out raids over the Dnepr and were told that 'the results will be important for the course of the winter offensive'. Sidor Artemovich Kovpak wrote: 'We had instructions to advance towards Zhitomir and Kiev. Our mission was to sabotage key railway lines to the Volga and the Caucasus, where important battles were then being fought.' The central partisan headquarters in Moscow sent in dozens of planes with rations, weapons and radio sets. Two field-guns were provided.

Saburov's group, for its part, faced a 500 km journey through the forests of the Ukraine. Its raid started on October 26, 1942, and involved 1,620 partisans, most of them on horseback. The ground had been well prepared. On the march they attacked transport convoys, blew up bridges and destroyed railway lines. They reached their target area in 30 days. The appearance of such a strong partisan force greatly encouraged the people of the region to mobilize in the resistance movement.

South of Stalingrad

November 17, between the Don and the Volga: temperatures were around zero, and thick fog alternated with icy rain and snow. The German reconnaissance planes were frozen up and remained grounded. 'The Russians cleverly made full use of the bad weather situation once again,' wrote General von Richthofen, commander of the German 4th Air Force.

At 5 AM on November 19, the Russians began their grand offensive, from the bridgeheads of Kletskaya and Serafimovich on the Don. A day later the troops south of Stalingrad also went into the attack. Cavalry and armoured units were sent into the breaches in the German front. In the north, the Corps of Cavalry Guards under General Pliev made attacks, and in the south, the cavalry of General Sapkin thrust forward.

The full force of the Soviet offensive was met by Romanian cavalry units which had been sent into action on this sector of the front. At Kletskaya the attackers struck at the left wing of the Romanian 1st Cavalry Division. In the Bol'Shoy the German Army Group hoped to stave off the attack by sending in the Romanian 7th Cavalry Division, which had orders to prevent the enemy forcing its way through to the Zuzkan valley at all costs. On the boundary position of the 6th Army High Command, the Romanian 1st Cavalry Division, with the support of the Lepper Group, resisted heavy attacks by the Soviet 65th Army. The artillery of the 12th Cavalry Regiment had been out of ammunition since noon, and the regimental commander, Colonel Lucca – who fell the next day in a counter-attack – announced that it was impossible to hold the position with the weak forces at his disposal. The regiment was no longer able to close up the breach south of Melo Melovsky; it was having to cover a front of between 7 and 8 km with only four squadrons, each only about 40 men strong.

... Cavalry surrounds the 6th Army

On the evening of November 19, the leading Soviet armoured units had already penetrated 50 km through the German front, near Blinov. At 4 AM, Soviet armour began to move along the east bank of the Zety. Troops of the Soviet 51st Army then succeeded in breaking through towards Kalach on the Don.

The troops of the Romanian 8th Cavalry Division, covering the 20 km gap between the two Romanian Corps, were surrounded. Next morning they fought their way through to the southwest but suffered heavy casualties. Most of the 3rd Romanian Army was falling apart in panic; in the first four days of the offensive it had already lost 75,000 men, all the heavy weapons of five divisions, and 34,000 horses.

Meanwhile, Soviet Cossack cavalry units advanced to the south of the Stalingrad front. This cavalry, together with the armoured units which had been sent in through the breach, destroyed the German reserves positioned in the area. On November 23, the cavalry units reached the west bank of the Don north of the town of Kalach, at the same time as General Podin's armoured troops and General Volski's motorized units arrived there. Thus the Soviet pincer move was complete, and General Paulus' 6th Army was surrounded. The 260,000 soldiers trapped in Stalingrad were doomed, and with them a total of 51,000 horses.

A captain's inspiration: the revival of the German cavalry

'Fine, Boeselager . . .'

The city of Smolensk, where the German Army Group (Centre) was based, seemed dead and deserted in the last days of December 1942. Deep snow covered all traces of the fierce battles of the summer of 1941, and people were kept off the streets by the sub-zero temperatures. In the town's army headquarters, people shook their heads in wonder when a captain laid his papers on the table and declared that he had come from Germany to spend his leave there.

It was Cavalry Captain von Boeselager – the man who had been the first to cross the Seine one sunny day in June 1940, during the French campaign. He was now an instructor on tactics at an army school in Potsdam. This gallant young man, then just 27 years old, had for some time been stirred with the vague idea of putting the German cavalry back into action.

The headquarters of the Army Group (Centre) was situated in a wood on the outskirts of Smolensk, and it so happened that Boeselager's brother, Philipp, was ordnance officer to the Group's supreme commander, Field-Marshal von Kluge. One evening, during conversation by the fireside, the Field-Marshal, with a shrewd understanding of human nature, said: 'Fine, Boeselager, I shall have the cavalry squadrons withdrawn from the front and you can use them to form a cavalry force – the Boeselager Mounted Force.' And so the new German cavalry units were born. But first, a mass of complications had to be overcome. The divisions were anxious to retain every available man and weapon, and were reluctant to carry out the Army Group's order. It was only after long delays and with poor equipment that the squadrons finally assembled at their appointed rendezvous at Novosselki, 20 km west of Smolensk. The horses were unbroken and in poor condition; they had no harness or saddles, and for the time being, plaited ropes had to be used to tie them up. But a squadron of the 15th Reserve Cavalry Battalion was recruited and 350 Cossacks were added; and the Boeselager Mounted Force could be regarded as officially constituted by the end of February 1943.

Kovpak and his horsemen

Extended sorties behind the German lines were typical of the operations of the mounted Russian partisan groups in the winter of 1942/43. On horseback and on horse-drawn sleighs, they continued their activities in defiance of all the troops sent into action against them. The region most favoured by the partisans was a wilderness between Mosyr and Pinsk, known as the Polessye swamp – which was accessible only in winter. At other times of the year, the wide trackless marshes were impenetrable to friend and foe alike. In winter, the partisans set up bases in the forests from which they launched their lightning raids.

The few railway lines which crossed through Polessye were of great strategic importance to the Germans and naturally attracted the partisans like a magnet. The partisan commander Kovpak noted:

'On January 3, 1943, our group, having used up nearly all its ammunition in the fighting of the last few days, managed to reach the bank of the fairy-tale lake Kniaz, after crossing the snow-covered marshes. This is one of the most remote corners of Polessye, where people still lived the primitive life of olden times. While we stayed on lake Kniaz, we sent scouts out on long-distance patrols to reconnoitre the provinces of Rovno, Zhitomir and Kiev. From the information they gathered we drew up a plan for our later operations.'

After a month, as the battles of Stalingrad were drawing to a close, the Kovpak partisans moved off towards the west on February 2. 'We were about to leave the Polessye marshes and to move round in a broad curve through the three Ukrainian provinces which our patrols had covered. After travelling for several days southwards through the forests, we reached the Pinsk–Luninets railway line one night, and a fierce clash with the Germans flared up. One part of our group engaged the enemy while the others stormed the railway track. The line was lit up with a hail of tracer bullets and the draught-horses used for the sleighs pawed the ground in fright and huddled together. Bullets whistled past and to prevent a great blockage building up I had to post several men at the foot of the embankment. They whipped on the obstinate horses which were refusing to budge. If a horse fell to the ground either dead or wounded we had to move it rapidly away by sledge and throw it down the slope to clear the way for others. Some of the companies were able to cross the railway line at a gallop.'

In the course of the Russian winter of 1942/43, a large number of the German horses perished 221 from exhaustion and starvation. But it was actually after conditions had improved along their winter positions, when supplies of fodder were gradually returning to normal, that the majority of the horses died off. It was only then that the extent of their weakness became apparent. The horses had lost so much strength that they were scarcely able to digest their food. It was not only the Germans, however, who were suffering from the onset of the muddy season. It also presented problems for the partisans, who were equally at the mercy of the quirks of nature. Kovpak takes up the story once more:

'The season was now upon us when all the roads were transformed into a morass. While other people living in the endless forests were overjoyed by the sight of the first spring flowers, for us it meant a total readjustment. For a start, it was now impossible to use the sledges which had been so invaluable in the winter months, so we tried to exchange them with the kolchozniks – the collective farmers – for carts and waggons. They balked at the idea because they needed the carts themselves. But in the end they let us have at least half the number we needed. And with the horses which were left over as a result, we formed a new cavalry squadron, though we had to improvise their saddles and stirrups ourselves.

Trooper Lyosha
'Lenkin, the former accountant, known by the partisans as "Whiskers", became the commander of the new squadron. His moustache did indeed surpass all others in both size and elegance – it was even better than that of the famous Budenny. The accountant turned out to be a born cavalryman and incomparably keen and resolute as a commander. As for the troopers of the new squadron, they suited Lenkin ideally: their very appearance was enough to terrify the Germans. I will never forget Trooper Lyosha – you should have seen him racing towards you as the squadron's dispatch rider. His horse was of an incredible size, with a tail that blew in all directions. Lyosha wore an enormous straw hat, decorated with hen's feathers, and he was laden with shoulder-straps, bags, water-bottles and field-glasses, and carried a sabre of fabulous size. Apart from his Cossack forelock, all these were trophies taken from the enemy.'

Around Rostov
During January and February 1943, Soviet Cossack cavalry units in the southern sector of the front pursued the enemy from the foothills of the Caucasus to the river Mius, forced them to cross the Don, and advanced to the area of Semerniki and Gnilovskaya, west of Rostov. From there, they rode out with the aim of liberating the city of Rostov. In the course of a single month, the fighting Cossacks covered a distance of more than 700 km. They demonstrated conclusively how effective

cavalry could be when used in the proper circumstances. But after fighting tenaciously, the Germans succeeded in halting the Soviet advance outside Rostov. The remainder of the Romanian 3rd and 4th Armies, now withdrawn from the front, proceeded to cross the Don. Captain Ion v. Emilian, an officer of the 2nd Calarasi Regiment, was among them:

'On our arrival, the Don was frozen over and strewn with a mass of abandoned vehicles, torn harnesses, guns, and corpses – but what disturbed us most was the monstrous carnage among the horses. Between two and three thousand of them must have been killed on the river. Many had been hit by bullets or grenades after breaking a leg, while others had died of disease, exhaustion or starvation. As we watched, the people of Rostov were walking in small groups on the frozen river, which was now more like a giant rubbish tip. They were using hatchets to chop off the stiffly-frozen horses' limbs. The beautiful beasts splintered like marble under the axe blows. A valuable thoroughbred suffered the same fate.'

The new tactics
As time went on, the Soviet Union had developed the tactics of their cavalry forces to near perfection. General P. I. Batov writes:

'As we were planning our assault on the river Dvina positions we debated the problem of how to put the cavalry corps to their most effective use. In modern warfare, with extensive use made of tanks and automatic weapons, the cavalry is highly vulnerable. After analysing the difficulties from all points of view we decided to protect them against the enemy armoured attacks with a diamond-shaped formation of armoured units. Two brigades from each armoured corps were to advance through the breach in the enemy front in a wedge-shaped movement. As they moved forward, the base of the wedge would be broadened. Then, in the area cleared by the tanks, the cavalry corps divisions would advance, followed by the armoured corps' third brigade, whose units would be broadly dispersed to form the rear part of the diamond. The tasks of the tanks, and those of the cavalry, were precisely defined: the former were to crush the enemy's technical resources and the cavalry would pursue the enemy infantry. When tanks and cavalry had reached their operational area, the rifle divisions would be left to engage what remained of the German forces. These tactics ensured a high speed of attack. The tanks were able to advance rapidly without worrying about the units immediately to their rear. And in places where the enemy had left behind forces armed with effective automatic weapons, the cavalry, ill-suited to fight on roads, would be halted only until our infantry came in to follow up the attack.' Once again the Soviet armies showed how well they understood the possibilities of cavalry.

The Boeselager Cavalry

Although the Boeselager Mounted Force was still short of horses, weapons, and much additional vital equipment, Field-Marshal von Kluge proposed to have it enlarged to form a reinforced regiment which could be used as a swift-moving reserve for Army Group (Centre). At the end of March, the complement of the first new cavalry regiment was established: about 130 officers, 5,000 NCOs and troopers – including 650 Cossacks – and 5,000 horses. After its proposed strength had been approved, it was recommended on April 7, 1943, that the Boeselager Mounted Force should be expanded and designated 'Cavalry Regiment (Centre)'. And von Boeselager's ideas were carried beyond his own cavalry force. He urged that the northern and southern Army Groups should follow the central Group's example and set up their own cavalry regiments. Soon, the Cavalry Regiment (North), under Lieutenant-Colonel Prince zu Salm, and the Cavalry Regiment (South), under Colonel Prince zu Sayn-Wittgenstein, were brought into being.

The primary task of the new cavalry regiments was to fight the partisans. Captain von Boeselager had his own individual way of fighting these small-scale campaigns: he formed patrols carrying rifles with silencers, radio sets and special rations, which would ride off as night fell. The horses would be brought back the same night, dragging brushwood behind them to wipe away their tracks. Meanwhile the patrol would remain for between five and eight days, heavily camouflaged in a promising position, mostly at a forest crossroads, lying in wait to ambush any partisan units which might pass by.

Kalmytski Kavaleriyski Korpus: the Calmucks

Surprisingly enough, the German retreat on the eastern front was an advantage to one cavalry group on the German side: the number of Calmucks available for the cavalry actually increased with the withdrawal, because of the influx of refugees capable of bearing arms. There were so many that new Calmuck cavalry units were still being set up in February 1943. Dr Doll was able to create a reinforced cavalry regiment; at first this was divided into three groups. In the files of the Supreme Armed Forces Command (*Oberkommando der Wehrmacht* – OKW), these were called the 'Dr Doll Kalmuck force' – though they were known by the Calmucks themselves as the *Kalmytski Kavaleriyski Korpus* (KKK).

In February, the KKK was attached to the 3rd Armoured Division and together with the von Jungschulz Cossack Regiment, was sent to the Tagenrog area to guard the coast of the Sea of Asov. By the end of April, it had been enlarged to four divisions, and was sent to the area of Dnepropetrovsk, to guard important arterial routes on both sides of the Dnepr.

Germany's new horsemen – the Cossacks

The volunteer horsemen

In autumn 1941, a few German commanders on the eastern front had set up small 'private' troops of Cossacks on their own initiative. These were known as 'Hiwis' or volunteers, and were formed from the mass of turncoats and prisoners-of-war. The weak German security forces behind the front took on these adventurous horsemen with no complaints and used them against the Soviet partisans.

When the Soviet counter-offensive was launched and the German Army was forced to retreat, it had too many other problems to bother about besides the volunteer horsemen, and the Cossack groups, which had been organized in a rather irregular manner, spent their time wandering about the countryside rather than actually taking part in the fighting. Although plans had been made to set up a Cossack division in August 1942, it was only in December 1942 that Major Graf Stauffenberg (who later carried out the attempt on Hitler's life) managed (in spite of the Führer's flat refusal) to gain the approval of the Supreme Armed Forces Command for the formation of a big eastern volunteer force. At the time, the major was an officer in the organizational department of the General Staff.

There was now no further obstacle in the way of the creation of a Cossack cavalry division.

Colonel Helmuth von Pannwitz was selected as the division's commanding officer. A former estate manager for Prince Radziwill of Poland, he was a keen horseman and was serving as official adviser to the general for mobile troops in the Army High Command. Von Pannwitz was a stockily-built man with Slav features; he had a poor command of Russian, and only really spoke German and Polish. He managed, however, to win the sympathies of the Cossacks with amazing speed.

The Cossack Division

Von Pannwitz had already set up a reception camp for Cossacks and their families in 1942, at Kherson in the Ukraine. The district town of Mlawa, north of Warsaw, was used as the base for setting up the 1st Cossack Division. It was particularly suitable, because of its extensive barracks for the men and horses and the flat areas nearby for manœuvres.

Between 10,000 and 15,000 eligible Cossacks must have come to Mlawa from Kherson for the formation of the division. In addition to these were the Cossacks which General Schkuro, in charge of the recruiting headquarters of the Army High Command, had sent out from prisoner-of-war camps and workers' hostels in the east. Their dependants were housed in the nearby camp at Mochowo, where they took their own cattle and vehicles by road. During the first half of 1943, the Cossack units in Mlawa included the Von Jungschulz and Lehmann Regiments of Army Group (South) and the Kononov and Wolff Regiments of Army Group (Centre), together with some smaller formations. The core of the Cossack Division was the Kononov Cossack Regiment which moved into Mlawa in June 1943.

The Cossack officer corps was a motley bunch. There were émigré officers from the old Tsarist army together with Cossacks who had served as officers in the Red Army – and in addition, individuals who had been promoted independently in earlier Cossack groups fighting on the German side. There were also a few German officers, who were supposed to instil discipline and order.

The Cossacks still wore their old traditional uniforms – tall fur hats made of best Persian lamb with red badges, and crossed cartridge belts over their chests. There was a whiff of the Orient about them, mounted bolt upright on their small, shaggy, but amazingly tough little horses, which trotted through the streets with remarkably short regular paces. Though the horses might not be to everyone's taste, their riders were passionately attached to them. They seemed more concerned about their horses' well-being than about themselves. They would always try to find them reasonable stabling or a sheltered corner. As for fodder, the Cossacks always found something, even in villages which had been totally destroyed. They would share their last crust with their horses.

'... against Bolshevism'

In autumn 1943, around 60 per cent of the division consisted of Cossacks from the Don, Kuban, and Terek rivers and of the Transbaykal and Ussuri Cossacks from Siberia; the remaining 40 per cent were volunteers from the prisoner-of-war camps. Von Pannwitz already envisaged himself as the leader of big Cossack forces supported by divisions equipped with captured Russian T34 tanks, operating in the same style as the Soviet cavalry armies and which could, perhaps, have brought about a change in fortunes on the eastern front. Nothing came of this, however: for on September 12, 1943, a cable from the Chief of General Staff, General Zeitzler, arrived in Mlawa. The Cossack Division was ordered to Yugoslavia to fight Tito's forces.

The Cossacks were extremely reluctant to comply with this order. They were quite willing to fight for Hitler – but only on their home ground. At the prospect of being sent to the Balkans, the whole camp at Mlawa began to seethe with anger. But von Pannwitz was not credited with 'an innate

sympathetic understanding of the peculiarities of the east European peoples' for nothing. Pyotr N. Krasnov, the venerable Tsarist Cossack general and former commander-in-chief of the forces of the Kerensky régime, was hastily fetched from Berlin.

The old man, dressed in a fantastic uniform and wearing a German general's cap, was greeted by Von Pannwitz at the gate of the camp with all pomp and ceremony, and the trumpeter corps sounded a brilliant fanfare as he strode towards the cavalry ranks lined up on the parade ground for inspection.... Krasnov lectured the Cossacks in a fiery speech: 'It's a question of the fight against Bolshevism. And in this struggle it's not important where you are sent into battle ...' The special visit ended with the Tsarist hymn 'Bozhe Tsarya Khrani'; the 1st Cossack Division was the only unit in the German forces allowed to sing it on official occasions. Krasnov's speech was a decisive factor in ensuring that the departure of the Cossacks for the Balkans went ahead smoothly a few days later, on September 25.

In Yugoslavia

The Cossacks made their way via Warsaw, through Czechoslovakia to Yugoslavia. Their journey ended in the area of Ossiek and Ruma, where they were immediately sent into action against Tito's People's Liberation Army. This campaign lasted until the end of November 1943, when the division was again transferred, this time further west to the area around Brod on the Sava river.

The districts taken over by the Cossacks were rapidly cleared of partisans. The natural instincts and crafty fighting style of the Cossacks – and above all their capacity to move through the most difficult terrain – were the source of their success. Whereas the normal German units were unable to make any appreciable headway against Tito's irregulars, the Cossacks immediately won their respect. The riders from the Steppes were given the most critical assignments, such as guarding the only railway line from the north to Sarajevo, which supplied the German troops as far as Greece.

One Cossack auxiliary regiment under Lieutenant-Colonel Stabenov was transported to the Plateau de Langres in the French departement of Haute-Marne, where it engaged in 'security operations.' The Cossacks supported the SS in combat with the Maquis – the French resistance fighters. The brutality of the Cossacks soon became a byword.

2,500 kilometres behind the front line

In the early summer of 1943, Sidor A. Kovpak started preparing a new campaign. This time, his 1st Ukrainian Partisan Division was to advance from near Kiev to the oilfields of Galicia in the Carpathians, with the aim of blowing up the oil refineries, derricks, and giant oil storage tanks which provided so much of the Germans' fuel. The journey there and back would mean travelling 2,500 km through German-occupied territory.

They set out on June 12. German security units and police commandos occasionally encountered squads from the partisan division, but were far from suspecting their overall strength.

'A police commando came upon us near the town of Skalat,' wrote Kovpak. 'We had broken our journey there and were encamped on the edge of the forest. The German gendarmes probably thought they were facing no more than a small group of paratroopers and went into the attack, little realizing that we were a partisan unit of around 2,000 men. We let those brave lads come fairly near so that we could see their expressions suddenly change when the undergrowth abruptly came to life. The partisans fell upon the enemy like an avalanche, and the squadron galloped out of the wood led by "Whiskers" Lenkin, closely followed by the picturesque figure of Lyosha, the "cavalier", on his gigantic warhourse. The gendarmes were scattered as if by the wind. Only the trucks which had brought them from Skalat were left behind.' The 4th and 13th SS-Police Regiments and the gendarmerie task forces were concentrated at all possible crossing points over the Dnepr. But the partisans were quicker.

'During the night of July 14, Lenkin's cavalry had made its way along hidden paths to a bridge near the village of Sivka. With a great roar, the riders suddenly appeared out of the darkness, and galloped over the bridge, shooting the bewildered sentries before they had a chance to open fire. Our division was already on the far bank before dawn.'

Step by step
From Manyava, Kovpak's partisans began the ascent to the oilfields of Bitkov and Yablonov in the middle of the Carpathians. This turned out to be more arduous than had been suspected. The stony, narrow tracks led straight upwards over the wooded hills. The partisans had more than 300 loaded waggons and the horses were soon pouring with sweat. Everyone had to lend a hand to haul the baggage-carts over the worst parts. The moment a horse fell to the ground with exhaustion, the whole column had to come to a halt; for it was impossible to overtake the waggons on the narrow tracks. Even the mounted dispatch riders managed it only with difficulty.

'15-year-old Ivan Ivanovich, who had already swapped horses several dozen times since the beginning of the campaign, was still on the lookout for one which would suit his slim figure. Finally he found a lively little horse the size of a pony and on it he was the only rider able to gallop swiftly through the closely-packed column.'

Despite the immense efforts of the German troops in the region to locate the big partisan force, the horsemen managed to elude them and to reach the mountains. They were in the middle of the Carpathians when they were first sighted by spotter planes. It was not difficult to trace them, for the summer nights were so short that they had to ride on in daylight. Some German fighter planes were sent after them and attacked the long column with machine guns.

'We had just managed to drag the dead horses to one side and to clear a way past the wrecked carts when the planes returned and the whistle of the bombs began anew. The men were always able to find enough cover, as we were surrounded by tall forests – but the waggon-horses were at the mercy of the bombing and machine-gun fire. In order to save the animals, we unharnessed them every time the planes appeared and took them down the steep slopes into the woods. And so, step by step, we edged towards the tall peaks of the Carpathians which dominated the horizon. The horses were continually being harnessed up and then unharnessed. Using spades and axes, we cut our way along the track, which was blocked by fallen trees and boulders and pitted with bomb craters. Sometimes we had to bury comrades who had been hit in the air raids. Then finally, on July 19, dozens of oil derricks appeared on the horizon: we had reached the oilfields of Drogobych.'

Cavalry against paratroopers
On July 10, 1943, the Italian cavalry was involved in one of its last actions of World War II. This was in Sicily, against the British and American paratroopers who had landed at various points on the island, but were dispersed by the heavy winds. If they happened to come down in a poorly-accessible country area anywhere near an Italian cavalry troop, the paratroopers would be met by a full charge as the horsemen threw themselves into the fray, sabre in hand, before the paratroops knew what was happening or could form up into a combat unit. And during the first days of 'Operation Husky', the allied invasion of the east coast of Sicily, the cavalry of the Italian 6th Army (General Alfredo Guzzoni) often obstructed the paratroops as they tried to contact the seaborne forces. The Italian cavalrymen were always prompt to reach the scene of any action and also often managed to stop the invaders in their attacks on the strategic points which constituted the target of their mission.

The ELAS horsemen
On the afternoon of September 8, General Eisenhower announced that a ceasefire agreement had been concluded with Italy. Thereupon the German counter-measures which had been prepared some weeks before under the code-name 'Fall-Achse' took their course: the immediate disarmament, imprisonment or demobilization of the Italian troops. As a result of all this the ELAS partisans, the combat group of the Communist underground

movement in Greece, EAM, acquired a truly formidable cavalry unit. Colonel Berti, commander of the Italian cavalry regiment *Lancieri di Aosta*, was stationed in Greece to deal with partisans there. When faced with the alternative of either going into German captivity or remaining in the Greek mountains, he decided to choose the mountains and went over to ELAS with almost his entire regiment, men and horses alike.

Two American liaison officers, Captain Ehrgott and Lieutenant Ford, both former cavalrymen, happened to fly to Greece with the EAM delegation which was returning home in mid-September after talks with the western allies in Cairo. When they heard that ELAS was about to set up a cavalry force, using the Aosta people and their own partisans, the officers were fired with enthusiasm.

'They were passionately keen to help and wanted to have the cavalry specially well organized and equipped. But they met constant opposition from the British. The present authorities in Cairo were unwilling to provide air transport for the cavalry equipment ordered by the Americans.' But one of the leaders of the United States military mission attached to ELAS, Lieutenant-Colonel Chris, himself a keen rider, helped the red partisans. 'At his request we even changed the name of the 3rd Cavalry Regiment to 3/7th to commemorate his own regiment in the United States Army, the 7th Cavalry, and made him honorary commander. Chris made many people angry in his efforts to help our cavalry and provide it with equipment. The British placed many obstacles in his way and finally, in December 1943, had him recalled.'

In the course of mopping-up operations in autumn 1943 on the Nevropoli plateau, the ELAS Cavalry Brigade forced the Germans to withdraw to their base at Kardhitsa with heavy losses.

'That winter the cavalry brigade found it impossible to find fodder for its horses in the mountains. So we decided to hand some of the weaker and wounded horses over to the farmers, so that they could feed them, use them for their own work and then give them back in the spring. We also gave back the horses we had requisitioned from the peasants to form the 1st Cavalry Brigade. Thus the brigade was reduced to a single regiment.'

In the Panther Position

At the beginning of July, Captain von Boeselager's Cavalry Regiment (Centre) was transferred to the Bryansk area. Operation Citadel, the offensive to be launched from the districts of Orel and Belgorod against the arc-shaped Soviet front round Kursk, was just about to begin. As the Army Group lacked sufficient reserves, the Cavalry Regiment (Centre) was also thrown into the battle north of the Bryansk–Orel road. After weeks of heavy fighting, the regiment was withdrawn in August.

In September, the regiment fought in the approaches of the so-called 'Panther Position', a scanty defence line from Melitopol over the Dnepr and Desna stretching as far as Vitebsk. And in October, there was more tough fighting when the Russians broke through the eastern Panther position north of the Dnepr. Casualties were heavy; and among those who fell was Captain Philipp von Boeselager, the commander of the 1st Battalion. The area came under artillery fire of a hitherto unknown intensity. It was possible to retain contact between the regimental battle headquarters and the 1st Battalion only by using tanks. Russian patrols advanced past the regiment and on both left and right flanks. The enemy again renewed his attacks in the early afternoon of October 23, but was repelled. The Cavalry Regiment (Centre), however, was by then reduced to around 120 men. It was a bitter day for the cavalry commander von Boeselager. His best officers had fallen, and among them was his brother. Two days later, the rest of the regiment was withdrawn and posted to Staiki. And on October 28, it was taken back to the Minsk district as an Army Group reserve.

The massacre of the horses

A bloodbath

On January 10, 1944, the Cavalry Regiment (North) was ordered by Field-Marshal von Küchler to retake the old stronghold of Novgorod, and to use all the means at his disposal to crush an enemy thrust which had cut deeply between the 16th and 18th Army High Commands (AOK). The Cavalry Regiment (North) was sent in to Novgorod as rapidly as possible, as the only Army Group reserve force.

Two of its squadrons were the first German army units on the eastern front to be fully equipped with sub-machine guns. By coincidence, the enemy force they encountered in this sector was a Russian ski division, likewise armed completely with sub-machine guns. The confrontation erupted in a hideous bloodbath for both sides. In less than 48 hours, the German regiment was almost entirely wiped out; only the hand-led horses could be saved. The other squadron of the Cavalry Regiment (North), unknown to the regimental commanding officer, was unloaded on the open track to clear up local enemy-held positions and in the course of this operation also suffered considerable losses. On the following day, with the remains of all three squadrons, the Cavalry Regiment (North) struggled successfully to re-form the link to the north, thus closing up the gap between the 16th and 18th Army High Commands. No sooner had this task been achieved when the regiment was suddenly ordered to evacuate Novgorod, the town it had taken at such grave cost.

Hitler's new 'wonder weapon'

In the first year of their existence, the Cavalry Regiments Centre, North and South had proved their value so clearly that the German leadership could not contemplate managing without them. It became gradually apparent that the employment of cavalry on the eastern front was essential because of the fall in the number of troops, the long retreats and the campaign against the partisans. Moreover, bottlenecks in the tank production lines emphasized the importance of the horse. And finally the Führer, after his long search for every possible 'wonder weapon' which could extend the agony of his Reich, turned his thoughts towards cavalry.

At the beginning of the New Year, the Cavalry Regiment (Centre) was sent into the district of the Rokitno marshes, to the east of Pinsk, and was put under the command of the XXIII Army Corps, based in Horodno. Each individual battalion covered a sector of front about 20 km long. Patrols were sent far into the Rokitno marshes to points which were accessible only with amphibious vehicles. With the exception of a few clashes in the district of Horodno, things remained quiet that winter; the weather was relatively mild and so the time was used for reorganization and training.

Tragedy in the Crimea

Since the evacuation of the bridgehead on the river Kuban in October 1943, the Crimean peninsula – that strategic key point in the centre of the Black Sea – had been defended against a superior enemy force by the 17th Army. After only a short time the Germans were forced to withdraw from a series of positions to the stronghold of Sevastopol. But it was not until late evening on May 8, 1944, that Hitler finally gave the order for the evacuation of the Crimea.

The Bay of Severnaya, in which the enormous harbour of Sevastopol lies, was to witness one of the biggest mass slaughters of horses in the whole of history. About 30,000 horses – the entire stock of the 17th Army – were 'liquidated', to prevent them falling into the hands of the Soviets.

The veterinary company of the 17th Army arrived in the first week of May at the point on the cliffs where the animals were standing in long rows awaiting their fate. Each man was supposed to shoot his own horse himself, but very few of them were willing to carry out the death sentence on the animals which had served them so loyally. So they led the horses to the place of execution where the vets took over this gruesome duty. There they went, the soldiers' brave, trusty servants, and as the shots rang out, many a soldier was moved to tears.

Each horse was taken in turn, with one man from the veterinary company holding it by the curb while another held the muzzle of a rifle to its ear and pressed the trigger. Then the carcases were pushed over the cliff, falling 100 m down into the sea. The bay was afloat with thousands upon thousands of horses' bodies, surging in a gruesome tide in rhythm with the waves. By the afternoon, the 227 scene of execution was ankle-deep in blood, and the remaining horses, lined up in the field, were becoming increasingly restive. As time was now becoming short, machine guns were brought in, and the animals were driven to the edge of the cliffs. The men opened fire, and kept up a continuous barrage until not a single horse remained.

The death of 'Paprika'

Among those thousands of horses of all breeds, shapes and colours was an insignificant-looking white horse named Paprika, who remains to this day unforgotten by her master, who loved her dearly:

'I had to hide behind a mask of anger, so as not to seem too tender-hearted. But I had to be alone to say farewell to my Paprika. She looked at me with those enormous eyes which always seemed to convey a feeling of melancholy. She nuzzled her head against my chest and finally laid it in her favourite position, on my shoulder.

'Do you remember, Paprika, how we first met? There you were, in June 1941, in Barlad, standing among a big crowd of horses bought in from Romania. No-one wanted to take you, your trot was too short and hard, really dreadful – what's more, you were a biter. No horse could stand near you without you going for him. Oh yes, Paprika, you were a real beast. Neither of us knew what name the army gave you. I called you Paprika, and Paprika you've remained. We got on well together from the very first day. You were clever, and you had spirit. You reacted to the lightest pressure of my leg. Of course your trot was appalling. Why did you have to throw your forelegs so high? Don't be angry with me, Paprika, but I often suspected that you might have come from the wanton world of the circus. But your gorgeous, incomparable gallop, your speed, and jumping were famous!

'Do you remember, Paprika, those long rides through Bessarabia, through the Ukraine, through the Crimea, when we passed the company at the slowest canter, imperceptibly faster than the rest of the column? When I slowly slackened the reins and you finally performed that trick on the long rein? And what about that habit of yours of lying down flat with all four legs stretched out whenever we took a break from the ride? My, how often I've taken a nap using your belly as a pillow. Both of us sneered when our comrades warned that the beast would roll over and crush me one day!

'And do you remember, Paprika, that time when we were both the laughing stock of the whole company? Of course it was my fault. I'd tied you to a fence in the pitch darkness, not realizing that the soft ground underfoot was in fact a quagmire of cow-dung. What a lovely time you had wallowing in the soft warm muck, you beast! Everyone had a good laugh the next morning about the white horse which had turned green! Yes, and how did you manage to get onto the roof of that house in Biyuk Syuren to get the grass you enjoyed so much – remember the trouble we had to bring you down again? Then there was our special trick, with you taking a little bit of bread from my mouth – that gave everyone a shock, didn't it? Well, you didn't look all that beautiful, Paprika, leaning down over my face with your great yellow teeth. "That beast'll bite your nose off one day," they said. We loved each other, we really did, Paprika, and the whole company knew it.

'You know how we won the Iron Cross with our dispatch-riding, Paprika? Can you remember, how we came upon minefields on the Kerch peninsula and your reins were shot to ribbons. You managed to make your way, really slowly, back over your own tracks – with your ears pricked up and panting gently. I never told you, Paprika, that I wanted to buy you a happy retirement after the war and had already found you a place to live in Berlin with some good people. But now we must go our separate ways, torn asunder by the merciless fortunes of war.

'Once more I drew in the scent of Paprika's warm breath, and laid my face on her silky soft nostrils. I watched her until the wall blocked my view.'

Towards the end

Hot summer

After the successful battle in White Russia of summer 1944, the Russian cavalry units played a decisive role in the breakthrough on the heavily-defended German lines at Lvov, in the battles on the Dnestr, and in the Kishinev area as well as in other sectors of the German–Soviet front. Once the initial assault through the frontal defences had opened up a breach, then the cavalry could press onwards, harassing the retreating Germans.

On July 2, the 4th Corps of Cavalry Guards under General Pliev advanced towards Slutzk. From there, it continued on to Siedlce, to cut off the enemy troops as they retreated towards Warsaw. The 2nd Corps of Cavalry Guards under General Kryukov was fighting in the same direction. But General Pliev had little luck. His 4th Corps of Cavalry Guards was surrounded northwest of Brest-Litovsk. It was only by making use of the old Soviet frontier defences that he managed to ward off the German attacks. During the night, aircraft supplied the Corps with ammunition.

The Harteneck Cavalry Corps

It had already been announced at the New Year that the central, northern and southern Cavalry Regiments were to be combined to form a cavalry brigade attached to Army Group (Centre). But as it turned out, orders were issued at the end of May to the effect that the 3rd Cavalry Brigade would be formed from the central Cavalry Regiment, with another cavalry brigade – the 4th – being formed from the southern and northern Cavalry Regiments combined. By the end of June, the formation of the 3rd Brigade had to all intents and purposes been completed. And it was von Boeselager who commanded it.

Meanwhile a headquarters corps linking the cavalry brigades was created. This was the 1st Cavalry Corps (known as the 1st Harteneck Cavalry Corps); it was a combination of the German army cavalry with the 1st Hungarian Cavalry Division – and in this fresh reorganization both the new cavalry brigades, the 3rd and the 4th, had to be redesignated as divisions.

The situation had deteriorated considerably in the summer months of 1944, with the collapse of Army Group (Centre). Only the 2nd Army remained in the central Army Group's assigned territory, as a defence guard for the East Prussian frontier. The 2nd Army, and with it the Harteneck Cavalry Corps (consisting now of the new 3rd and 4th Cavalry Divisions and the 1st Hungarian Cavalry Division), had to be withdrawn to the north-west of the Bug and the Narew, to ward off attempts by the Russians to break through the German border. It was the cavalry corps' task to ease the retreat of the infantry by engaging the enemy in delaying skirmishes. The war correspondent, A. Haas, has described these battles:

'The soldiers of the cavalry division were as adaptable as Red Indians over this terrain. The marshes were parched by the sun to such an extent that they presented no difficulties for the horses. The recce patrols stalked through the fields wearing camouflage clothes, and gym-shoes or rubber boots. The cavalry squadrons would gallop up close to the advancing Soviet columns, dismount and lie in ambush, catching the enemy by surprise and strafing them from the cover of the undergrowth – then they would rapidly remount, to be ready for more surprise raids. A baggage column defended itself successfully against no less than 18 tanks and three battalions. Near Kobrin, 70 horsemen with three assault guns secured such an advantageous position, anticipating the advance of two enemy divisions, that they were able to wipe out these forces when they attacked.'

Around August 10, the Germans managed to form a defence line, albeit a thin one, along the Narew and Bug rivers. But then the Red Army advanced in force once more. The battles were intensified, and the horsemen of the cavalry divisions were forced to dismount as they went into action. The Russians had had supremacy in the air for some time; in order to escape the dreaded attacks of the Soviet ground attack aircraft and artillery, guided by the air force, the Germans attacked by night.

Around Ossowiec, north-east of Warsaw, major defensive battles took place. The war journal of the 3rd Cavalry Division under von Boeselager recorded heavy casualties daily: 'August 13, 1944 – Gazewo, 20 km north-east of Makow – of the 85 men who went out from our squadron, only one man survived. All the others were lost.'

Von Boeselager's death

August 28 was a radiantly sunny summer's day. At 8.05 AM, the 3rd Cavalry Division launched an attack on enemy concentrations near Lomza. From a high point in the village of Lady, von Boeselager decided to drive over to the squadron forming the unit's right wing, in order to supervise an attack by the 104th Tank Brigade which was also under his command. He was perched on the running board of his scout-car so as to get a better view of the area when he was shot down by a burst of machine-gun fire. Despite the chaos of the general retreat, his loyal horsemen carried the corpse to Heimerzheim, the home of the Boeselager family, disregarding all check-points and controls.

The Hussars on the Vistula

The 1st Hungarian Cavalry Division attached to the German 1st (Harteneck) Cavalry Corps, was a hussar unit *par excellence*. The Hungarian hussars, with a riding tradition spanning a quarter of a millenium, represented what was probably the best example of the dashing daredevil spirit of light cavalry. In the days between July 14 and August 2, the Division was engaged in running battles north-east of Warsaw. It scored a notable success in a plucky encircling operation near Siedlce; however, the Hungarians were exhausted and running short of ammunition, and because of this, the Russians managed to withdraw behind the Bug at the last minute. After these exhausting battles, the Hussar Division was sent north-west of Warsaw for a rest in mid-August. There it was re-equipped with German supplies and equipment. Meanwhile, the divisional command was taken over by Major-General Vitéz Mihály Ibrányi.

Here, too, came a graphic illustration of the character of the hussars: when the Germans expressly demanded that their allies should take part in suppressing the Warsaw uprising and they were ordered into action against Polish partisans, the divisional commanding officer refused categorically. 'Our two peoples are traditionally linked by a deep-rooted mutual sympathy,' he said. Likewise the Commander-in-Chief of the 9th Army, General von Vormann, failed, on August 27, to persuade the general in command of the II Hungarian Reserve Corps – who had been Hungarian military attaché in Warsaw until 1939 – to open negotiations with the rebels to force their surrender.

The Germans were well aware of the value of the Hussars. On September 14, 1944, it was announced in the bulletin of the Supreme Armed Forces Command: 'In the fierce battles north-east of Warsaw, the Royal Hungarian 1st Cavalry Division under the leadership of Major-General Ibrányi especially distinguished itself with its stern resistance and brave counter-thrusts.' Their involvement continued until the middle of September. The Hussar Division was then transported back to Hungary, where the position had become increasingly critical since the *volte face* by the Romanians. Incidentally, the Cossack units sent in to crush the Polish uprising were responsible for some particularly gruesome atrocities and left Warsaw with a legacy of hatred.

The royal stud horses of Trakehnen

The Red Army's summer offensive gradually began to wane. The Germans stepped up their resistance and slowed down the tempo of their retreat.

It was a glorious autumn of unprecedented splendour, as East Prussia gradually took its leave of a way of life which had altered little in 800 years. The predominant colours were brilliant red shades, with flashes of silver shimmering through the forests from the waters of the Mansurian lakes. From the little villages huddled along the lake shores, the fishermen were still sailing out with their nets. The mansions of the old families remained in a dream world among the mighty trees of their enchanted parks. The horses of the country's noble pedigree stock could still be seen hunting over the broad fields.

The Trakehnen royal stud, founded in 1732 by the soldier king Frederick William I, had played a prominent role among the studs of East Prussia and won universal acclaim for its breeding stock. The Trakehners, known also as East Prussians, were not only the noblest and most elegant hot-blooded animals in Germany, but also the fastest. When they were used for courier service between Königsberg and Berlin, it was found that they arrived at their destination a full 24 hours earlier than other horses. Those of the lighter breed were used as riding horses, and the heavier stock as artillery draught-horses. In the previous century, the Trakehners had already shown themselves to be much faster than the horses of all other armies. But the fact that they seemed tailor-made for warfare, was a grim fate. They were hideously decimated during Napoleon's campaigns and sacrificed in all subsequent wars; but thanks to the efforts of East Prussia the stock was again and again replenished. Even in the fifth year of World War II, the German Army still had a large number of Trakehners which, though more than 20 years old, still faithfully carried out their duties. This fact was the best proof that the East Prussians had succeeded in breeding a tough and outstanding army horse which could hold its own whatever was required of it, whether in the heat of southern France or in the sub-zero temperatures of a Russian winter.

A race against tanks

In autumn 1944, the Russians launched a daring attack against East Prussia. After heavy clashes, the advancing troops came to a halt at the Mansurian lakes, but the Russians then repeated their thrust with stonger forces. The East Prussian stud-farms could have been evacuated many months before, but the Nazi *Gauleiter* (district-controller) Koch had forbidden it up to then. The director of the Trakehnen stud complained: 'When I spoke personally to the *Gauleiter* by telephone at the beginning of September, he told me that if the Russians should advance "temporarily", the Trakehners would have a chance of proving their efficiency in a race against the Soviet tanks.'

During the tragic flight of refugees in January 1945, a large proportion of the Trakehners died because of the immense exertions forced on them. They were shot down by the pursuing Russian tanks, or collapsed in the freezing waters. The bulk of the stock of the Trakehnen stud fell into the hands of the Soviets. Nearly 800 mares and 45 stallions were saved, however, and taken to the west, where they were used to form a new stud at Schloss Erichsburg.

The XV Cossack Corps

In autumn 1944, the German position in the Balkans had again worsened. Army Group 'E' (General Löhr) retreated north through Macedonia and Bosnia, amid continuous heavy fighting, encountering enormous difficulties in finding supplies. Even before the Army Group's forces had reached the region north of the Sava, a particularly threatening situation had developed on the Danube and Drava front, especially after the Russians captured Belgrade on October 18, 1944.

On November 30, what had been the Cossack Division with its two old brigades and one new one was reconstructed to become the XV Cossack Cavalry Corps under General von Pannwitz; it now incorporated the 1st and 2nd Cossack Cavalry Divisions, and the Plastun (Rifle) Brigade comprising two regiments. This brigade, under Colonel Kononov, remained in the Kutina area to guard the railway line and the main road to Agram. General von Pannwitz had his XV Cossack Cavalry Corps attached formally to the SS; he was persuaded to do this because of the prospect of using their help to obtain extensive replacement personnel from the prisoner-of-war camps run by the SS units and also of getting better weaponry than the army could provide. In December 1944, the Cossacks were shooting at their own compatriots: the Red Army had reached the Drava.

Tito's horsemen

In autumn 1944, the People's Liberation Army in Yugoslavia, led by Josip Broz Tito, already numbered 500,000 men. From September 15, 1944, it had a complete cavalry formation at its disposal – the *Prva Konjicka Brigada*, or 1st Macedonian Cavalry Brigade. After a short posting near Rumi, the brigade was incorporated into the 21st Serbian Division of the 1st Proletarian Army Corps, on December 1, 1944. The brigade was a well-equipped cavalry force prepared for all prospective assignments.

At the beginning of December, the 34th German Army Corps was holding the strongly-fortified front near Srem, between Dunava and Sava. The 1st Proletarian Army Corps went over to the attack on December 3, to force the enemy westwards. The 21st Serbian Division attacked the left wing of the Army Corps along the front between the villages of Calma and Martinici. The *Prva Konjicka Brigada* advanced from the village of Gibarac taking the shortest way to Vrbanja and Gunja.

After the 1st Proletarian Division had broken through the enemy defence ring on the slopes of the Fruska Gora on December 4, with the 11th Division occupying the village of Erdevik at the same time, the 21st Serbian Division succeeded in driving out the German units from the Martinici district on December 5. While one part of the division pursued them, the others covered the *Prva Konjicka Brigada* as it formed up. The cavalry passed

the forward lines of the 21st Serbian Division and continued in pursuit of the Germans, reaching the village of Gibarac at around 7 PM. Meanwhile, however, strong German forces had been sighted in Sida, so any further advance had to be called off. Because of this the brigade stayed in the village to await the vanguard of the 21st Serbian Division.

A Christmas surprise

At dawn on December 6, the cavalry units rode on into Adaseuci. Here they received the news that the Sava and Bosuta rivers had overflowed their banks and that an advance through the forests of Bosutsk was impossible. The plan of action was changed and the brigade headed towards Batrovci and Lipovac, where the cavalry's unexpected attack caught the Germans so much off their guard that they offered no resistance. A large number of soldiers drowned as they attempted to escape across the river Bosuta. The brigade captured a vast quantity of weapons, ammunition and equipment.

The cavalry then took over the defence of the left flank of the 21st Serbian Division, guarding against a possible enemy attack from the forests of Bosutsk. In view of the importance of the Vinkovac junction for the retreat of the German troops from Greece, the German 34th Army Corps called in reinforcements to hold on to it against any possible threat.

The *Prva Konjicka Brigada* was posted to Novo

The Balkans autumn 1944: the actions of mounted Yugoslav and Greek partisans.

231

Selo, from where it was able to control the Bosutsk forests as a mobile reserve. The brigade acted as a cavalry vanguard, and also protected the left flank of the main force of the 1st Proletarian Army Corps on the Sremsk front. On December 22, the 5th Brigade of the 21st Serbian Division carried out a surprise attack on German troops along the railway line south of the village of Otok. The German defences were really weak in this sector of the front because of the floods. So the 5th Brigade succeeded at their first try in taking the railway embankment and advanced at least 0·5 km. The horsemen noticed this breach at around 7 PM. Taking advantage of the darkness and the wooded and partly flooded terrain in which the enemy were prevented from using motorized forces and had to confine themselves to infantry, the *Prva Konjicka Brigada* pressed through to the village of Vranjevo, 5 km behind the enemy lines, meeting no resistance.

At dawn on December 23, a squadron of the 1st Battalion advanced into the village of Gradiste. The unexpected appearance of the cavalry caused panic among the Germans, and in the ensuing battle, which lasted about two hours, they suffered heavy casualties. A squadron of the 2nd Battalion pursued the enemy on horseback for a full 24 hours, as far as the village of Zupanji. There, they surprised the German troops who were celebrating Christmas, believing themselves to be safe in enemy-free country. The prisoners later confessed that they had assumed the attack by the mounted partisans to be an airborne landing by the Russians!

After spending three days behind the German lines, the *Prva Konjicka Brigada* returned in the night of December 25/26 and was ordered to Sid for a break.

The last hurrah...

The Soviet offensive

Winter drew in with a vengeance, bringing blizzards and icy-cold weather such as had not been experienced for years. On January 12, 1945, at 1.30 in the morning, hundreds of Soviet heavy guns opened up with a barrage of artillery fire lasting five hours. Towards 7 AM, the firing eased off for a short while, then intensified with colossal force. Close behind the curtain of bursting shells, the Soviet infantry advanced in storm columns many ranks deep, headed by mine-sweeping 'delinquent' battalions and sappers. They pounded forward unchecked over the German positions, with fast-moving armoured divisions protecting their flanks. By Sunday, January 14. the Soviet advance on a single front from the Baltic to the Carpathians had been set in motion. Coinciding with the advance, a migration of unprecedented proportions began. Millions of people from the eastern part of Germany were leaving everything that was dear to them in an attempt to escape the clutches of the Red Army.

The great trek

'It was rare indeed to see such beautiful horses,' enthused an article in the Nazi magazine *Das Reich*. 'At the head of the group rode an old grey-bearded man with rather tired eyes, yet stiff and upright in posture and clad in a short fur coat with a mink hat, his legs enclosed in finely-worked riding boots; with him was his wife, riding side-saddle, and finally a boy, probably their grandson, cheerfully chattering away to himself. Their horses were stallions of irreproachable Arabian stock, white and dappled-grey. They were followed by waggon after waggon, drawn by mares—also mainly white, fine-limbed, noble animals. The waggons—about nine of them—were loaded with people, sacks of food, bundles of hay, with pots and pans, beds and crates, and were followed by a few foals on rope halters. Bringing up the rear were farm-hands, riding the powerful tough little horses of the east. The local lord of the manor rode aside from the head of the little column and allowed it to pass by. He had an encouraging word for everyone. "Soon we'll be in Doberschütz and we'll be able to take a rest there for a few days," or: "Do you think, Wilhelm, that the mare will manage the ride?" Then they rode on, a glorious picture of noble horses, setting the final aesthetic touch to the aus-tere lines of the landscape–yet in the destiny of every person, every vehicle, and every piece of baggage was a touching reminder of this merciless war which tore up everyone and everything in its path – civilization and destiny, man and beast, and even the landscape itself!'

The overall picture was not so idyllic as the Nazi magazine would have its readers believe: the lines of refugees were edging forward at a painfully slow pace as snowdrifts became almost impassable obstructions. A horseman galloped past one of these refugee columns with the news: 'The Russians will be here in half an hour!' Those on foot fled over the fields through the deep snow; but the carts were wedged together and could scarcely budge. Suddenly grenades exploded close to the road; a machine gun firing from the darkness raked the column. For a moment all was quiet again. Then heavy tanks thundered forward, followed by soldiers in white camouflage uniform stamping through the snow. One of the monster tanks blundered along the road, pushing waggons to one side or crushing them like a steamroller. More tanks followed. Wounded horses lay in the ditches, whinnying with pain. Dozens of carts were smashed, and humans were ground to mincemeat beneath the tracks of the tanks.

In Pomerania

General Oslikovski's Cavalry Corps, sent on well ahead of the main Russian advance, burst into Allenstein, catching the Germans by surprise. Several trainloads of tanks and artillery had just arrived in the town, and bitter fighting followed. The cavalry and its accompanying tanks were only saved from defeat by the timely appearance of the troops of the 48th Army. On the night of January 27, German infantry and armoured divisons launched a thrust out of the Heilsberg area towards Elbing, to help the troops engaged in the fighting there. The Germans succeeded in forcing units of the Soviet 48th Army about 20 km back.

Marshal Rokossovsky reported: 'We reacted promptly and sent in a large proportion of the forces of the 5th Army Tank Guards, as well as those of the 8th Armoured Corps and the 3rd Corps of Cavalry Guards. The commanding officer of the 5th Tank Army, General Volski, telephoned me to say that the enemy was approaching his forward headquarters. Some time later, the Corps of 233

Cavalry Guards galloped past Volski's headquarters towards the breach.'

The battles intensified. Around January 19, the Soviet advance was stopped along the line between Mewe, Czersk and Konitz. Progress was also halted on the Belorussian front. And the neighbouring 2nd Corps of Cavalry Guards remained where it was in the sector of Landeck and Rederitz. A few days later, however, the Soviet offensive was resumed once more. Rokossovsky:

'I entrusted the commander of the 3rd Corps of Cavalry Guards with the task of capturing Neustettin and at the same time of protecting the left flank and rear of the assault grouping on the White Russian front. The 3rd Corps of Cavalry Guards lived up to all our expectations: Oslikovski's horsemen surrounded Neustettin with air and artillery support, battered the enemy in a toughly-fought battle and proceeded to occupy the town. General Verschini's air force units were of great help to the cavalry. They supplied them with information about the German positions and bombarded strategic points.'

'Forward – follow me!'

West Pomerania on the morning of March 1, 1945. A chill wind was sweeping low, heavy, threatening clouds across the rolling countryside; small lakes sparkled among the dark forests and, here and there, patches of dirty snow could still be seen. In a village near to the small town of Schönfeld, the military band was playing the Polish national anthem 'Poland is not yet lost'.

Two cavalry squadrons were trotting in front of a group of senior officers. One of the squadrons, under Lieutenant Spisacki, wheeled round to the right towards the forest as the other, under Lieutenant Starak, moved straight ahead towards the railway line. A few kilometres further on, in a valley, lay Schönfeld, behind flat meadows criss-crossed like a chessboard with irrigation canals. The town was divided by the railway line with a trunk road running directly parallel; on both sides were lakes, while beyond were more meadows and woods. It was here that the Pomeranian 'wall' was situated – the last German defence line between the Oder and Berlin.

The horsemen of the *1. Samodzielna Warszawska Brygada Kawalerii* – a cavalry brigade fighting on the side of the Soviet Union as part of the *1. Armia WP*, the 1st Polish People's Army – had a tough nut to crack: they were to break through the Pomeranian wall if at all possible. The Poles had already been trying to storm the German lines for two days. The tanks and infantry storming party had got stuck in the boggy fields the previous day and was then wiped out in a hail of anti-tank grenade fire from powerful tank-busters, well camouflaged in the irrigation ditches. The infantry was forced to withdraw with heavy losses under heavy machine-gun fire. The task which the T-34

tanks and the assault infantry had failed to achieve was now to be undertaken by two cavalry squadrons supported by the remaining tanks. The cavalry could only hope that the Germans would direct their anti-tank gunfire at the T-34s and not at the horses.

A few tanks moved in line towards the trunk road, and a red very-light soared into the air in a high arc: this was the signal for the cavalry to launch its attack. The squadron commander, Lieutenant Starak, raised his sabre and ordered: 'Forward – follow me!' Yelling 'Hurrah' they galloped off and rapidly crossed the road. Thick billows of smoke from the burning tanks formed a protective blanket. They were quickly upon the horrified and astonished anti-tank gunners: 'Russian Cossacks, Russian Cossacks!' The gunners had probably thought it impossible that cavalry would be accompanying the tanks. Behind the German positions, the horsemen dismounted and attacked from the rear.

The 2nd Squadron, under Lieutenant Spisacki, had assembled in a small copse and was soon in difficulty. Even before their charge, a section of the tank force had got stuck in thick mud and was now in flames, hit from the side by German anti-tank fire. The exploding tanks made the horses shy, and the thick black smoke caused confusion. They galloped blindly through. In the trenches ahead of them all was quiet, then suddenly shooting broke out. Possibly the Germans had been disconcerted momentarily by the sight of the cavalry galloping towards them. The squadron's horsemen jumped over the forward German positions, found cover in a hollow a short distance from Schönfeld, and dismounted. It was the last Polish cavalry charge in history.

Both squadrons fought their way nearer to the town. And by evening, with tank and infantry support, Schönfeld, which was fortified with a few dugouts, had been captured. The infantry losses were 370 dead and wounded, but the cavalry lost only seven uhlans.

A lucky escape

Extraordinarily, the influx of Cossack volunteers persisted, despite the hopelessness of the position for the Germans. Only five months before the German capitulation, both Cossack brigades – the 1st and the 2nd – had been converted into divisions, which together formed the XV Cossack Cavalry Corps. Von Pannwitz, now a lieutenant-general, retained command of the corps.

At the beginning of March 1945, the 2nd Cossack Division, supported by some units of the 1st Division, was fighting in the Papuk mountains of Yugoslavia and in the Bila Gora. The Cossacks on the Drava front were at the time engaged in fierce fighting against the Red Army and the Bulgarians. Sasha Volkin, an NCO in the Red Army, was among those who experienced a Cossack attack in the Yugoslav mountains.

'Visibility was no greater than 300 m. Shortly before dark, the sentry announced: "Fascist Cossacks – several hundred of them – are attacking." Two machine guns were hurriedly moved into position. "Scouts to reconnoitre ahead!" yelled the lieutenant – but they were already galloping towards us on a broad front. About 150 Cossacks. They were shooting wildly with their sub-machine guns. Then both our machine guns opened fire, catching them off guard. Nearly half the riders fell to the ground in the first burst of fire, and the riderless horses raced on ahead. We were just starting to breathe more easily when a second wave of cavalry appeared – a stronger force this time. Our positions were being hammered by the Cossack tommy-gun fire. Suddenly one of our machine guns jammed. But the attack collapsed shortly afterwards, before the horsemen reached the trenches. Only one machine gun was now in action and with the crackle of fire from their tommy guns and the roared 'hurrah' of the Cossack battle cry they charged forward again – but this attack, like the others, petered out under the fire from our lines. Luckily, there was no fourth attack. We would not have had the ammunition to withstand it.'

'Za prava – za Kuban!'

On the evening of March 7, the 1st Battalion of the 4th Kuban-Cossack Regiment rode off over a pontoon bridge, protected from the Soviet air force by darkness and the pouring rain. The battalion spent the rest of the night well camouflaged, with its horses and vehicles in the forests along the Drava river. A part of the German bridgehead had been cut off the day before, and an infantry company was to burst through the enemy encirclement round the bridgehead that night. Through this opening, the 1st Battalion of the 1st Don Cossack Regiment was to gallop ahead to regain contact with the isolated German troops and then to force the Soviets back as far as possible with a cavalry attack.

At 12.45 AM, a red very-light went up: the infantry had launched its attack. And 30 minutes later a green flare gave the signal for the cavalry to mount and ride off. On the road ahead, the first mines exploded. The hollow thunder of hundreds of horses' hooves drowned even the shots which were crackling through the night air. The Cossacks galloped off into the darkness. 'Za prava – za Kuban!' resounded the Cossacks' battle cry. One squadron got caught up in an entanglement of barbed wire, but the other squadron, yelling 'Hurrah!' as it forged ahead, reached a Soviet gun-emplacement without hindrance. The Cossacks turned the captured guns around and fired on the enemy. The target line was reached even before sunrise.

The Cossacks, fighting abroad in Yugoslavia against the Red Army and Tito's partisans, had no inkling of the fact that their fate had actually been sealed some time before. In fact, in Yalta on the Crimea, Churchill and Roosevelt had decided on February 10 to put them in the hands of their ally, Stalin, by handing over to the Russians – if necessary using force – all those who had been citizens of the Soviet Union on September 1, 1939; and also all those who on June 22, 1941, had been members of the Red Army and were now in German captivity, wearing German uniform, or serving as voluntary collaborators. Thus ran the text of the secret clause. 'I do not think these people have much of a future left,' said the American General Omar Bradley later.

As far as the Elbe

On April 15, General Romanovski of the Soviet 10th Army relieved the 3rd Corps of Cavalry Guards on the coast of the Baltic; they still had the long ride to the Oder in front of them. Oslikovski's 3rd Corps now formed the reserve of the 2nd White Russian front and took up a position on the left wing of the 49th Army. A few days after crossing the Oder, the 3rd Corps, skirting Berlin in a broad arc, advanced through to the Elbe. The corps was to cut off the German troops as they marched towards Berlin.

To maintain the colonies

The XV Cossack Cavalry Corps reached the districts of Slov and Varazdin on the evening of May 8. That evening, one of the officers of the 1st Cossack Division received a message from Tito's 8th Partisan Army: Germany had capitulated, and from 11 PM no further operations were to be undertaken by the German forces. Von Pannwitz had the Cossack units fall in at 11 PM ready to move off, and urged them to 'force their way through to the Austrian frontier to the British Army under Lord Alexander'.

For several weeks, attempts had been made to establish contact with Field-Marshal Alexander, the British Commander-in-Chief in Italy. Lieutenant-Colonel von Rentelen, who had taken part in battles on the Baltic in 1919 with the then Captain Alexander, fighting against the Bolsheviks, was sent to the Field-Marshal to remind him of this fact. Moreover he was '... to tell him that the Cossacks could once more become valuable allies of the British in maintaining their colonies'. Later yet another comrade-in-arms of 1919, Captain von Gudenus, was sent to the British headquarters to convey the same proposal. Neither of these gentlemen was given the chance to make representations to Field-Marshal Alexander. They were sent to prison camp on the first available transport. Of course, this was unknown to von Pannwitz.

Fighting to both sides as they pressed on, the Cossacks managed to get half-way through the mountains into Austrian territory.

... handed over to the Soviets

In the early morning of May 9, it seemed that the worst must be over; around 10 AM two Cossack officers reached the outposts of the British 11th Armoured Division. Von Pannwitz immediately gave himself up to the British divisonal staff. A few hours later the 1st Cossack Division was marching along the Lavamünd–Völkermarkt road when suddenly a convoy of cars came towards them. Von Pannwitz sat in the leading vehicle with British officers behind him. The regiments turned off the road and formed up in a line. The order was passed from regiment to regiment – '1st Cossack Cavalry Division, parade for inspection!' The bugler corps fell into line in front of von Pannwitz and the British officers; and the division, regiment by regiment, rode past the disconcerted British as if in old times. After this introduction, the captured Cossacks believed in the first few days that the British would allow them considerable freedom within their camps.

They were then ordered to give up their motley selection of weapons, 'so that they could be equipped with standard British models'. After the Cossacks, blindly trusting the British, had surrendered their arms, their officers – 1,475 of them – were persuaded to assemble at Spittal, with the intimation that 'important matters were to be discussed with them there'. But they were overpowered and handed over to the Russians.

The 20,000 Cossacks, Calmucks, Caucasians and their families at the camp near Lienz, now bereft of their leaders, were herded together by the British, with bayonets and rifle-butts. They were then forced into trucks and taken to the nearby railway station, from where they were brought to the Soviet authorities.

British enthusiasm

Apocalyptic scenes were enacted during the course of the handover to the Russians: women leapt with their children into the rushing waters of the river Drava, men shot their families and then committed suicide themselves. Many slashed their wrists or hanged themselves, while others who struggled or resisted were shot dead by the British. Altogether more than 50,000 Cossacks – soldiers and their dependants – were deported from Austria to Russia in the last days of May.

The meticulous British left no stone unturned in their efforts to carry out their promise to Stalin as smoothly as possible. And in their enthusiasm they even delivered many Russian émigrés of long standing and German employees – people who in no way came under the Yalta agreement. Von Pannwitz and most of the Cossack officers were hanged after being handed over to the Russians. Most of the other Cossacks disappeared for years in the mines of Siberia. The horses were the luckiest; the most valuable of them, having lost their masters, were seized by horse connoisseurs and the majority of these were brought to Great Britain.

The end of the German cavalry

On the evening of May 8, 1945, the 4th German Cavalry Division, which had been fighting in Hungary, was south of Knittelfeld. A short while before, it had successfully warded off Russian tank forces. And now, defying the orders which banned further movement by German troops from midnight on May 9 onwards, the division decided to break through to the west that same night, by a forced march. On the morning of May 10 its scouts came upon a British unit on the bridge of Tamsweg. After lengthy negotiations, the cavalrymen were allowed to pass the British lines and told to await further orders. The division – a large self-contained unit of 22,000 men and 16,000 horses as well as all their associated equipment – then proceeded across the bridge over the Mur, to the astonishment of the British who in recent days had seen only the ruined remnants of a defeated army. The last German cavalry unit capitulated to the British 8th Army on May 11, 1945. Horses and men were interned in the Mur valley.

After the meadows had been grazed bare, it appeared that the 4th Cavalry Division with its large complement of horses could no longer be accommodated in the Mauterndorf area, and it was decided to move them to the American-occupied zone. On June 9, 1945, exactly a month after the German forces' unconditional surrender, the squadrons of the 5th Cavalry Regiment of the 4th Cavalry Division fell in for parade in the Mur valley, near the Styrian town of Saint Michael. The Colonel rode along the front of the regiment, more slowly than was customary, as if he wanted to drag out the final moment which was now inevitable. And through the valley, the last 'Hurrah!' resounded as it floated up to the snow-capped mountains above . . . the German cavalry had at last ceased to exist.

Appendix: the cavalry forces of World War II

Bulgaria

In summer 1932, there were two cavalry divisions of 42 squadrons in the 70,000-strong Bulgarian Army. On the outbreak of war, this number was doubled, and from 1941 on the army, under German leadership, took part in the campaigns on the eastern front.

China — the communist forces

Spread over the territory dominated by Mao's troops in China, in 1940/41 there were 11 cavalry divisions on the northern front, and three on the central front – a total of about 100,000 horsemen. Mao Tse-tung spoke of the role of the mounted reconnaissance unit in a speech at a reception for delegates representing recruits from regiments of the army of the interior (September 8, 1944):

'Reconnaissance is aimed at establishing the presence, characteristics, and strength of the enemy. The reconnaissance service is essentially the concern of the cavalry of the People's Liberation Army and includes a wide range of important activities. Skill and cunning, tactical insight, the capacity to grasp a sitation rapidly, courage and decision – all these are the qualities required of a cavalryman. Most important of all, the enemy cavalry must be beaten off at as early a stage as possible so as to gain an absolute psychological advantage over them.'

Finland

Finland's most famous cavalryman, the legendary General C. Mannerheim, was named Field-Marshal in 1935. Between 1935 and 1945, he was Commander-in-Chief of the Finnish Army, and with the exception of the Soviet Marshal Budenny was probably the only Field-Marshal anywhere from the cavalry. In 1920 there had been three different Finnish cavalry units: the Uudenmaan-Rakuuna Regiment (URR), the Karelian Mounted Rifle Regiment (KRJR) and the Hämeen Cavalry Regiment (HRR). As a result of reorganization, the Karelian Mounted Rifle Regiment was disbanded and its troopers assigned to the Hämeen and Uudenmaan-Rakuuna Regiments. These two regiments then formed a cavalry brigade, which was stationed in Lappeenranta.

Before the beginning of the winter war of 1940/41, the Cavalry Brigade consisted of a headquarters section, the Uudenmaan-Rakuuna Regiment, the Hämeen Cavalry Regiment, the 1st Mounted Rifle Battalion, a battery of horse-drawn artillery, an NCOs' school, a tank squadron and an engineers' company. From 1929–41, Major-General Georg Palmroth was its commander.

Shortly before the Winter War, each infantry division was given a light squadron, which included cavalry. The composition of the light squadrons was: headquarters detachment, a battalion with sub-machine guns, a mounted squadron and a motor-cycle company. At the beginning of the Winter War, the Finnish cavalry numbered 8,000 men.

Uusimaa/Häme Cavalry Regiment

Establishment, 1939/40.
Commander, staff, headquarters squadron, four squadrons each of three sections, one support section, one squadron leading section, one machine-gun squadron, and transport unit.

France

The French Army had one of the greatest traditions of horsemanship in Europe, but little of its renowned cavalry remained at the outbreak of war. Three cavalry divisions were still in existence, however, and from these, the five light cavalry divisions – the *Divisions Légères de Cavalerie* – were formed in May 1940. All five were organized on similar lines. They were mixed groups of varying mobility: a mounted cavalry brigade of two regiments with horse-drawn artillery and a mechanized brigade of two motorized regiments (one machine-gun regiment with 36 armoured personnel carriers and one dragoon regiment consisting of riflemen carried in trucks). The *Divisions Légères de Cavalerie* (DLC) had a combat strength of around 10,000 men with 2,200 horses, including mobile infantry. Besides these, there were also one independent *Brigade de Cavalerie à Cheval* (BC) and three *Brigades Spahis* (BS). In addition each Army Corps and Infantry Division had a reconnaissance battalion (*Groupement de Reconnaissance*).

The Cavalry consisted of regiments of: *Cuirassiers, Dragons, Dragons montés, Chasseurs à cheval* and *Hussards*. In the North African colonies, the mounted troops were divided into: five *Régiments de chasseurs d'Afrique*; seven *Régiments de spahis algériens*; one *Régiment de spahis tunisiens* four *Régiments de spahis marocains*; one *Régiment étranger de cavalerie* of the Foreign Legion, and six *Companies de remonte*.

One special unit of the French Cavalry was the *Groupement Collet*, stationed in Syria – an independent mounted group of Circassians, named after their commander, Colonel Collet. The group had light desert scout cars, 12 R-39 tanks and 75 mm and 25 mm field artillery.

The Spahis Brigade (commander Colonel Jouffrault) won unforgettable fame in the campaign of 1940 in spite of the defeat. These élite units were stationed in Compiègne and Senlis. Their officers enjoyed great prestige in the French Army because of their extensive training and their success in equestrian sports. The Brigade consisted partly of French volunteeers and partly of natives of North

Africa from the warlike Bedouin tribes. The fighting strength comprised 80 officers and 2,200 other ranks, of which 930 were Frenchmen; they had over 2,000 horses and 150 vehicles of various sorts. In the campaign of 1940, Jouffrault's Spahi Brigade moved in like a fire brigade to all flashpoints where they were needed to check the enemy advance; they were in action on May 13 in Longwy (Luxembourg), on May 15 on the Aisne near Sissonne, then on the Somme; at the beginning of June they were on the lower Seine and later on the Loire. While the ceasefire was being signed, the Spahi Brigade was fighting on indefatigably in the Rhone valley. When Jouffrault learned of the armistice, he declared: '*Les hostilités ont cessé ce matin, à minuit 30. L'armistice qui consacre notre defaite, est signé. C'est une humiliation que la 1ère Brigade de Spahis n'a pas méritée ...!*' After the end of the campaign, Jouffrault and his Spahi Brigade were named as the only unconquered force in the general collapse ('*le seul invaincu de la débâcle*').

After the ceasefire, the Pétain administration's force, the so-called *Armée de l'Armistice*, was organized in the unoccupied part of France. It was formed into eight divisions, and was given the same names as the former units which were now in occupied territory: these were the *7e Division militaire*, at Bourg-en-Bresse; the *9e Division militaire*, at Châteauroux; the *12e Division militaire*, at Limoges; the *13e Division militaire*, at Clermont-Ferrand; the *14e Division militaire*, at Lyon, the *15e Division militaire*, at Marseille; the *16e Division militaire*, at Montpellier, and the *17e Division militaire*, at Toulouse. The army staff under the leadership of General Verneau was based in Vichy. Each of these divisions had a cavalry regiment; these were composed of two mounted squadrons, three motor-cycle squadrons, and one squadron of Panhard armoured cars.

In 1943/44, the so-called *Goumiers* – the soldiers of the mounted Moroccan supply columns – fought in Italy as part of the *Corps expéditionnaire Français* (General Juin). In the difficult terrain of the Apennines, their pack-horses gave them great mobility. In May 1944, the *Goumiers* of General Guillaume were also among the first to advance to Monte Cassino. They proved their fighting ability in the desperate combats there.

Germany

In 1914, the German Imperial Army had more than 110 active cavalry units. In the 100,000-man postwar army (the *Reichswehr*) there were 18 mounted regiments, later divided into three cavalry divisions. In 1935 these three divisions were disbanded. Most of the mounted regiments were redesignated and converted into motorized cavalry regiments, and when war came they were used as reconnaissance units for the infantry divisions. In East Prussia, however, the 1st Cavalry Brigade survived to form the only remaining unit of the Army

Horse Cavalry. It consisted of two mounted regiments, the 1st and the 2nd. These, broadly speaking, retained their old structure of five squadrons apiece, and kept their old names.

The combat strength of the 1st Cavalry Brigade, dismounted, corresponded broadly to that of an infantry regiment. Though it lacked the heavy 15 cm infantry cannon, the firing power of its artillery was actually rather greater. It had more light cannon and more heavy weapons than an infantry battalion, and was especially manœuvrable across country. The 1st Cavalry Brigade proved its value in the Polish campaign, although its lack of modern heavy weapons was a handicap.

The army's mounted units [the 1st Cavalry Brigade, later to become the 1st Cavalry Division; and the Cavalry Regiments (North), (South) and (Centre) which were later to become the 3rd and 4th Cavalry Divisions] were the least numerous part of the German cavalry. The major part consisted of motorized divisional reconnaissance battalions serving as divisional cavalry for the infantry, light and also mountain divisions. In this role the cavalry had no independent strategic value but was very useful because of its mobility.

1st Cavalry Brigade

Establishment, September 1, 1939. C.O.: Colonel Feldt;

1st Mounted Regiment: C.O.: Lieutenant-Colonel Wachsen;

2nd Mounted Regiment: C.O.: Colonel von Saucken;

1st Mounted Artillery Battalion: C.O.: Lieutenant-Colonel Holste.

The 1st Cavalry Brigade was redesignated the 1st Cavalry Division on October 25, 1939, and reinforced with the 2nd Mounted Brigade (formed on December 7, 1939) which consisted of:

21st Mounted Regiment: I 1st–5th, II 6th–10th (formed from the 8th, 28th, 162nd; and 7th, 54th, 14th Reconnaissance Battalions);

22nd Mounted Regiment: I 1st–5th, II 6th–10th (formed from the 3rd, 17th, 173rd, and 21st, 30th 156th Reconnaissance Battalions).

2nd Mounted Artillery Battalion (Batteries one-three) and headquarters 202nd Mounted Artillery Regiment.

On February 2, 1940, the Division was reorganized, the II/21st disbanded and the three other regiments thus brought to an equal strength of two battalions, each of four squadrons, nine heavy infantry guns, and a 10th headquarters squadron.

The former 2nd Mounted Brigade became the 1st Mounted Brigade on April 2, 1941. This consisted of:

1st Mounted Regiment, I, II; 2nd Mounted Regiment, I, II; 21st Cavalry Regiment (1st–5th squadrons); a motor-cycle battalion (with five supporting batteries); 1st Mounted Artillery Regiment I, II and (from autumn 1940) III; and the 40th Battalion divisional units (86th Battalion Cavalry Signals).

1st Mounted Regiment

Establishment, September 1, 1939.

Structure:

C.O.: Lieutenant-Colonel Wachsen.

Regimental headquarters with a mounted and a motorized unit.

Signals section:

One radio unit (a) motorized: one motorized telephone unit, and three portable radio units (b) mounted: one mounted telephone unit, and one NF4 horse-drawn signals waggon. Strength: One officer, 29 NCOs and men, 25 horses (17 saddle-, four pack-, four draught-), one NF4 signals waggon, two no. 15 vehicles, and one radio truck.

1st Squadron:

One headquarters troop; three mounted troops split into one headquarters group and three sections each (each section consisted of two rifle groups, and one machine-gun crew; 13 other ranks and 14 horses; the 1st and 2nd section were equipped in addition with one ammunition pack-horse and groom); each troop had one officer, 44 other ranks, 50 horses, and three light machine guns. There was one heavy machine-gun troop consisting of one officer, 39 other ranks, 48 horses, and four heavy MG34 machine guns; a sanitary patrol; a hand-led horse squad, and the regimental sergeant-major; a baggage section of 28 other ranks, 35 horses, one field canteen, four HF2, three HF1 vehicles, and one motor-cycle and side-car.

Total strength: five officers, about 216 other ranks, about 254 horses. Dismounted the squadron's firing power was: four heavy MG34 machine guns, nine light MG34 machine guns, 14 MP38 sub-machine guns, and about 68 98k rifles.

2nd, 3rd, and 4th Squadrons:

As 1st Squadron.

5th (Heavy) Squadron:

Headquarters troop; one heavy mortar troop (split into one headquarters group and three sections each with two mortars of 8 cm calibre, mounted on carriages drawn by six-horse teams, with the mortar commander and two mounted riflemen, and four riflemen on the limber); two cavalry-gun sections (consisting of a headquarters group, each with two cavalry guns of 7·5 cm calibre with a six-horse team and one ammunition squad, riflemen on limber, and a mounted gun commander); two field canteens, and a baggage section.

Total strength: four officers, 226 other ranks, 225 horses, 20 vehicles, six 8 cm mortars, and four 7·5 cm cavalry guns.

Headquarters Squadron (motorized):

Headquarters group; armoured scout-car troop (two four-wheeler armoured scout-cars with MG34 machine guns, one radio truck of old design); anti-tank troop (three sections each with one MG34 machine gun and rubber dinghies); baggage section.

Total strength: three officers and 150 other ranks.

Light cavalry column:

11 HF1 waggons with four-horse teams (five ammunition waggons, five fodder-carts and one blacksmith's waggon).

Total strength: 39 other ranks and 50 horses.

The regiment also had sanitation vans and several supply trucks.

Fire power: 42 MG34 light machine guns, 16 MG34 heavy machine guns, six 8 cm mortars, four 7·5 cm cavalry guns, and three 3·7 cm anti-tank guns.

Theoretical strength: 39 officers, two clerical officials, 204 NCOs, 1,195 men, 1,421 horses, 91 horse-drawn vehicles, one trailer, 21 cars, 12 trucks and 27 motor-cycles (nine with side-cars).

The horsemen were armed with sabres and 98k rifles; section leaders had '08' pistols. The bicycle squadron and machine-gun crews were motorized with motor-cycle and sidecar combinations. Sabres were no longer used after 1940, and rifle-holsters were phased out. The horsemen carried their rifles on their backs from then on, while group commanders were armed with sub-machine guns.

The 1st Cavalry Division saw action in eastern Holland and also in the French campaign, riding 1,000 km in forced marches and fighting from Aix to Bordeaux. On June 22, 1941, they crossed the Bug south of Brest with General Guderian's armoured units. In the Pripet marshes they fought on difficult terrain, and were engaged in pursuit battles as far as the Berezina; they then fought defensive battles on the Dnepr and near Gomel. Horsemen and horse-drawn artillery were later involved in the battle around Bryansk.

On November 3, 1941, the feast-day of St Hubertus, the patron saint of cavalry, the 1st Cavalry Division dismounted for the last time. Finally, during the winter of 1941/42, they were retrained near Paris to become the 24th Armoured Cavalry Division and attached to the 6th Army which was in Stalingrad. In recognition of their previous services, the old regiments retained the yellow insignia on their uniforms and cavalry nomenclature – such as the 'squadron' unit and the ranks of '*Rittmeister*' (for captain) and '*Wachtmeister*' (for sergeant-major). Today it is no longer possible to establish the reasons for disbanding the self-contained cavalry units; it cannot have been because of the lack of horses, however, for at the same time, under Hitler's future brother-in-law, Fegelein, the SS Cavalry was being formed into a division, modelled on the dissolved Cavalry Division in structure, equipment, and designed to fulfil the same tasks.

After mechanization, the cavalry regiments, with their long history, were converted partly into armoured and assault-gun units and partly into motor-cycle and light infantry battalions. These groups were attached to infantry divisions as reconnaissance units.

Structure of a divisional reconnaissance battalion with mounted squadron: headquarters with motorized signals detachment, one mounted squadron, one motor-cycle squadron and one motorized heavy squadron. Headquarters: C.O., 239 adjutant, ordnance officer, quartermaster, battalion medical officer, battalion veterinary officer, paymaster, and ancillary headquarters clerical staff (orderly, typist etc.), combat transport, food supplies transport and baggage transport (the C.O. and adjutant each had two horses, the ordnance officer, M.O. and vet. each had one horse); motorized signals section: section commander, one motorized radio unit for divisional communications, one morotized radio unit for communication with armoured or scout parties, one radio unit for communication with the three mounted radio troops and three mounted radio troops with knapsack-radio sets.

From this point, mounted squadrons only saw sustained action when used as reconnaissance parties by the infantry divisions. The formation of these partly-motorized recce battalions, divided into one mounted squadron, one motor-cycle squadron, and one motorized heavy squadron had little point and it was barely possible to organize them in action as self-contained units. The 25 or so recce battalions which had mounted squadrons were worn out by the divisional commanders on the eastern front, who used them as 'firemen' in crisis situations.

As this was out of keeping with the character of the force, the Army Supreme Command finally decided to convert the mounted squadrons into cavalry regiments once more, so as to form a reserve which was mobile at all times. Thereupon various cavalry units were established in the years 1942 and 1943 as part of the Army Group (Centre). On the orders of General Model, commander of the 9th Army [the left wing of the Army Group (Centre)] the Special Operations Army Cavalry Command was set up. This was formed from the Reconnaissance Battalions of the 6th, 23rd, and 27th Army Corps, reinforced by mounted infantry sections. It was sent into action in forest areas in the district of Rshev, in operation 'Seydlitz' (July 2, 1942) and used in other similar operations, where it was quite successful.

Special Operations Army Cavalry Command
C.O.: Colonel Holste;
1st Army Cavalry Regiment – C.O.: Major Laubner;
2nd Army Cavalry Regiment – C.O.: Major Briegleb;
3rd Army Cavalry Regiment – C.O.: Lieutenant-Colonel von Baath;
1st Squadron (formerly Mounted Squadron, 26th Reconnaissance Battalion) C.O.: Captain Bräuning;
2nd Squadron (formerly Motor-cycle Squadron, 26th Reconnaissance Battalion) C.O.: Lieutenant Dresing;
3rd Squadron (formerly Motor-cycle Squadron, 6th Reconnaissance Battalion) C.O.: Lieutenant Dresler;
4th Squadron (Heavy, from 6th and 26th Recon-

naissance Battalions) C.O.: Lieutenant Massmann;
5th Squadron (Mounted Squadron, 6th Reconnaissance Battalion) C.O.: Lieutenant Begeré.
Entirely unexpectedly, the Special Operations Army Cavalry Command was disbanded on July 24, 1942, and the reconnaissance battalions were returned to their original divisions.

Another unit, the Von Winnig Mounted Force, set up in 1942/43, was disbanded in spring 1943. Their designation as 'Light Troops' was changed to 'Armoured Troops' on March 31, 1943. Thus the cavalry formations and motor-cycle troops, as well as the reconnaissance and light infantry battalions of the infantry divisions, lost the title of 'Light Troops' which they had hitherto shared with the armoured troops, motorized rifle-regiments and anti-tank gun battalions – from then on, they became simply 'Infantry'.

Spring 1943. The Von Boeselager Mounted Force, whose establishment had been supported by Field-Marshal von Kluge of Army Group (Centre) – who had gathered together the remaining reconnaissance battalion units and had given von Boeselager priority in selecting staff and material from the supplies transport sections – became the Cavalry Regiment (Centre). Von Boeselager succeeded in forming a cavalry unit from the widely-dispersed squadrons of the divisional reconnaissance battalions and from riders who had been posted elsewhere. This unit lasted until the end of the war, proved itself remarkably efficient in action.

It was the 6th Reconnaissance Battalion and the 1st Mounted Squadron which von Boeselager had led until the beginning of 1942, which now formed the basis of the new mounted force. In addition, the Von Boeselager Mounted Force had the following:
2nd Squadron, from the 3rd Squadron of the 34th Reconnaissance Battalion – later the 34th Motor-cycle Battalion of the 34th Infantry Division.
3rd Squadron, from the 1st Squadron of the 35th Reconnaissance Battalion of the 35th Infantry Division.
4th Squadron, from the 1st Squadron of the 102nd Light Battalion of the 102nd Infantry Division.
5th (Heavy) Squadron, from the 'Trubtshevsky' Mounted Force – 350 Cossacks.
6th Squadron, from the Mounted Squadron of the 186th Light Battalion – formerly the 186th Reconnaissance Battalion.

The mounted squadrons were equipped with M42 machine guns and a mortar group. The heavy squadron had a heavy machine-gun section with four machine guns, a mortar section with six heavy mortars, and a section of 10·5 cm light guns. The total establishment of the five squadrons consisted of 28 officers, 160 NCOs, 920 men and 1,123 horses. It was also planned to add an armoured battalion (of three assault-tank squadrons) and a horse-drawn artillery battalion.

Cavalry Regiment (Centre)

Establishment, March 1943.

Structure:

Regimental headquarters: partly-motorized signals squadron; three mounted battalions with: headquarters and signals section; three mounted squadrons, each with 18 light machine guns, two heavy machine guns and two mortars; one heavy squadron with eight machine guns; one motorized heavy squadron; one motor-cycle reconnaissance section with three light machine guns; one armoured scout-car section with three heavy anti-tank guns, and three light machine guns; one artillery battalion; a headquarters battery; three batteries of four light guns each; one rocket-launcher battery planned with six motorized rocket launchers; one motorized anti-aircraft battery with 12 2 cm anti-aircraft guns; one heavy squadron consisting of an anti-tank squadron, an engineers' squadron, one partly-motorized supplies battalion, one motorized ambulance section with medical group; one veterinary field hospital unit, and one cavalry repair-shop section.

Strength: 6,199 men, 5,967 horses, 237 motor-vehicles, 115 motor-cycles, 308 waggons (horse-drawn), 495 sub-machine guns, 188 light machine guns, 42 heavy machine guns, 36 mortars, three heavy anti-tank guns, 12 light 10·5 cm guns, six rocket launchers, 55 radio sets, eight armoured scout-cars.

The combat strength of a squadron, dismounted for battle, was intended to be 168 men (one man to every four horses); experience showed however that this proportion could be reduced to one man to every two horses. The relatively smaller squadron could be led so easily that with all its light machine guns in action, its firing power was just as effective. The ratio of one man to two horses also had the advantage of leaving more hand-led horses for exchanging after being allowed to rest. On the front, single squadrons were used mostly in an infantry role in the trenches. The horses were generally kept protected from air attack two or three km behind the front lines.

In spring and summer 1943, the Cavalry Regiments (North) (Prince Karl zu Salm-Hordtmar) and (South) (Prince zu Sayn-Wittgenstein) were set up in Russia as part of the other Army Groups.

On November 23, 1943, the former 1st Mounted Squadron of the 12th Reconnaissance Battalion was established as the 9th Mounted Squadron in the Cavalry Regiment (North). Equipment and armament were excellent, and the horses were well above average. One 'white horse squadron' was even given Barbs from the former French colonial troops. The horsemen were all equipped with M44 automatic rifles. The central mortar sections of the heavy squadrons were conveyed on peasant carts. At the end of 1944, the Cavalry Regiment (North) was renamed the '5th Cavalry Regiment' in honour of Field-Marshal von Mackensen, and decorated with an arm-band inscribed '*Generalfeldmarschall von Mackensen*'. By tradition, the regimental headquarters and the 1st battalion, with the exception of the 3rd and 11th squadrons, wore the death's head of the *Leibhusaren* hussar regiment on their peaked caps and forage caps, beneath a wreath of oak-leaves surmounted by the national emblem. In the middle of 1944, the 3rd and 4th Cavalry Brigades were formed from the Cavalry Regiments (North), (Centre) and (South).

3rd and 4th Cavalry Divisions

In July 1944, the 3rd Cavalry Brigade and the 4th Cavalry Brigade were combined with the 1st Hungarian Cavalry Division to form the Harteneck Cavalry Corps; and in March 1945, without any noticeable restructuring, they were renamed the 3rd and 4th Cavalry Divisions. Both forces were posted to Hungary in late autumn 1944.

Structure: Divisional headquarters with map section and field-gendarmerie troop, two mounted regiments, one artillery regiment, one heavy cavalry battalion, one anti-tank battalion, one engineers' squadron, one signals battalion, one commander of supplies troops, one sanitary company, one veterinary company, one field reinforcement battalion.

Uniform: Yellow service-colour badges, shoulder straps and forage caps. Riding boots with spurs worn with riding breeches. Those divisional reconnaissance battalions formed from the 5th and 13th Cavalry Regiments still wore the death's head emblem on their caps, while those from the former 6th Cavalry Regiment still wore an eagle insignia. Later the eagle was also worn by various other members of the 3rd Cavalry Division, while in the 4th Cavalry Division the newly-formed 5th Cavalry Regiment wore the death's head of the *Leibhusaren*, and the 41st Mounted Regiment wore the death's head of the Brunswick Hussars.

In February 1945, the 3rd Cavalry Division reached its establishment strength of 11,333 men. The division was captured by the Americans in May 1945 near Graz. The 4th Cavalry Division was captured by the British in May 1945.

SS Cavalry

The SS Mounted Regiments (*Standarten*), which came into being early in 1940 from a single SS Death's Head mounted battalion of stormtroopers, were modelled on the army mounted regiments, but had an additional motor-cycle battalion and a mounted battery.

The SS 1st Death's Head Mounted Regiment was formed on May 21, 1940, in Warsaw from parts of the SS Death's Head Regiment, seven squadrons and a mounted battery.

The SS 2nd Death's Head Mounted Regiment was formed on May 21, 1940, in Lublin from parts of the SS Death's Head Regiment, with seven squadrons.

The SS 1st Cavalry Regiment was formed on February 25, 1941. Instead of the death's head, its men wore the markings of the Waffen-SS; in 1942 it gave up its 6th and 7th Squadrons to the Engineers' Battalion, and the motor-cycle battalion to the SS Cavalry Division. It was redesignated the SS 15th Cavalry Regiment on October 22, 1943.

The SS Cavalry Brigade was reconstructed from December 22, 1941, to April 18, 1942, as the SS Fegelein Mounted Brigade near Moscow (Rshev) – and then from September 1942 became the SS Cavalry Division, Central Russia. From February 25, 1941, the SS 2nd Cavalry Regiment wore the S-runes of the Waffen-SS as its collar badge instead of the death's head. In 1942 the 7th Squadron was given to the motor-cycle reconnaissance battalion of the SS Cavalry Division and became the SS 16th Cavalry Regiment on October 22, 1943. The SS Cavalry Regiments established in 1941 were clearly modelled on the 1st Cavalry Brigade of the army, as was the SS Cavalry Brigade.

In 1942, the Waffen-SS Cavalry Division was formed from the brigade. In structure, equipment and basic combat characteristics it still owed much to the prototype of the former army cavalry divisions, and like these it incorporated an additional motor-cycle reconnaissance battalion. Correspondingly, it also had nearly all the short-comings and faults which had limited the combat value of the 1st Cavalry Division. The 8th SS Cavalry Division, reinforced with an armoured reconnaissance battalion, assault guns, anti-aircraft and anti-tank guns as well as heavy weapons and special units, was reorganized into an effective modern combat force. In spring 1944, the SS Volunteer Cavalry Division was formed as a sister unit; in autumn 1944 it received the name 'Hungary' and at the end of the year became known as the 22nd Division. It was also termed the 'Maria Theresa' Division. Both the SS divisions were crushed in the battles around Budapest.

SS Volunteer Division Lützow. On the orders of SS *Reichsführer* Himmler, a start was finally made on the establishment of the 37th SS Volunteer Division Lützow, to be formed from the remains of both SS divisions on February 19, 1945. The Commander was SS Colonel Karl Gesele. The unit was established in the area of Pressburg, but as the front moved westwards it had to be transferred to the area of Znaim and Raab. It incorporated ethnic Germans from Hungary – mostly as recruits – and also Romanian volunteers. On the orders of the Supreme Army Command, the divisional commander and the divisional staff, together with army units (one motorized regiment, one machine-gun battalion and one Hungarian honvéd division), were sent into action in March and April 1945 to cover the gap between the 6th Panzer Army and the 8th Army north of Vienna, where they were to fight against the pursuing Soviet forces. Meanwhile still in the early stages of its formation, the division was posted to the area of Pisek and further equipped and replenished.

Structure:
Establishment, April 1945.
Headquarters Divisional staff.
SS 92nd Cavalry Regiment: Headquarters, 1st Battalion, 2nd Battalion.
SS 93rd Cavalry Regiment: Headquarters, 1st Battalion, 2nd Battalion; 37th SS Artillery Battalion; 37th SS Engineers' Battalion; establishment began in February 1945.
37th SS Field Reinforcement Battalion: with headquarters and four companies.
The division capitulated on May 5, 1945, and was taken captive by the Americans.

German Cossack units

The army cavalry was further boosted in 1943 by the creation of a Cossack Cavalry Division under the leadership of Lieutenant-General von Pannwitz. Later it became the 2nd Division, and was subsequently combined with the 3rd Division, which was being formed during the later stages of the war, to become the XV Cossack Cavalry Corps. In structure, weaponry and equipment, the Cossack units all shared many of the characteristics of the old 1st German Cavalry Division. The Cossacks, however, thought nothing of text-book riding-school techniques or of German riding regulations. The horses were controlled by weight of pressure and the *Nagaika* – the Cossacks' thick plaited whip. The officers wore spurs as they had in the time of the Tsars. Curbs were scarcely used at all; the snaffle alone was suited to the Cossack style of riding. The horses were superbly trained. They would obey one rider alone, his voice or his whistle. There were about 160 Germans on the staff of a Cossack regiment of about 2,000 horsemen. There were also 'welfare officers' who looked after the Cossacks. The cultural and welfare detachment in the divisional headquarters produced a newspaper, '*Kasatschi Klitsch*'.

1st Cossack Division

With the Von Pannwitz Mounted Force (formed on November 15, 1942, as a part of Army group A) as the headquarters staff, two units were added on August 4, 1943, to form a division. These were the Cossack Platow Cavalry Regiment and the Von Jungschulz Cavalry Regiment (formerly Prince von Urach), both of which had been established from 1942 on and had been ready for divisional use since May 13, 1943.

1st Brigade. C.O.: Colonel Wagner. 1st Don Cossack Regiment, 4th Kuban Cossack Regiment, 2nd Siberian Cossack Regiment, Caucasus Artillery Battalion.

2nd Brigade. C.O.: Colonel von Schulz. 3rd Kuban Cossack Regiment, 5th Don Cossack Regiment, 6th Terek Cossack Regiment, Caucasus Artillery Battalion.

These two brigades were converted into

divisions during the later months of 1943, with a fresh distribution of divisional troops, and later formed the Cossack Corps with Lieutenant-General von Pannwitz as commanding general. Both divisions saw action in 1944 in Croatia against Tito's partisans. The divisional command of the 2nd Division, which included the Cossack troops of the former 2nd Brigade, was stationed at Novo Gradiska. Except for the 5th Don Cossack Regiment, which was led by the old Cossack General Kononov, all the regiments had German commanders; moreover about half the officers and some of the NCOs were also German staff on attachment. The language of command used in all regiments was Russian.

In December 1944, the Cossack Division was taken over by the Waffen-SS and converted by the SS Command to form the 1st and 2nd Cossack Divisions of the XV SS Cossack Cavalry Corps, on April 30, 1945.

At the beginning of 1945, General von Pannwitz was nominated by the All-Cossack Congress at Virovititza in Yugoslavia as Supreme Ataman (commander) of all the Cossack armies – an honour formerly reserved for the Tsars.

2nd Cossack Cavalry Division

The 2nd Cossack Cavalry Division – formed from the 2nd Cossack Cavalry Brigade – was taken over by the Waffen-SS. It included the 3rd Kuban Cossack Regiment; the 5th Don Cossack Regiment; the 6th Terek Cossack Regiment and the 2nd Divisional units.

Uniforms. There were two types of Cossack headdress: *Kubankas*, the traditional fur caps of the Kuban and Terek Cossacks, and *Papaschas*, the taller caps of the Don Cossacks. Officers' fur caps were made of astrakhan or black lamb's skin, with the badge of the German Army in front. The Siberian Cossacks wore white fur caps. The fur was topped by cloth, in each case in the appropriate colour for the army the man came from. All ranks wore a silver embroidered cross on top of their caps. The Cossacks spurned the use of steel helmets, even in action.

From 1944, the 2nd Division wore the uniform and badges of the German Army – that is, normal service blouse with braided collar; shoulder straps and national emblem, and the badge of the appropriate army unit. For the Cossack regiments, the service colour was yellow-gold for the cavalry and bright red for the artillery. Badges and symbols of rank were German, with Cossack NCOs and sergeant-majors wearing silver-braided collars.

Various members of the Cossack regiments wore a special badge on their left sleeve – a diagonally quartered shield in two colours, with a field-grey strip on its upper edge adorned with the Cyrillic initial of the relevant army in light grey. Officers wore officers' brown belts, and other ranks had normal army belts. Often they would carry a *Shashka* – the Cossack sabre with a brass handle but no hand-guard, and black leather sheath. They wore either field-grey or dark blue riding breeches with a stripe down the outer seam, plus black riding boots with strap-on spurs.

Both in and out of service the Cossacks wore *Purkas* – stiff capes of black pressed camel's hair. The purka was held by a buckle at the neck. When riding, it would cover the horse from the saddle to the croup, providing protection from damp and cold. The so-called *Baschlyk*, a big hood with two long scarf-like ends, worn round the neck and tied with a cord, would flutter from the shoulders during the ride.

From 1942, the Cossacks had been eligible for a decoration for 'bravery and merit of the peoples of the east', and later they were also awarded the normal German medals.

The Calmuck Cavalry Corps

This was originally the 103rd Defence Troop, set up by the Panzer Army High Command within the 6th Army around Stalingrad to close up gaps in the line through the steppes of the Calmucks.

As a result of the efforts of the counter-intelligence officer, *Sonderführer* Dr Doll, with the aid of only two other Germans as driver and radio operator, it was expanded and divided into two brigades, each of two regiments after August 1942.

In August 1943, the Calmuck Cavalry Corps was organized as follows: 1st Battalion – five squadrons. 2nd Battalion – five squadrons. 3rd Battalion – five squadrons. 4th Battalion – five squadrons. A further five squadrons remained behind in the steppes fighting against the Red Army. Each battalion had a pursuit squadron made up of hand-picked men. The strength of each squadron was 120–150 men.

The position of the CCC in the armed forces was unique. In composition and function it resembled a free corps. Because of its special status, the Calmuck cavalrymen did not regard themselves as reinforcements for the Germans, but rather as an independent allied force. Germans in the Corps had no jurisdiction over the Calmucks; they were there only to deal with administrative affairs, for instance the sanitary service and other purely functional matters.

On all levels apart from the corps headquarters staff, the leadership of the battalions and squadrons was exclusively in the hands of the Calmucks themselves. As in Russian units, each commander had an assistant (*pomoschnik*) and a chief-of-staff (*nashtaba*). Most of the officers came from the Red Army cavalry. So there were a few senior people who had graduated from the Soviet war academy.

The horses

In the course of the campaigns against Soviet Russia, a few interesting conclusions about horses were made. Brown horses were prone to go lame more than average, and suffered especially from bruises. Black horses were the most susceptible to fatigue. It was the white horses which were the most trouble-free. Their casualties from fatigue were well below average, and other complaints were limited.

Of those horses which were killed or died, about 75% fell as a result of enemy action – especially from artillery or air raids – while around 17% died of exhaustion or heart failure. For the horses, nourishment in the form of concentrated foods was more important than rest. They were especially fond of an army fodder-ration which came in cakes weighing about 5,000 gm, made from a mixture of 2,000 gm oats, 300 gm yeast, 1,300 gm potato flakes, 750 gm chopped hay, and 650 gm chopped straw.

Veterinary Hospitals

Among the veterinary troops in the field, both behind the lines and at home, was employed a permanent staff of 5,650 vets and veterinary officers in, amongst other things, the veterinary companies, hospitals and horse depots; in addition to these, there were 250 line officers, 700 medical officers, 400 officers on special troop service, 8,100 NCOs and crews, as well as 3,700 blacksmiths.

In all about 13,000 men served in the veterinary service of the armed forces. Their work consisted primarily of treating sick and wounded horses. Smaller, easily transportable hospital squadrons were set up near the front. The big formations were equipped with mobile veterinary hospitals so that they could treat several hundred sick animals at a time. On the home front there were permanent veterinary hospitals equipped with the most up-to-date aids. Many veterinary hospitals had isolation units. In the early years of the war at least, horses recovering from illness or injury were allowed a period of convalescence before being sent back into active service. The duties of the veterinary service also included the supply of relief horses, tools and equipment for shoeing horses, and dressings.

Horsewomen of the German Army

Because the officers and NCOs of the armed services' riding and driving schools were urgently needed on the front, women were used for the training of remounts. Their task was to break in the remounts as saddle- and draught-horses for the infantry and horse-drawn units (the cavalry relied on the remount squadrons of their own reserve units). The women were also there to teach pupils from unmounted units to ride, and gave short courses for regimental, battalion and contingent commanders. A horsewoman would often have to ride eight to 10 remounts, and then one or two riding-school horses in a day. The women were mostly aged 18 to 40, and were not given ranks. They wore the uniform jacket of a headquarters assistant, and riding breeches with boots.

German cavalry bands

The origins of cavalry music went back to the days of knights and minnesingers. It remained virtually unchanged for nearly 600 years, before its brilliant development in the 19th and 20th centuries which saw both its zenith and its demise. The greatest reviver of German cavalry music was the Prussian royal chamber musician Friedrich Wilhelm Wieprecht, who became musical director of the Prussian Corps of Guards and the royal Prussian Army's first musical inspector. His reform work remained a key factor in the development of the Trumpeter Corps right up until the end of World War II. The Trumpeter Corps was quite popular because of the close links individual trumpeters and buglers had with the cavalry troops for whom they signalled commands in the field.

Great Britain

By the outbreak of war, only the 5th Cavalry Brigade – composed of three regiments, the Cheshire Yeomanry, the North Somerset Yeomanry and the Yorkshire Dragoons – had been spared the process of mechanization into armoured units. The Cheshire regiment, or the Earl of Chester's Yeomanry, was posted to the Near East under Lieutenant-Colonel D. E. Williams, M.B.E., T.D., to take part in the Syrian campaign of June 1941. It was the last action seen by a mounted unit of the British Army. The Yeomanry cavalrymen were armed with sabres and rifles; each squadron had a Hotchkiss machine-gun section, and in the headquarters squadron there was a Vickers machine-gun section. The horses were mainly hunters. The Yeomanry Regiment acquitted itself well, and Churchill noted that 'this successful campaign in Syria' notably improved the strategic position in the Near East. Shortly afterwards the regiment was dismounted and became a dispatch unit for the Royal Signals. Lieutenant-Colonel Williams observed: 'There was no actual farewell mounted parade; but the whole regiment had a cross-country race of four miles, which finished with swimming the River Jordan. It was very much enjoyed by all.'

Greece

The Greek cavalry scored astounding successes during its war of five months and 27 days against Italy, Germany, Hungary, Romania and Bulgaria. It is also worth noting that this was the biggest Greek cavalry force since the downfall of the Byzantine empire, and that the commander-in-chief of the Greek Army was General Alexandros Papagos, himself a former cavalry officer.

Greece was attacked by Italy on November 28, 1940, and the Greek 1st Cavalry Division under Major-General Georgios Stanotas was involved in the early defensive operations. This large force was mobilized in Langada, and belonged to the supreme commander's general reserve. On November 29, 1940, some of its units were

detached to form the 1st Cavalry Brigade (commander Sokrates Dimaratos), which became a self-contained part of Army Corps B in Thessaloniki.
Structure of the 1st Cavalry Brigade:
1st and 3rd Cavalry Regiment each with four squadrons, one machine-gun battalion (12 machine guns) and one mortar squadron (four 8·1 cm mortars); one motorized regiment with a reconnaissance squadron; three machine-gun squadrons (12 machine guns) and one mortar squadron (four 8·1 cm mortars); one mounted squadron with three machine-gun detachments (12 machine guns); one horse-drawn artillery unit, consisting of two batteries (eight 7·5 cm guns); one mountain battery (four Skoda 7·5 cm guns); one engineers' squadron; two communication squadrons.

The 1st Cavalry Brigade was a self-contained force and one of the largest formations in the Greek–Italian war of 1940. On January 2, 1941, it was disbanded and attached to the Cavalry Division once more.

In addition there were the following mounted units: the reconnaissance battalions of the Army Corps and the divisional reconnaissance battalions. The four Army Corps reconnaissance battalions consisted of two squadrons, one machine-gun company (12 machine guns) and one mortar section (two 8·1 cm mortars). The 5th Reconnaissance Battalion had only one squadron with one machine-gun section (four machine guns) and one mortar section (two 8·1 cm mortars).

The reconnaissance battalions of the Army Corps and the Divisions were formed from what had been Cavalry Regiments A, B, C and D, and the 5th Cavalry Squadron. Each of the divisional reconnaissance battalions had two squadrons and one machine-gun section (with four guns) except for the 11th Reconnaissance Battalion, which had only one squadron and one machine-gun group (with two guns).

The Greek cavalry consisted of 47 cavalry squadrons, four motorized squadrons, 10 machine-gun squadrons, 15 machine-gun sections, three mortar squadrons and five mortar sections. A good deal of reorganization was necessitated by the operational demands, the nature of the terrain, unfavourable weather conditions, and difficulties in replacing horses. A few cavalry units were disbanded and others newly established.

In September 1943, ELAS, the armed wing of the Greek underground communist movement EAM, formed a mounted partisan battalion, the 1st Cavalry Brigade.

Hungary

Hungary was the land of the hussars, those dashing soldiers who had fought so bravely on the battlefields of Europe during the previous century, as well as featuring prominently in operettas. In 1939, the Hungarian hussar regiments were organized into two cavalry brigades.

The hussar regiments, with their 12 *Eskadrons* apiece, were extremely cumbersome formations. Each *Eskadron* consisted of more than 300 riders, since the Hungarians wanted to keep their impact and firing power when dismounted as the equivalent of an infantry company. The *Eskadrons* had only about 100 troopers and saddle-horses in peacetime, so, to make them ready for combat, the extra 200 horses had to be requisitioned from farmers and were not broken in. This circumstance on the one hand delayed the mobilization and combat-readiness of the cavalry, while on the other, the untrained horses, unaccustomed to carrying saddles, were simply incapable of lengthy rides and were a considerable handicap.

The Hungarian Light Corps, *Gyorshadtest*, consisting of two motorized brigades and one cavalry brigade – in all 44,444 men – advanced from the eastern Carpathians towards the Dnepr on June 27, 1941. There it was attached to the German 17th Army, Army Group South, and used to protect the river in the sector between Dnepropetrovsk and Saporshye. In 1942, when the cavalry units of the Light Corps were withdrawn from the eastern front, it was time for a reorganization: the result was a single division of three hussar regiments, which was still being converted into a modern combat unit up to 1944. The establishment of the 1st Cavalry Division was part of the SZABOLCS organization plan and was put into effect in late autumn 1943. Between May 1 and about the middle of September 1944, a new Hungarian occupying force was stationed on the eastern front. It consisted of the 2nd Reserve Army Corps and included three infantry divisions and one cavalry division. Its operational zone was to the east and south of Warsaw.

The new 2nd Hungarian Army was organized in August 1944 in Hungarian North Transylvania. On September 5, it carried out an operation against Romanian troops, but after a concentrated counter-attack on combined Soviet and Romanian forces (the 2nd Ukrainian Front) it had to withdraw from Transylvania at the end of October. The 3rd Hungarian Army, formed from a few replacement and reserve divisions and the 1st Cavalry Division, was set up in the middle of September 1944 in great haste, for the Red Army had already infiltrated Hungarian territory. The 1st Cavalry Division fought along the Hungarian–Romanian border and in October–November withdrew between the Danube and Theiss towards Budapest.
Structure:
The reconnaissance battalions of the infantry divisions each had a mounted company. Until 1942 there were two cavalry brigades each with two hussar regiments. They still bore the traditional historic names:
1. Jasig-Kuman Regiment 'Franz Josef'
2. Hussar Regiment 'Prince Arpad'
3. Hussar Regiment 'Count Nadasdy Ferenc'
4. Hussar Regiment 'Count Hadik Andras'

Each of these hussar regiments was organized into: two half regiments; one hussar battery; one bicycle battalion; one motorized battery with 10·5 cm howitzers; one engineers' and signals company; three batteries of mounted artillery, and supply troops.

In 1942 both cavalry brigades were combined into a single cavalry division. The three hussar regiments were subdivided into:
two half regiments; one hussar battery; one bicycle battalion; one motorized battery with 10·5 cm howitzers; one battery of anti-aircraft tanks; one reconnaissance battalion (with two armoured scout-car companies of 14 armoured scout-cars); one mounted artillery battalion; one motorized artillery battalion; one anti-aircraft battalion; one motorized engineers' company, and one motorized signals company.

Italy

The Italian cavalry had a long history, and its officers enjoyed great social prestige, but at the beginning of the Thirties, the cavalry units were considerably reduced, and were equipped with modern infantry weapons. The designation 'light divisions' (*Corpe d'Armata Celere*) was introduced to emphasize their new function. During World War II, the Italian cavalry had 13 cavalry regiments, some squadron groups with light tanks, and five transport squadrons.

Each cavalry regiment consisted of two squadron groups each of which comprised two squadrons. A squadron consisted of three mounted troops, and each troop was subdivided into three sections. There would also be one machine-gun squadron of four machine-gun troops. A cavalry regiment totalled 37 officers, 37 NCOs, 798 men, 818 horses, 39 bicycles, six motor-cycles, 16 trucks, one motor-car, 26 sub-machine guns and 12 machine guns.

In Libya, there were the following native mounted units; a Spahi police troop, the Savaris, the regular Libyan cavalry and the irregular mounted troops, or Sapties.

The Italian cavalry regiments 1939–1943

1. Divisione Celere 'Eugenio di Savoia'
Regiment *Cavalleggeri di Saluzzo* (1848) Motto: '*Quo fata vocant*'.
C.O.: Colonel Barone Emilio Guidobono.
Regiment *Cavalleggeri di Alessandria* (1850) Motto: '*In pericula surgo*'.
C.O.: Colonel Antonio Ajmone-Cat.
I motorized group *S. Giusto*.
Regiment *Lancieri di Firenze* (1753) Motto: '*Con l'animo che ogni battaglia.*'
C.O. Colonel Guiseppe Ferrari.

2. Divisione Celere 'Emanuele Filiberto Testa di Ferro'
Regiment *Lanciero di Vittorio Emanuele II* (1859)

Motto: '*Per la gloria del nome.*'
C.O.: Colonel Spartaco Casciotti
II Motorized group *S. Marco*.

3. Divisione Celere 'Principe Amadeo Duca d'Aosta'
Regiment *Savoia Cavelleria* (1692) Motto: '*Savoye! Bonnes nouvelles*'.
C.O.: Colonel Weiss Poccetti.
Regiment *Lanciero di Novara* (1829) Motto: '*Albis Ardua*'.
C.O.: Colonel Egidio Guisiana.
III Motorized group *S. Giorgio*.

1. Armata
Regiment *Cavalleggero di Monferrato* (1850) Motto: '*Semper ut quondam*'.
C.O.: Colonel Pado Tarnassi.

2. Armata
Regiment *Piemonte Reale Cavalleria* (1692) Motto: '*Venustas et audax*'.
C.O.: Colonel Oscar Gritti.
Regiment *Genova Cavalleria* (1683) Motto: '*Soit a pied soit a cheval, mon honneur est sans egal*'.
C.O.: Colonel Carlo Cheriana Majneri.
Regiment *Cavalleggeri Guide* (1859) Motto: '*Alla vittoria e all'onor son guida*'.
C.O.: Colonel Gaetano Pelligra.

4. Armata
Regiment *Nizza Cavalleria* (1690) Motto: '*Nicea Fidelis*'.
C.O.: Colonel Conte di Bergola.

Comando Superiore Albania
Regiment *Lancieri di Aosta* (1774) Motto: '*Aosta d'Fer*'.
C.O.: Colonel Giovanni di Francavilla.
Regiment *Lancieri di Milano* (1859) Motto: '*Sic personat virtus*'.
C.O.: Colonel Giorgio Morigi.

In Sardinia
Gruppo *Cavalleggeri di Sardegna*.

In 1937, San Giorgio was named the saint who protected the cavalry of Italy. In 1939 a new training regiment, the *Reggimento di Formazione*, was formed from the 2nd Squadron group and the machine-gun detachments of the *Genova Cavalleria* and the 1st Squadron group of the *Lancieri di Aosta*. Under Colonello Pelligras, the *Reggimento di Formazione* took part in the occupation of Albania. The cavalry formation for Italian East Africa – *Raggruppamento di Cavalleria per l'Africa Orientale Italiana* – was set up in 1940. It consisted of the *Cavelleria Coloniale* and *Cavalieri di Neghelli*. In the same year, three Light Divisions were redesignated as the Light Army Corps. The Regiments *Lancieri di Aosta*, *Lancieri di Milano* and *Cavalleggeri Guide*, together with the Army Corps of Ciamuria, *Rag-*

gruppamento Celere del Litorale (light coastal group), took part in the campaign of October 1940 on the Greek–Albanian front. On July 20, 1941, the regiments *Savoia Cavalleria* and the *Lancieri di Novara* with their light divisions were formed into the Expeditionary Corps for Russia (*Corpo di Spedizione*, CSIR) and transferred to the eastern front. The 14th Group of *Cavalleria Coloniale*, as the last mounted unit of the Italian forces in East Africa, was involved in fighting near Gondar. During the period from July to August 1941, the daily bulletins of the *Comando Supremo* still mentioned the battles in which the 14th Cavalry Group was engaged; but it was then destroyed.

Japan

Before 1939, the army had four cavalry brigades, and in each of the 17 infantry divisions there were eight light mounted batteries. There was also a cavalry regiment belonging to the Imperial Guard, stationed in Tokyo to guard the Imperial Palace. In the 'China' Army group there were a few cavalry battalions forming part of the Mongolian Army. In the 'Kwantung' Army Group in China, the 4th Cavalry Brigade's 6th and 10th Mounted Regiments fought under the 6th Division.

The 5th Mounted Reconnaissance Battalion (Colonel Shizuo Saeki), took part in the landing operations on the Malayan peninsula and the advance towards Singapore in December 1941 as part of the 5th Division.

Manchuria

The cavalry, consisting of about 25,000 men divided into 10 large formations, was recruited for the most part from the Mongolian border tribes, whose outstanding horsemanship and tough horses were well known. Manchuria was a puppet state, its emperor Kang De the last representative of the 300-year-old Manchu dynasty.

When the Japanese invaded Manchuria in September 1931, there was no single united army in the entire country. Each provincial governor had his own private army on which his power was based. After several revolts by these warlords, the Japanese disbanded all the military units in Manchuria and began to build a new army, with an organization similar to that of the Japanese Army. The groups of Manchurian cavalry served together with the Japanese 'Kwantung' Army in battles in northern China, captured the important town of Kalgan and conquered Inner Mongolia, which was occupied by Chinese troops.

Norway

In 1940, Norway's cavalry consisted of the cavalry Chief-of-Staff with his headquarters group, three dragoon regiments and the reserve officer school Skolee squadrons. The cavalry was regarded as a reconnaissance force which could be used in emergencies as a mobile reserve for the general staff; it was expected to fight dismounted. The reserve officer school served throughout the year; but for the regiments there was only a summer cavalry-training course lasting 84 days. For the rest of the year, only the regimental headquarters staff was operational. The German attack in April 1940 threw the mobilization scheme into chaos and the course of action taken by the cavalry worked out quite differently from what had been planned. The cavalry had been intended to carry out attacks on the enemy's flanks and rear, and subsequently to disappear into the forests. In the event, however, the German forces thwarted this entire plan of action.

What happened to the individual cavalry regiments was as follows: some sections of the 1st Dragoon Regiment–sent into action in a very rough and ready fashion near Gardemoen north of Oslo – were taken prisoner by a detachment led by the German Air-Attaché Spiller. The 2nd Dragoon Regiment, motorized, fought on as an infantry battalion. The 3rd Dragoon Regiment had already been mobilized and made combat-ready at the beginning of April but its structure was altered – instead of two mounted squadrons, it now had only one, and its machine-gun detachment was enlarged to become a machine-gun squadron.
Structure of the Dragoon Regiments
Establishment, September 15, 1939.
Headquarters Squadron; two mounted squadrons; a machine-gun squadron; two bicycle squadrons and one mortar troop.
The 1st and 2nd Dragoon Regiments also had: one motorized machine-gun squadron, two machine-gun sections, one rifle section and one training troop.
The 3rd Dragoon Regiment was strengthened by a motorized machine-gun section.

Poland

The Polish cavalry tradition survived through 125 years of foreign rule, and when the nation finally became independent on November 11, 1918, a new Polish cavalry emerged. A mere year-and-a-half later its achievements were already being acclaimed: in August 1920 it launched a surprise attack on the Red horsemen of Marshal Budenny, who had reached the outskirts of Warsaw and were advancing on towards Thorn. The cavalry's intervention saved Poland.

There were 37 mounted regiments – as against 90 infantry regiments – a good indication of the importance attached to the horse and rider on the Vistula from that point on. In fact, the Polish cavalry was a wholly self-contained strategic service. But paradoxically, there was no up-to-date doctrine to govern the use of the cavalry units, of which there were so many. The infantry, for instance, instead of being given the job of holding a position, was launched into wide-ranging mobile manœuvres – even though it was not motorized; the highly mobile cavalry meanwhile would be used for defensive tasks, where its superior manœuvrability was useless. The second grave mistake was that the cavalry was not arranged into large formations – into divisions for example or even better into corps – which would have given it a significant combat strength. On the contrary, the existing brigades were weakened by the detachment of entire regiments for secondary assignments. All 11 cavalry brigades were concentrated along the German border. The mass of Polish cavalry, around 70,000 horsemen, were spread over the whole enormous front – a distance of 1,500 km – and in consequence could play neither a strategic nor a tactical role in 1939. The only exception was the *Wolynska Brygada Kawalerii*.

The firing power of a cavalry regiment was equivalent to that of an infantry battalion, but the cavalry had no mortars. In numbers, a dismounted cavalry regiment had the strength of two infantry companies. Military service in the cavalry lasted 23 months. The cavalry officers were mainly recruited from the landed classes.

A characteristically historic survival in the Polish cavalry was the lance – a thrusting weapon consisting of a tubular steel shaft about 3 m long with leather straps. Beneath the four-edged sharpened blade was a small pennant with the regimental colours, about 20 cm wide and 50 cm long; the lance weighed about 2·10 kg. Although the lance had not been used as a weapon, even on manœuvres, since 1934, and after being banned was carried only on baggage-waggons, strangely enough cavalry troops re-adopted this seemingly outmoded weapon on the battlefield in September 1939. In addition, every rider had a rifle, a sabre, a bayonet, a short shovel, gas-mask, knapsack and cooking utensils and a round French steel helmet. Officers and NCOs were distinguishable from the ranks at a glance by their elegant well-cut riding boots, which proved a sure identification for the German snipers. The saddles of the cavalry and horse-drawn artillery often dated back to the days of the old monarchy.

The cavalry of Poland was the last complete strategic cavalry force to retain its original form. And with the end of the German–Polish war of 1939 came the demise of a service which differed only in trifling details from the cavalry units of the 19th century. The deep loyalty of the troopers to their regiments and the long regimental traditions made the cavalry the most respected arm in the Polish forces.

Structure and strength of *Samodzielna Byrgada Kawalerii* (independent cavalry brigade)
Brigade Headquarters
Reconnaissance Battalion
One bicycle squadron; one mounted machine-gun section; one armoured-car battalion with one armoured-car squadron, seven Citroën-Kegresse armoured cars and one squadron with 13 light reconnaissance tanks, Type TKS (2·65 tonnes).
Infantry and cavalry
One rifle battalion (not found in all cavalry brigades) and three or four cavalry regiments.

Cavalry Regiment
Regimental headquarters
One signals section (with two horse-drawn N2 radio-waggons); one engineer troop; one bicycle squadron; one anti-tank section (with horse-drawn 437 mm guns); four mounted squadrons each of three sections with one machine gun and one anti-tank rifle, of 50 to 60 men; one heavy machine-gun squadron (12 heavy machine guns: eight on pack-horses, four on light horse-drawn carts) and one horse-drawn supplies unit.
In the reserve squadron, the young remounts purchased each year for the regiment were broken in. During the war, the squadron also took over the training of the reserves. In all, a cavalry regiment could send between 230 and 250 troopers into battle.

A *Samodzielna Brygada Kawalerii* also included the following:
One horse-drawn artillery regiment, of three or four batteries each with four field-guns (M 02/06, Russian model of 1900/14) of 75 mm calibre, and a range of 8·5 km.
Anti-aircraft
One motorized detachment, battery-type B with two 40 mm guns.
Engineers
One horse-drawn engineers' squadron.
Signals Battalion
One squadron with two N1 type radios and an RKD radio, partly motorized; six horse-drawn baggage columns.
Total strength: about 6,350 men and 5,400 horses.

Poland's large-scale cavalry formations
September to October 1939
'Mazowiecka' Cavalry Brigade – attached to the 'Modlin' Army
C.O.: Colonel Jan Karcz (Warsaw).
1st Light Cavalry Regiment, 'Josef Pilsudski' (Warsaw), 7th Uhlan Regiment, 'Lubelskich' (Minsk Mazowiecki), 11th Uhlan Regiment, 'Legionowych' (Ciechanow), 1st Mounted Artillery Regiment (Warsaw) and 3rd Light Infantry Battalion (Rembertow).

On the outbreak of war the *Mazowiecka Brygada Kawalerii* fought around Krzynowloga Mala on the East Prussian frontier, then, as the rearguard, delayed the German advance on the Przasnysz–Pultusk axis. From September 5–7, the brigade defended the line of the river Narew from Pultusk to Serock, and then the river Bug line. It broke through the encirclement of the 'Kempf' armoured division and was incorporated into the 'Polnoc'

(North) Front grouping. On September 24, the brigade was defeated near Suchowola.

'Wolynska' Cavalry Brigade – attached to the 'Lodz' Army.

C.O.: Julian Filipowicz (Rowne).

12th Uhlan Regiment, 'Podolski' (Krzemieniec), 19th Uhlan Regiment, 'Wolynskich' (Ostrog), 21st Uhlan Regiment, 'Nadwislanskich' (Rowne), 2nd Mounted Light Infantry Regiment (Hrubieszow), 2nd Mounted Artillery Regiment (Dubno) and 11th Light Infantry Battalion.

On September 1, 1939, near Mokra, the *Wolynska Brygada Kawalerii* engaged the German 4th Panzer Division in battles lasting throughout the day and scored some notable successes (the Poles destroyed 76 tanks and 74 other vehicles). On the next day, the brigade halted the enemy near Ostrowy and in the night of September 3/4, at Kamiensk, launched a successful raid on the armoured columns of the 1st Panzer Division. During the retreat of the 'Lódź' Army the brigade distinguished itself in the battle near Cyrusowa and Wola. Later the brigade joined up with the *Nowogrodzka Brygada Kawalerii* (General Anders) and took part in the battle near Minsk-Mazowiecki on September 13, and later in the battle of Krasnobród on September 23. Both brigades fought their way towards the Hungarian frontier, and were then heavily defeated by the Soviets on September 27.

'Wilenska' Cavalry Brigade – attached to the 'Prusy' Army.

C.O.: Colonel K. Drucki-Lubecki (Wilno).

4th Uhlan Regiment, 'Zaniemenskich' (Wilno), 13th Uhlan Regiment, 'Wilenskich' (Nowa Wilejka), 23rd Uhlan Regiment, 'Grodzienskich' (Postawy) and 3rd Mounted Artillery Regiment (Podbrodzie).

The *Wilenska Brygada Kawalerii* took part in the battle near Piotrkow, then withdrew to the central sector of the Vistula and suffered a crushing defeat at the river crossing near Maciejowice on September 8 and 9. The remains of the brigade joined the *Pomorska Brygada Kawalerii*. The 23rd Uhlan Regiment, cut off from the brigade, withdrew into the mountains around Kielce and carried on guerrilla warfare there for a few days.

'Suwalska' Cavalry Brigade – attached to the *Samodzielna Grupa Operacyjna 'Narew'*.

C.O.: Brigadier-General Z. Podhorski (Suwalki).

3rd Light Cavalry Regiment, 'Mazowieckich' (Suwalki), 1st Uhlan Regiment, 'Krechowiekich' (Agustow), 2nd Uhlan Regiment, 'Grochowskich' (Suwalki), 3rd Mounted Light Infantry Regiment (Wolkowysk) and 4th Mounted Artillery Regiment (Suwalki).

Until September 4, the *Suwalska Brygada Kawalerii* was stationed in the Suwalki area on the East Prussian frontier, from where the brigade launched a few raids into East Prussia with units of the 3rd Light Cavalry Regiment. The brigade was then transferred to the Zambrów area, where it was involved in fighting with elements of the 'Kempf' armoured division on September 9 and 10. It succeeded in breaking out of the encirclement of Zambrow into the Bialowieza forest (September 18), where it was reorganized into a cavalry division with two brigades (the 'Plis' and the 'Edward'). On the march to the Hungarian frontier it was incorporated into the *Samodzielna Grupa Operacyjna 'Polesie'* (General Kleeberg) with which it surrendered near Koch on October 6.

'Kraków' Cavalry Brigade – attached to the 'Kraków' Army.

C.O.: Brigadier-General Zygmunt Piasecki (Kraków).

3rd Uhlan Regiment, 'Slaskich' (Tarnowskie Gory), 8th Uhlan Regiment, 'Prince Jozef Pontiatowskiego' (Kraków), 5th Mounted Light Infantry Regiment (Debica) and 5th Mounted Artillery Regiment (Oswiecim).

The *Krakowska Brygada Kawalerii* was involved in heavy fighting in the Mozniki area on September 1 and 2. During the retreat on September 4, it acted as rearguard for the northern army wing, and its 8th Uhlan Regiment took part in the battle of Szczekociny against the German 2nd Motorized Division. The brigade then moved to the right bank of the Vistula to cover the river crossing. On September 16, near Farnogrod, it was heavily engaged with superior enemy forces, and then took part in the so-called first battle of Tomaszów, but did not surrender with the 'Kraków' Army. The 8th Uhlan Regiment had detached itself from the brigade at Szczekociny and then fought in the so-called second battle of Tomaszów as a part of the 'Lublin' Army.

'Podolska' Cavalry Brigade – attached to the 'Poznan' Army.

C.O.: Colonel Leon Strzelecki (Stanislawow).

6th Uhlan Regiment, 'Kaniowskich' (Stanislawow), 9th Uhlan Regiment, 'Malopolskich' (Trembowla), 14th Uhlan Regiment, 'Jazlowieckich' (Lvov), 6th Mounted Artillery Regiment (Stanislawów) and 7th Light Infantry Battalion.

The *Podolska Brygada Kawalerii*, whose main task had been intended to be the conquest of Berlin, was brought by railway to the Poznan area, where on September 3, it guarded the town from the west. In the first phase of the battle of the Bzura it advanced to Uniejow and Wartkowice as the vanguard of the main Polish force, and fought a battle at Ozorkow. On September 14, the brigade was thrown onto the left wing at Brochów, and on September 17 marched through the Kampinos forest towards Warsaw as a unit of General Abraham's operational group. On September 19, the 14th Uhlan Regiment launched a cavalry attack against the main German front at Weglowa Wolka, and reached Warsaw.

'Wielkopolska' Cavalry Brigade–attached to the 'Poznan' Army.

C.O.: Brigadier-General Dr Roman Abraham (Poznan).

15th Uhlan Regiment, 'Poznanskich' (Poznan), 17th Uhlan Regiment, 'Gnieznieskich' (Leszno), 7th Mounted Light Infantry Regiment, 'Wielkopolskich' (Poznan), 7th Mounted Artillery Regiment and 10th Light Infantry Battalion.

The *Wielkopolska Brygada Kawalerii* guarded the Leszno–Rawicz area from September 1–3 and made two insignificant raids over the German frontier. In the battle of the Bzura, it was on the left wing of the main force and had the task of taking the town of Główno. On September 14, the brigade was transferred to Brochów, where it defended the river-crossing over the Bzura in two days of heavy fighting against the German 4th Panzer Division. During the march to Warsaw on September 16 and 17, the brigade was engaged in heavy fighting in the Kampinos forest and later near Sierakow and Laski. In the night of September 20 it broke through the German lines to the beleaguered city of Warsaw and took part in the defence of the capital until its capitulation.

'Nowogrodzka' Cavalry Brigade–attached to the 'Modlin' Army.

C.O.: Brigadier-General Wladyslaw Anders (Baranowicze).

25th Uhlan Regiment, 'Wielkopolskich' (Pruzana), 26th Uhlan Regiment (Baranowicze), 27th Uhlan Regiment (Nieswiez), 4th Mounted Light Infantry Regiment, 'Ziemi Leczychiej' (Plock), 9th Mounted Artillery Regiment (Baranowicze) and 5th Light Infantry Battalion.

The *Nowogrdzka Brygada Kawalerii* protected the left wing of the 'Modlin' Army around Dzialdowo and Lidzbark until September 4. On September 5 and 6 it moved via Plock and Modlin to Wiazowna, where it formed the core of the Cavalry Brigade of General Anders. On September 13, it made its way to Minsk-Mazowiecki with the *Wolynska Brygada Kawalerii*, before withdrawing through Laskarzew and Ryki to the district of Lubartów as the reserve of the commander-in-chief. It took part in the so-called second battle of Tomaszów with General Anders' Cavalry Brigade, and on September 23, fought its way past Krasnobrod as far as Kajdan Sopocki. On September 27, the brigade was heavily defeated by Soviet forces near the Hungarian frontier and effectively finished as a fighting force.

'Pomorska' Cavalry Brigade–attached to the 'Pomorze' Army.

C.O.: Brigadier-General Stanislaw Grzmot-Skotnicki (Starogard).

16th Uhlan Regiment, 'Wielkopolskich' (Bydgoszcz), 18th Uhlan Regiment, 'Pomorskich' (Grudziadz), 8th Mounted Light Infantry Regiment (Chelmno), 11th Mounted Artillery Regiment

(Bydgoszcz) and 2nd Light Infantry Battalion (Tczew).

The *Pomorska Brygada Kawalerii* originally had the task of launching a *coup de main* against the free city of Danzig. Its 18th Uhlan Regiment carried out the first cavalry charge of World War II, at Krojanty. The brigade was later nearly wiped out during its attempts to break out of the enemy encirclement at Swiecie. The remaining regiments joined the artillery of the 'Poznan' Army, which undertook an advance to the river Ner. On September 12, the remaining regiments and two batteries fought at Ozorków. The brigade formed the western rearguard of the 'Poznan' Army, and broke through the Campinos forest to Warsaw. Here it joined two other brigades which had likewise reached the capital, to form the Wielkopolska–Pomorska–Podolska Cavalry Brigade, and defended the city until the capitulation.

'Kresowa' Cavalry Brigade–attached to the 'Lódż' Army.

C.O.: Colonel Stefan Kulesza (Brody); from September 5, 1939, Colonel Jerzy Grobicki.

20th Uhlan Regiment (Rzeaszow), 22nd Uhlan Regiment, 'Podkarpakkich' (Brody), 6th Mounted Light Infantry Regiment (Zolkiew), 1st Cavalry Regiment, border defence group, 13th Mounted Artillery Regiment (Brody) and 4th Light Infantry Battalion.

The *Kresowa Brygada Kawalerii* protected the northern army wing on the Warthe from September 3. During the retreat, it was divided into several groups and partly wiped out. The remnants were incorporated into General Anders' cavalry group and covered the group during their operation at Minsk-Mazowiecki on the bank of the Vistula. During the second withdrawal they shared the fate of General Anders' cavalry group.

'Podlaska' Cavalry Brigade–attached to the *Samodzielna Grupa Operacyjna 'Narew'*.

C.O.: Brigadier-General Ludwik Kmicic-Skrzynski (Bialystok).

5th Uhlan Regiment, 'Zaslawskich' (Ostroleka), 10th Uhlan Regiment, 'Litewskich' (Bialystok), 9th Mounted Light Infantry (Gryjewo) and 14th Mounted Artillery Regiment (Bialystok).

The *Podlaska Brygada Kawalerii* protected the frontier with East Prussia up until September 4, and on the night of September 3/4 launched a raid into East Prussian territory near Belczece. On September 6, the brigade withdrew behind the river Narew and remained in the commander-in-chief's reserve. One of the brigade's smaller units, under Captain Skarzinskj, was overrun and carried on fighting behind the enemy's lines for a few days. On September 9, the brigade advanced on Ostrów Mazowiecki and Brok. On September 18, it fought its way out of the enemy encirclement at Zambrów through to the Bialowieza forest, where the brigade joined the *Samodzielna Grupa Operacyjna*

'Polesie', sharing its fortunes until capitulating at Koch on October 6.

Brigade of Colonel Adam Zakrewski – attached to the 'Lublin' Army. This brigade was set up on September 10 in the area of Garwolin. Most of its officers and men were from the Grudziadz cavalry school. On September 12, the brigade joined the improvised cavalry group of Colonel Komorowski (later the commander of the Home Army AK and leader of the Warsaw uprising) and parts of four different dispersed cavalry formations of varying size. The brigade was beaten in the battle of Krasnobród on September 21; remnants managed to reach the Hungarian frontier after heavy clashes with the Red Army on September 22 and 23.

'Wolkowysk' Reserve Brigade (101st, 102nd, 110th Uhlan Regiments and 103rd Light Cavalry Regiment).

Formed at Vilna in north-east Poland on September 17 from the central cavalry reserve, after the Red Army invasion, this formation was intended to take part in the expected battles against the Soviets. The 102nd Uhlan Regiment crossed the Lithuanian border, and was interned. The brigade withdrew to the south-west, but did not encounter German forces. The 110th Uhlan Regiment went back to Warsaw to help in its defence. Among its ranks was Major Dobrzanski, later to become the legendary partisan leader, Hubal.

Romania

After the Soviet Union and Poland, Romania was one of the biggest cavalry powers in the world. The Romanian cavalry formations were based on the so-called 'Roşiori' and 'Calarasi' regiments. These had a long tradition and had formerly been a sort of militia, founded by the landed gentry and free farmers in Wallachia and Moldavia for their own protection. In summer 1939, the Romanian cavalry was issued with standardized equipment, including Czechoslovak ZB rifles and light and heavy guns; at the same time it was restructured into six cavalry brigades, of which three were partly motorized (one regiment in each of those three brigades received half-track Skoda vehicles).

5th Cavalry Brigade
7th Roşiori Regiment; 8th Roşiori Regiment; 6th Roşiori Regiment (motorized); 2nd Mounted Artillery Regiment; one motorized squadron; one mounted engineers' squadron; one motorized signals squadron, and one motorized anti-aircraft company.

6th Cavalry Brigade
5th Calarasi Regiment; 9th Roşiori Regiment; 10th Roşiori Regiment (motorized); 4th Mounted Artillery Regiment; one motorized squadron; one mounted engineers' squadron; one

signals squadron and one anti-aircraft company.

8th Cavalry Brigade
2nd Calarasi Regiment; 4th Roşiori Regiment; 3rd Calarasi Regiment (motorized); 3rd Mounted Artillery Regiment; one motorized squadron; one mounted engineers' squadron; one signals squadron and one motorized anti-aircraft company.

7th Cavalry Brigade
9th Calarasi Regiment; 12th Roşiori Regiment; 11th Roşiori Regiment (motorized); 5th Mounted Artillery Regiment; one motorized squadron; one engineers and signals squadron, and one anti-aircraft company.

1st Cavalry Brigade
1st Roşiori Regiment; 2nd Roşiori Regiment; 13th Calarasi Regiment; 1st Mounted Artillery Regiment; one motorized squadron: one engineers' and signals squadron and one anti-aircraft company.

9th Cavalry Brigade
3rd Roşiori Regiment; 5th Roşiori Regiment; 11th Calarasi Regiment; 6th Mounted Artillery Regiment; one motorized squadron; one engineers and signals squadron, and one anti-aircraft company.

Mounted Regiment (Roşiori or Calarasi)
One headquarters squadron (*Escadrun de Commando*) with a signals section; one engineers' section with flame-thrower group; four rifle squadrons with four sections, and 13 light machine guns (total strength of squadron was 178 men); one heavy weapons squadron (one section with 16 60 mm mortars, one section with 12 heavy machine guns) and four batteries with 75 mm Krupp guns.

The 5th, 6th and 8th Cavalry Brigades, together with the Mountain Corps, formed the 3rd Romanian Army (General Dumitrescu) until the end of 1941. At the end of June 1941 the 7th Cavalry Brigade was also sent into action on the front; at the end of August 1941 the 1st Cavalry Brigade was sent in and in mid-July 1942 the 9th Cavalry Brigade followed suit.

The Calarasi regiments 1st, 4th, 6th, 7th, 8th, 10th and 12th bore the name Cavalry Corps (*Regimente de Corp de Armata*) and provided the mounted reconnaissance battalions of the Infantry Divisions and the Army Corps.

Mounted Divisional Reconnaissance Battalions
One rifle squadron with one heavy machine-gun section.

Mounted Reconnaissance Battalions

Two rifle squadrons; one heavy weapons squadron with one heavy machine-gun section; one 80 mm trench mortar section; one section of 33 mm anti-aircraft guns.

On March 1, 1942, all six brigades were redesignated as divisions, but their structure remained unchanged. After the defeats in the winter of 1942/43, the 5th, 7th, and 8th Cavalry Divisions were transferred to their home base for re-equipping and reorganization. The Romanian 1st Cavalry Division remained with the German 6th Army in Stalingrad. At the beginning of 1944, the 1st Cavalry Division was newly assembled and sent into action in southern Bessarabia. The 6th and 9th Cavalry Divisions fought on the Kuban bridgehead and in the Crimea until the evacuation of the peninsula in May 1944, during which they suffered heavy casualties.

The Soviet Union

At the beginning of World War II, the Red Army was the only force using large cavalry formations apart from Poland and Romania. The former sergeant-major of dragoons, Budenny, who had once been one of the best riders in the Tsarist cavalry, had set up the Red Cavalry Army during the 1917 Revolution. Organized in a few weeks and led with an iron hand, this force quickly conquered the Ukraine and southern Russia. In the war against Poland, they were halted only a short distance from Warsaw and Thorn. Soviet strategists were well aware of the role of cavalry. Voroshilov declared at the 17th Party Congress in 1934: 'It is necessary once and for all to put an end to the theory of replacing the horse with the machine.'

The Cossacks proved indispensable for the creation of a cavalry – both as soldiers and as horse breeders. But Stalin had already liquidated or deported a large part of the Cossack population. They had been dispossessed of their lands, the best part of the Cossacks had been branded as 'Kulaks', and even military service in the Red Army was prohibited for this race of horsemen. On March 17, 1936, however, Marshal Budenny held a cavalry parade in Rostov to inaugurate a new policy towards the Cossacks. In fact, in the very same year, five cavalry divisions of the Red Army were renamed Cossack Divisions. They were, moreover, the only troops who were given colourful parade uniforms: the old Tsarist style with the new national and rank badges. Thus the Cossack divisions came to form the core of the mounted troops of the Red Army.

At the 18th Party Congress on March 13, 1939, the last before the outbreak of war, Marshal Voroshilov said: 'The mounted troops can serve as an example of discipline and military skill. Our cavalrymen are efficient in the use of technical combat weapons.' And in the cavalry combat regulations of 1941/42, the basis for the use of cavalry in the forthcoming conflict with the German forces, much stress was laid on the mobility and versatility of mounted troops. The value of the cavalry in flank and rear attacks or for harassing the enemy was also emphasized. Large-scale formations had already been created in 1937/38 as 'strategic cavalry' which could be used in its own right as well as in conjunction with other arms of the service. And the firing power of a cavalry division could be altered to suit requirements.

The standard division comprised three cavalry regiments; one reconnaissance squadron; a unit of something between battalion and regimental strength of tanks, and one artillery regiment with three batteries of 76 mm guns and two batteries of 120 mm mortars (howitzers); one light anti-aircraft battery; one engineers' squadron; half a signals squadron and supply troops.

The cavalry regiment was looked upon as a small but mobile combat force. Though in numbers it was half the size of a Red Army infantry regiment, it had almost the same firing power as a result of its support weapons. A cavalry regiment consisted of four mounted squadrons with eight machine guns, six anti-tank rifles and a large number of sub-machine guns, one squadron with 16 machine guns, one battery of 76 mm field guns, one battery of 45 mm anti-aircraft guns, one squadron with 12 82 mm mortars, one group with light anti-aircraft guns, one signals group, one reconnaissance group, one engineers' group and one 'chemical' group.

Though the big formations were really well equipped with powerful weapons, they were often reinforced with accompanying infantry, field-artillery, anti-aircraft and anti-tank artillery. They were regarded as a supplement, but not a replacement for armoured and motorized troops. The Budenny Academy catered for the creation of a cavalry officers' corps. And in order to cope with new recruits, in the first months of the war no fewer than nine cavalry officer schools were established.

The new cavalry won its first battle honours in the far east. There were six cavalry divisions in the 1st Independent Far East Army led by Marshal W. K. Blücher – of which two, the Mongolian 6th and 8th Cavalry Divisions, took part in the frontier battles against the Japanese from August 20–31, 1939. Here for the first time, the cavalry, with tank support, carried out an offensive operation.

One of the cavalry's first missions of World War II was on September 17, 1939, when the Soviet Union invaded Poland. The 3rd, 6th and 24th Cavalry Divisions were at the time on the 'Belorussian Front' commanded by General M. P. Kovalyev; in addition there was a self-contained motorized cavalry group led by V. I. Utshikov, and the 'Ukrainian Front' had a Cavalry Corps (4th and 5th Cavalry Divisions). The three Soviet armies which occupied the Baltic lands between June 12 and 17, 1940, also had cavalry units at their disposal – the 25th, 30th and 4th Cavalry Divisions, assigned to the 'North-West Front'. In June 1941, the Red Army had between 26 and 30 cavalry divisions in the European part of the Soviet Union. After Hitler's invasion of the Soviet Union on June 22, 1941, the cavalry took part in the Red Army's defensive battles, and Soviet mounted units played a decisive role in the battle of Moscow. By November 1941, four cavalry corps had been changed into cavalry guards corps. After their experiences of the first months of the war in 1941, the Russians went on to combine the cavalry divisions into corps, consisting of three cavalry divisions; these divisions were very strong, both in numbers and in the weaponry at their disposal.

Structure:

Divisional headquarters with NKVD (security) detachment; half a signals squadron; three cavalry regiments, headquarters, signals section, anti-aircraft section; four mounted squadrons, each with eight light machine guns, four light mortars, six bazookas; one machine-gun squadron with 16 heavy machine guns; one heavy squadron, an anti-tank section with four 4·5 cm anti-tank guns; an artillery section of four 7·6 cm guns; one mortar squadron of six mortars; one engineers' section; one gas-defence squadron; one motorized anti-aircraft battery of six 3·7 cm anti-aircraft guns; one artillery battalion; a headquarters battery; two batteries with four heavy mortars; one battery with four 7·6 cm cannon; one artillery column (part motorized); one motorized supplies column; one motorized sanitary squadron; one veterinary field-hospital.

Strength:

About 5,040 men; 5,128 horses; about 130 motor vehicles; three motor-cycles, and about three waggons.

Weapons:

447 sub-machine guns; 118 light machine guns; 48 heavy machine guns; 48 light mortars; 18 medium mortars; eight heavy mortars; 76 bazookas; 12 4·5 cm anti-tank guns; 16 7·6 cm guns; about 25 radio sets; 10 T70 tanks; 9 12·7 mm anti-aircraft machine guns, and six 3·7 cm anti-aircraft guns.

Switzerland

Despite its neutrality, the Swiss Confederation experienced World War II at close quarters – and at all events, mounted troops had a significant role in the Swiss military structure and the plans to resist any intrusion on Swiss neutrality.

The army regulations of 1936 for the first time abandoned the term 'cavalry' in defining the various arms of the service and instead introduced the designation 'light troops'. The force's first leader was Divisional Colonel Jordi (1936–1947). The cavalry brigades now became light brigades organized into three army corps; the dragoon regiments, two per brigade, became light regiments, consisting of three dragoon squadrons – the so-called horse-group – and of a bicycle battalion

whose fourth company was motorized.

Reconnaissance battalions were created from the dragoon battalions in the 1st, 2nd, 4th, 5th, 6th and 7th Field Divisions. Each of these consisted of a dragoon squadron and a bicycle company. The remaining six squadrons were directly at the disposal of the divisional commanders for communications purposes; then, during the course of service in 1939–1945, they too were formed into reconnaissance battalions. The cavalry machine guns were phased out; instead, however, the number of machine guns in the 30 remaining dragoon squadrons (whose complement was now slightly smaller) was raised from four to nine each. Thus grouped, and with considerably increased firing power, the dragoons entered service in World War II. One of the cavalry brigades, consisting of the 18 squadrons of the light regiments, was in service during the winter of 1944/45 in the Jura and on the northern frontier. One similarly hastily-established light division was formed in autumn 1940 on the Saane from the 1st and 2nd Light Brigades and the 5th Reconnaissance Battalion. From 1939 to 1945 the dragoon squadrons were engaged in almost 750 days of active service.

The United States

The American Army was the first in the world to become fully motorized. In the few cavalry regiments which remained after World War I, the horse gave way to the internal combustion engine.

The Chief-of-Staff General Douglas MacArthur had the 1st Cavalry Regiment dismounted in January 1933 at Fort Knox, Kentucky, to be mechanized. Later the 13th Cavalry Regiment was converted into a motorized brigade, and shortly afterwards the 4th and 6th Cavalry Regiment was reorganized into the Horse-Mechanized Corps Reconnaissance Regiment (HMCRR), which had the advantage of both methods of conveyance: a group of eight riders and horses with fodder, rations and complete equipment including heavy and light machine guns in their baggage could be loaded into a truck and trailer within five to seven minutes. If the truck came to an impassable obstacle, the riders would unload their horses, mount up and scout out the land ahead. As a result of the success of this experiment, the remaining cavalry regiments were converted into seven HMCRRs and co-ordinated with the existing corps. However, the necessary equipment for this conversion was not delivered before 1941 and therefore before Pearl Harbor there was no opportunity to measure its effectiveness. In 1940 two more cavalry regiments were motorized. That left the 26th Cavalry ('Philippine Scouts') as the only remaining mounted cavalry regiment. It was stationed at Fort Stotsenburg, Pampanga, 85 km north of Manila. Between December 1941 and April 1942, the regiment was engaged in a series of tough and dramatic battles.

The 26th Cavalry was divided into two squadrons each of two troops, one machine-gun troop and one headquarters troop. In late autumn 1941, the regiment was reorganized and reinforced to 789 men. Both squadrons were given an additional troop. Though still lacking in anti-tank guns and mortars and other modern equipment, the 26th Cavalry (PS) was one of the best regiments of the Army so far as training was concerned.

Establishment, December 1941:

C.O.: Colonel Clinton Pierce.
Executive Officer: Lieutenant-Colonel Vance.
Commander of 1st Squadron: Major Ketchum.
A-Troop: Captain Cramer. B-Troop: Captain Barker. C-Troop: Captain Praeger.
Commander of 2nd Squadron: Major Trapnell.
E-Troop: Captain Wherler. F-Troop: Captain Wriskle. G-Troop: Captain Fowler. Machine-gun troop: Captain Ford.
Headquarters-Troop: Captain Richards.
Special Staff.
Medical Corps: Captain Reed, Chaplain: Zerfas.

Yugoslavia

The peoples of Yugoslavia had been through an entire century of struggle for national liberation and unification into a single state – which they finally achieved in 1918. The basis of the Yugoslav cavalry was provided mainly by Serbian units: the 1st Mounted Division, the 1st Division of Guards and six other squadrons. The army cavalry regiments had been originally formed in August 1919. The Cavalry Headquarters Staff was founded in 1937 to provide a unified cavalry command. Each division was to have a cavalry battalion, and each army was to have a mounted regiment. Before the beginning of World War II, three cavalry divisions were set up. These contained motorized, so-called 'fast units' as well as mounted troops. The cavalry was armed with sabres, rifles, light infantry weapons, horse-drawn artillery, armoured scout-cars and light tanks.

During the German invasion of Yugoslavia in April 1941, the Yugoslav cavalry suffered heavy casualties. Only the 7th Cavalry Regiment near Kacanik and the 2nd Cavalry Regiment were able to offer vigorous, but short-lived resistance between the Drava river and Zagreb as the German troops advanced. Elements of the 2nd Mounted Division fought their last battle near Deligrad, before withdrawing behind the river Juzne Morava. A few stalwarts went into the mountains, where fighting flared up again soon after.

In 1941, the partisans of Ucick and Cacansk organized a mounted squadron for courier work and another for reconnaissance. Tito's People's Liberation Army at the same time planned to provide each brigade with a mounted detachment of 30 men. In April 1942, a mounted troop was formed in the partisans' Savinjal battalion in Slovenia, and a mounted squadron was set up in the same year as part of the headquarters of the 3rd operational zone in Croatia.

The growth and successes of the People's Liberation Army in 1944 led to the establishment of large-scale operational formations. At the end of 1944, Tito's troops numbered about half a million men, organized in 17 army corps. Individual divisions had their own cavalry detachments and a few local commanders raised small mounted units to guard their provinces. In September 1944, the Macedonian headquarters set up a cavalry squadron which was enlarged in November that year into a cavalry battalion with two squadrons and a machine-gun squadron.

The imminent liberation of the country made the creation of larger formations vital; so on September 15, 1944, the 1st Mounted Brigade, attached to the 1st Proletarian Army Corps, was established near Ljiga, 80 km from Belgrade. Apart from headquarters and transport staff, the brigade started out with two battalions, each consisting of two squadrons split into two troops. There were 450 horsemen, armed with rifles, sub-machine guns and machine guns. After flushing out scattered German and Cetnik units in the district around Valjev and Arandelovc, the 1st Mounted Brigade was posted to the Sremsk front on November 18, 1944; later, up till 1945 it covered the left flank of the 1st Army, and after the collapse of the German front it pursued enemy troops to Zagreb and Maribor.

Bibliography

von Adonyi-Naredy, F.: *Ungarns Armee im Zweiten Weltkrieg.* Neckargemünd 1971.

Andolenko, P.: *Recueil d'Historiques de l'Arme Blindée et de la Cavalerie.* Paris 1967.

Appelius, M.: *Una guerra di 30 giorni.* Mediolan 1942.

Batow, P. I.: *Von der Wolga zur Oder.* Berlin (East) 1965.

Behrens, W., Kuehn, D.: *Geschichte des Reiter-Regiments 1 (1919–1939).* Kameradschaft ehem. R.R.1.

Belov, I. B.: *Za nami Moskva.* Moscow 1962.

Ber, H. W.: *Kosaken-Saga.* Rastatt 1966.

Boldin, J. W.: *Stranizy schisni.* Moscow 1961.

Brinksy, A.: *Po tu storonu fronta.* Moscow 1961.

Central Committee of the Communist Party of the Soviet Union (publ.): *Istoriya velikoy otechestvennoy voyny Sovyetskogo Soyusa 1941–1945.* Moscow 1961.

Corbeiller: *La guerre de Syrie.* Paris 1967.

Darnóy, P.: *Organisation der kgl.-ung. Honvéd-Armee 1941–1942.* Freiburg 1955.

Derecki, M.: *Tropem majora 'Hubala'.* Lublin 1971.

Disselhorst-Loewe, M.: *Beurteilung des Pferdes.* Berlin 1940.

Elbin, G.: *Der Schimmelmajor.* Munich 1969.

Eltz-Erwein, K. G. zu: *Mit den Kosaken. Kriegstagebuch 1943–1945.* Donaueschingen 1970.

von Emilian, I.: *Rumänische Kavallerieverbände und Aufklärungsabteilungen im Zweiten Weltkrieg.* Munich 1966.

von Emilian, I.: *Les cavaliers de l'Apocalypse.* Paris 1974.

Epstein, J.: *Operation Keelhaul.* Connecticut 1973.

Franz, W., Raschdorf: *Im Land der Pferde – Trakehnen.* Leipzig 1937.

von Fürstenberg, H.: *Der Vormarsch de Divisions-Aufklärungsabteilung 26 während der Entscheidungsschlacht in Frankreich vom 9. bis 21. Juni 1940.* Münster 1941.

Gai-Lung, L.: *Kurze Geschichte des chinesischen volksbefrieungskrieges.* Berlin (East) 1957.

Genellis, M.: *Le Cheval dans l'Histoire.* Paris 1956.

Gontaut-Biron, L.: *Les Dragons au Combat.* Paris 1952.

Goodall, D. M.: *Die Pferde mit der Eichschaufel.* Munich 1974.

Gosztony, P.: *Die Kavallerie der Roten Armee im Zweiten Weltkrieg.* Österr. Militärzeitschrift 6 (1969).

Grampe, A.: *15. (Preuss.) Reiter-Regiment. Kavallerie-Regiment 15 und seine Kriegseinheiten. Regimentsverband ehem. 15. Reiter e. V. 1972.*

Haupt, W.: *Heeresgruppe Mitte 1941–1945.* Dorheim 1968.

Heling, S.: *Trakehnen.* Munich 1959.

Hillgruber, A.: *Die Räumung der Krim 1944.* Berlin–Fankfurt 1959.

von Hobe, C., Görlitz, W.: *Georg v. Boeselager – Ein Reiterleben.* Düsseldorf 1957.

Hoffmann, J.: *Deutsche und Kalmyken 1942–1945.* Freiburg 1974.

Höhne, H.: *Der Orden unter dem Totenkopf.* Gütersloh 1967.

Jacobsen, H. A., Philippi, A. (Publ.): *Kriegstagebuch des Chefs des Generalstabes des Heeres 1939–1942.* Stuttgart 1962.

Jarman, N.: *Var Kavalerihest – historikk.* Norsk Militart Tideskrift 1971.

Jouffrault, R.: *Les Spahis au Feu.* Paris 1952.

Kern, E.: *General Pannwitz und seine Kosaken.* Göttingen 1963.

Kovpak, A.: *Ot Putivlya do Karpat.* Moscow 1959.

Krasnow, N.: *Nesabywajemoje.* San Francisco 1957.

Krzeczunowicz, K.: *Ulani Ksiecia Józefa – Historia 8 pulka ulanów.* London 1960.

Kuehn, D.: *Geschichte des Reiter-Regiments 1 (1939–1941).* Kameradschaft ehem. R.R.1.

Kuusaari, N., Nitemaa, V.: *Finlands Krig 1941–1945.* Helsinki 1949.

von Lengyel, B.: *Die ungarischen Truppen im Russland-Feldzug, der Einsatz der 1. Kavallerie-Brigade.* Allg. Schweizerische Militär-Zeitschrift 1960.

Liddell Hart, B. H.: *Die Rote Armee.* Bonn 1951.

Mitkiewicz, L.: *Kawaleria Samodzielna Rzeczypospolitej Polskiej W Wojnie 1939 Roku.* Toronto 1964.

Moczulski, L.: *Ostatnia szarża.* Warsaw 1968.

Morton, L.: *United States Army in World War II. The War in the Pacific. The Fall of the Philippines.* Washington 1953.

Mościcki, L.: *Wypad polskiej kawalerii na tereni Prus Wschodnich.* WPH 1969.

Naumenko, W.: *Welikoje predatelstwo.* New York 1970.

Niessel, R.: *La cavalerie sur le front soviétique. Revue de défense nationale 1948.*

Petrowsky, A.: *Unvergessener Verrat!* Munich 1963.

Plijew, I. A.: *A Tisza völgyében.* Hadtörténelmi Közlemények 1965.

Pozdnyakov, V.: *Sovetskaya agentura v lageryach voennoplennych v Germanii 1941–1945. Novy Zurnal 1970.*

Pulkowski, F.: *Geschichte des 10. (Preuss.) Reiter-Regiments.* Tennenlohe o. J.

Roeingh, R.: *Freund Pferd.* Berlin 1941.

Roeingh, R.: *Ross und Reiter am Feind.* Berlin 1941.

Rogers, C. B.: *The Mounted Troops of the British Army 1066–1945.* London 1959.

Sawjalow, A. S., Kaljadin, T. J.: *Die Schlacht um den Kaukasus 1942/43.* Berlin (East) 1959.

Schönerstedt, K.: *Pferde und Soldaten.* Giessen 1959.

von Senger-Etterlin, F. M.: *Die 24. Panzer-Division, vormals 1. Kavallerie-Division 1939–1945.* Neckargemünd 1962.

Sobolev, L.: *Dorogami pobyed.* Moscow 1945.

Springer, B.: *Reiterkrieg.* Berlin 1944.

von Stein, H. R.: *Das Kavallerie-Regiment 5 und seine Entwicklungen von 1920–1945.* Off-print from Trad.-Verb. d. Kav.-Reg. 5.

Stolz, G., Grieser, E.: *Geschichte des Kavallerie-Regiments 5.* Munich 1975.

Szacherski, Z.: *Bój o Brochów.* WPH 1962.

Szacherski, Z.: *Wierni przysiedze.* Warsaw 1968.

Tanner, V.: *The Winter War.* New York 1955.

Telpuchowski, B. S.: *Die sowjetische Geschichte des Grossen Vaterländischen Krieges 1941–1945.* Frankfurt 1961.

Tessin, G.: *Formationsgeschichte der Wehrmacht 1933–39. Stäbe und Truppenteile des Heeres und der Luftwaffe.* Boppard 1959.

Tessin, G.: *Verbände und Truppen der deutschen Wehrmacht.* Frankfurt 1966.

Tyulanev, I. V.: *Sovetskaya kavaleriya v boyach za rodinu.* Moscow 1959.

Treguboff, J.: *Der Letzte Ataman.* Velbert 1967.

Verdin, R. B.: *The Cheshire Yeomanry.* London 1971.

Verschigora, P.: *Reyd na San i Vislu.* Moscow 1960.

Vorobjov, W. F.: *Boyevoi put sovyetskich vooruschonnych sil.* Moscow 1960.

Völz, A.: *Zur Geschichte des Kavallerie-Regimentes 5. Deutsches Soldatenjahrbuch 1970.*

Wagener, C.: *Heeresgruppe Süd. Der Kampf im Süden der Ostfront 1941–1945.* Bad Nauheim o. J.

Wainwright, J. M.: *General Wainwright's Story.* New York 1946.

Werner-Ehrenfeucht, M.: *Kavallerie-Fibel.* Berlin 1933.

Yeremenko, A. J.: *Na sapadnom napravlenii.* Moscow 1959.

Zawilski, A.: *Bitwa nad Bzura.* Warsaw 1968.

Zessarsky, A.: *Sapiski partisanskogo vratscha.* Moscow 1956.

Journals, magazines and pamphlets

Armored Cavalry Journal. Washington 1947.

Deutsch-tatarisches Nachrichtenblatt. Berlin 1943.

H. Dv. 299/1. Ausbildungsvorschrift für die Kavallerie. Berlin 1937.

H. Dv. 299/2. Ausbildungsvorschrift für die Kavallerie. Berlin 1938.

Kameradschaft ehem. 8 Reiter. Mitteilungsblatt 1965–1967.

Khalmag. Berlin 1943.

Komunikat Informacyjny. Kola Zolnierzy 7 Pulka Ulanow Lubelskich im. gen. K. Sosnkowskiego. London 1950–1975.

Der Meldereiter. publ.: Regimentsverband ehem. 15. Reiter e.V.

Nachrichtenblätter des Kav.-Reg. 15. July 1943–September 1944.

OKH-Verordnung 5000. Landeseigene Hilfskräfte im Osten – Hilfswillige. April 29, 1943.

Politischer Dienst für SS und Polizei. 1. Folge 1944.

Schilenkow, General/Bojarski, Oberst. Erfahrungen mit ihrer russischen Freiwilligeneinheit. Extract from January 15, 1943.

Der Schweizer Kavallerist 1948. Die Kosaken Russlands.

Völkischer Beebachter. Berlin–Munich 1939–1945.

INDEX

256